Always Being Reformed

Always Being Reformed

Challenges and Prospects
for the Future of Reformed Theology

EDITED BY
David H. Jensen

☙PICKWICK *Publications* • Eugene, Oregon

ALWAYS BEING REFORMED
Challenges and Prospects for the Future of Reformed Theology

Copyright © 2016 David H. Jensen. All rights reserved. Except for brief quotations in critical publications or reviews, no part of this book may be reproduced in any manner without prior written permission from the publisher. Write: Permissions, Wipf and Stock Publishers, 199 W. 8th Ave., Suite 3, Eugene, OR 97401.

Pickwick Publications
An Imprint of Wipf and Stock Publishers
199 W. 8th Ave., Suite 3
Eugene, OR 97401

www.wipfandstock.com

ISBN 978-1-4982-2152-8

Cataloging-in-Publication data:

Always being reformed : challenges and prospects for the future of Reformed theology / edited by David H. Jensen.

xiv + 258 p.; 23 cm—Includes bibliographical references.

ISBN 978-1-4982-2152-8

1. Theology. 2. Reformed church—Doctrines. I. Jensen, David H. II. Title.

BX9422.3 A44 2016

Manufactured in the USA.

Biblical quotations (except as noted) come from the New Revised Standard Version Bible, copyright ©1989, Division of Christian Education of the National Council of the Churches of Christ in the United States of America. Used by permission. All rights reserved.

For the Frierson family

Contents

List of Contributors | ix
Preface | *David H. Jensen* | xiii

PART 1: *What Is Reformed Theology?*

1. Reformed and Always Being Reformed: A Tradition of the Spirit? | *David H. Jensen* | 3

2. Reformed Identity and Relevance in Zambian Context: Motifs, Challenges and Prospects | *Lameck Banda* | 21

3. *Semper Reformanda* as a Confession of Crisis | *Jason A. Goroncy* | 43

PART 2: *Reformed Theology and Religious Diversity*

4. Barth and Thatamanil: Two Theologians against Religion | *Martha Moore-Keish* | 77

5. "What Is Jesus Doing among the Spirits?" Questions from a Mission Studies Scholar to Grassroots Caribbean Charismatic *Evangélicos* | *Carlos F. Cardoza-Orlandi* | 92

6. The Holiness of God as Reason for and Promise of a Theological Critique of Religion | *Margit Ernst-Habib* | 108

7. Stepping into the Madness: On Being Skeptical, Doing Justice, and Hoping against Hope | *Cynthia L. Rigby* | 133

PART 3: *Reformed Theology and Doctrine*

8. Spirit, Vulnerability and Beauty: A Pneumatological Exploration | *Deborah van den Bosch* | 151

9. Integrating Different Values: Beyond Literal vs. Oral, Word vs. Image in the Reformed Spirit | *Meehyun Chung* | 174

10. Jeffrey Stout, Original Sin, and Christian Faith | *William Greenway* | 187

CONTENTS

PART 4: *Reformed Theology and Practices of Faith*

11. Reformation and Bodily Properties: Disrupting Rituals of Hospitality | *Mary McClintock Fulkerson* | 213

12. Land, Exile, and the Spirit of God: Rebuilding Selves in a Globalized World | *Grace Ji-Sun Kim* | 226

13. Epistemological Transformation in Theological Education | *Henk van den Bosch* | 237

Contributors

Rev. Dr. Lameck Banda is Professor of Systematic Theology at Justo Mwale Theological University College in Lusaka, Zambia. In addition to numerous journal articles, he has contributed book chapters to the following volumes: *In Search of Health and Wealth: The Prosperity Gospel in African, Reformed Perspective*, and *Christian Identity and Justice in a Globalized World from a Southern African Perspective*.

Dr. Carlos F. Cardoza-Orlandi is Professor of World Christianities and Mission Studies at Perkins School of Theology, Dallas. His most recent publications include *To All Nations From All Nations: A History of the Christian Missionary Movement* with Justo L. Gonzalez, and "Interreligious Dialogue: Why Should Interreligious Dialogue Matter for our Academic and Grassroots Communities? Reflections from a Latino/Caribbean Scholar," in *A Companion to Latino/a Theology*.

Rev. Dr. Meehyun Chung is Associate Professor at the United Graduate School of Theology of Yonsei University, Seoul, Korea. She has served as Vice President for Ecumenical Association of Third World Theologians and worked as the head of the Women and Gender Desk at Mission 21, Protestant Mission Basel, Switzerland. Her publications include *Reis und Wasser; Liberation and Reconciliation*; and *Lillias Horton Underwood*.

Dr. Margit Ernst-Habib is Scholar and Lecturer in Systematic Theology. Her publications include: *But Why Are You Called a Christian? An Introduction to the Heidelberg Catechism*; "Chosen by Grace: Re-Considering the Doctrine of Predestination," in *Feminist and Womanist Essays in Reformed Dogmatics*; and "A Conversation with Twentieth-Century Confessions," in *Conversations with the Confessions: Dialogue in the Reformed Tradition*.

CONTRIBUTORS

Dr. Mary McClintock Fulkerson is an ordained Presbyterian minister who teaches theology at Duke Divinity School. She has written on a variety of women's groups in *Changing the Subject: Women's Discourses and Feminist Theology*; and a book titled *Places of Redemption: Theology for a Worldly Church*. Her book co-authored with Dr. Marcia Mount Shoop is *A Body Broken, A Body Betrayed: Race, Memory, and Eucharist in White-Dominant Churches* (Cascade Books, 2015).

Jason A. Goroncy is Senior Lecturer in Systematic Theology at Whitley College, University of Divinity, in Melbourne, Australia. He is author of *Hallowed be Thy Name: The Sanctification of All in the Soteriology of P. T. Forsyth*; and he has edited *Descending on Humanity and Intervening in History: Notes from the Pulpit Ministry of P. T. Forsyth* (Pickwick Publications, 2013); and *Tikkun Olam—To Mend the World: A Confluence of Theology and the Arts* (Pickwick Publications, 2014). He also writes at *Per Crucem ad Lucem*, a popular theology blog.

William Greenway is Associate Professor of Philosophical Theology at Austin Presbyterian Theological Seminary and is author of *For the Love of All Creatures: The Story of Grace in Genesis*; *Reasonable Belief: Why God and Faith Make Sense*; *Agape Ethics* (Cascade Books, forthcoming); and *Amazing Grace and the Spiritual Challenge of Evil* (forthcoming).

Dr. Grace Ji-Sun Kim is Associate Professor of Theology at Earlham School of Religion. Her publications include *Embracing the Other: The Transformative Spirit of Love*; *Colonialism, Han and the Transformative Spirit*; and *The Holy Spirit, Chi, and the Other: A Model of Global and Intercultural Pneumatology*. She is a co-editor ,with Joseph Cheah, for the Palgrave Macmillan series Asian Christianity in Diaspora.

Dr. Martha Moore-Keish is Associate Professor of Theology at Columbia Theological Seminary in Decatur, Georgia. Her publications include *Do This in Remembrance of Me: A Ritual Approach to Reformed Eucharistic Theology* and *Christian Prayer for Today*.

Dr. Cynthia Rigby is the W. C. Brown Professor of Theology at Austin Presbyterian Theological Seminary. Cynthia is a regular contributor to the Dallas Morning News, is the author of *The Promotion of Social Righteousness*, and is a general editor of the forthcoming "Connections" lectionary series.

CONTRIBUTORS

Dr. D. (Deborah) van den Bosch-Heij is Research Fellow in the Department of Systematic Theology, University of the Free State, Bloemfontein, South Africa, and Minister of the Harkema Congregation of the Protestant Church in the Netherlands. Her publications include: "Gezondheid, ziekte en genezing in zuidelijk Afrika"; "A Reformed Pneumatological Matrix: An Exploration," *Journal for Christian Scholarship*; and *Spirit and Healing in Africa: A Reformed Pneumatological Perspective*.

Dr. H. M. (Henk) van den Bosch, Protestant Theological University, Amsterdam/Groningen, the Netherlands. Dr. van den Bosch is involved in the development of programs for professional formation and continuing education for ministers, both in the Netherlands and abroad.

Preface

PERHAPS THE MOST MEMORABLE slogan of the Reformed churches, those denominations shaped by the legacy of Calvin and Zwingli, is that the church is "reformed and always being reformed by the Word of God." Over the centuries since the Swiss Reformation, this slogan has garnered countless commentary. The phrase has taken on different accents over time and probably no two Reformed theologians would agree on its precise meaning. This lack of unanimity is hardly surprising, since Reformed traditions have spawned numerous, even disparate, movements (for example, Protestant fundamentalism and theological liberalism). But amid the astonishing diversity of the Reformed project is an underlying conviction that the church stands in continual need of reform. Reformed Christians insist that they never quite "get it," that whatever theology or ecclesiology stands fast, it will always fall short of the fullness of God's self-disclosure in Jesus Christ, the fullness that awaits the church at the end of days. There is, in this sense, a continual restlessness in Reformed theology, a continual need to revisit what it means to be Christian, and the need to re-claim and re-interpret even the most cherished theological claim. The Word of God is continually reforming us, and it is one task of theologians to take up the work of reform, re-articulating the faith for *this* day, *this* time. Reformed theologians, thus, take the past seriously, while paying close attention to present context in anticipation of a renewed future.

The chapters of this book ask varied questions about the meaning of the Reformed project for today and articulate fresh perspectives for the future. The essays are the result of an inaugural conference hosted at Austin Presbyterian Theological Seminary in April 2014, devoted to topics in Reformed theology. These conferences were made possible by the generosity of the Frierson Family of Shreveport, Louisiana, longtime friends of Austin Seminary who are deeply concerned with how Reformed theology gets articulated in congregations, especially in adult education settings. The essays are as varied as Reformed traditions themselves, tackling a host of themes from doctrine to practice. The conversations at this particular conference were especially animated, owing to the broad geographic diversity of the participants. Unlike some gatherings of Reformed theologians in North America, which tend toward cultural homogeneity, this conference was comprised of nearly equal numbers of men and women, coming from five different continents. The result was a thoroughly international series of perspectives.

I have organized these essays into four broad groupings. The first section poses questions of Reformed identity, both in its historical trajectory and in varied cultural contexts. The second tackles the issue of Reformed traditions as they encounter the vibrancy of other religious traditions and skepticism about those traditions. The third turns attention to some classical Reformed doctrines—such as Spirit, Word, and sin—with an eye toward rearticulating them in light of contemporary challenges. The final section focuses on varied practices of faith (such as hospitality and theological education) in a Reformed hue. The topics of each essay are quite disparate, reflecting a diversity of ways of "doing" Christian theology. Together, however, the chapters offer promising directions for the ongoing reclamation of a living tradition. The future of Reformed theology, at least as judged by these essays, is bright.

This book is possible because of the splendid group of scholars who gathered at Austin Seminary in April 2014. Their work forms the backbone of this project. The conference was made possible by a chorus of voices: seminary president Ted Wardlaw, faculty colleagues, and the board of trustees, who consistently support research in service to the church. Most prominent in that chorus is the Frierson Family of Shreveport, Louisiana. Clarence Frierson, longtime board member and chair, and his wife Betty, were steadfast ambassadors and supporters of Austin Seminary at a critical time in the seminary's history. Their sons Archer, Chris, John, and Tannie; and their spouses Ivy, Paula, Christy, and Jennifer gave generously in creating a faculty chair in Reformed theology to honor their parents. Their gift ensures that Reformed theology will be sustained at Austin Seminary—and throughout the wider church—through regular conferences such as this. As the book was entering its final stages, Alison Riemersma provided abundant help with proofreading, formatting, and technical issues. Finally, I owe thanks to Molly, Grace, and Finn, the family I call home who make each day new.

PART 1

What Is Reformed Theology?

1

Reformed and Always Being Reformed

A Tradition of the Spirit?

David H. Jensen

REFORMED CHRISTIANITY FREQUENTLY ASKS questions about its own identity. What makes theology Reformed? Answers to this question have proven elusive, yet the search for distinctive marks of the tradition(s) continues unabated. Perhaps the one mark that has endured across the centuries among Reformed Christians is that this tradition continually is *in search of* an identity. The search, of course, is not unique to the Reformed churches. None of the heirs of the Protestant Reformers can claim to have arrived at an authoritative definition of their tradition. Hence, the quest for "distinctives" within Lutheranism, Anglicanism, and the various Anabaptist traditions goes on. But the heirs of Calvin face particular challenges in the question. Unlike Lutheranism, there is no common confessional/theological core (such as the Formula of Concord); unlike Anglicanism, there is no common liturgical/devotional text (*a la* the Book of Common Prayer); and, unlike Anabaptism, there is not a distinctive ethic centered on pacifism. Perhaps this lack of a "common core" has fed the quest for Reformed identity across the centuries. When one looks at the history of the Reformed churches, it can appear that Reformed Christians have devoted the *most* attention to questions of identity among their Protestant siblings. Despite the lack of a common confession, Reformed Christians have probably authored more confessions than any other body of Christians worldwide since the Reformation. Rooted in particular contexts and places (as varied as Edinburgh, Accra, Belhar, and Barmen), these statements of faith have not only sought to articulate Christian faith for a particular body of Christians, but to offer gifts to the broader church. Lack of common creed, in other words, has generated an astonishing, vital plurality of confession among Reformed Christians and provoked a large degree of ecumenism. Despite the lack of a common liturgical/devotional text, attention to the *ordo* of worship has fed much reflection on Reformed identity today and the renewal of its traditions surrounding Word and Sacrament. And, despite the lack of a common ethical framework (such as pacifism), many attempts at articulating a Reformed identity center on the witness and posture of Reformed Christians vis-à-vis the world. Most of these attempts stress a sensibility that "transforms" the world (H. Richard Niebuhr) or places special significance on Calvin's "third use of the law" as a means for making the world conform more nearly to the call of the Kingdom of God.

Attempts at forging a distinctively Reformed identity, in other words, are legion. The danger of such attempts, of course, is that they invariably flatten or eviscerate an otherwise vibrant tradition. But if one considers the attempt not to oversimplify a tradition, but to give some cast to the ongoing vitality of the tradition, I believe the search for Reformed identity to be well worth pursuing. The search, in other words, may be nothing less than the attempt to discern what gives this particular tradition its vitality. The point of this essay is to make one such attempt, and to probe an angle of Reformed identity that is often underdeveloped. After considering some other recent attempts at discerning distinctive theological marks of the Reformed tradition, I suggest a theology of the Spirit as a powerful (if often unarticulated) animating drive of the tradition(s), a theology that is inherently open to the confessional plurality that characterizes the Reformed churches and that animates its politically-engaged understanding of the Reign of God. By claiming Reformed theology as a tradition of the Spirit, I am not offering a definition or prescription for its varied theologies, but a heuristic for considering its ever-fragmentary confession of faith and its insistence that the Reign of God concerns people, places, and events in this world. The quest for Reformed identity, in short, is always incomplete, a recognition perhaps discerned most clearly through the lens of the Spirit.

Theological Essentials?

Some of the earliest attempts to describe the Reformed tradition have appealed to a cluster of distinctive or essential tenets. The English mnemonic TULIP, derived from the seventeenth-century Synod of Dordt is perhaps most famous in this regard (total depravity, unconditional election, limited atonement, irresistible grace, and perseverance of the saints). Another example would be the five central doctrines affirmed by the American Presbyterians in 1910 (biblical inerrancy, virgin birth of Christ, the validity of his miracles, his substitutionary atonement, and bodily resurrection). Such attempts appeal to beliefs that purportedly distinguish the Reformed tradition from others, and continue down to this day, even if the list of essential tenets remains undefined.[1] This approach, though it has endured across the centuries, has two significant shortcomings: First, the list of what is "essential" changes over time. Indeed, many tenets dubbed "essential" in past periods are now seen as dispensable or even mis-characterizations of Reformed theology (such as biblical inerrancy). A second weakness of an appeal to "distinctive tenets" is that it makes "central" what is most peculiar to the tradition. In other words, the "essential tenets" risk becoming beliefs that are not shared with the church catholic. Is what is most "essential" to the Reformed tradition its particular understanding of election, grace, or the atonement? Or is it that cluster of beliefs that is shared most widely and generously with the church catholic, such as the affirmation of God the Father as maker of heaven and earth, Jesus Christ as the Son of God, and the Spirit as the giver of life (to take a few affirmations from the Nicene Creed)? An insistent focus on "essential" Reformed tenets may, in the end, result in a rather idiosyncratic understanding of the tradition, one that becomes rather distant from other bodies of the Christian family.[2]

An appeal to essential tenets may even violate the intents of the Reformers. The early proliferation of Reformed confessions points to an essential distrust of any one confession as being binding and authoritative for all time. At the signing of the First Helvetic Confession, Heinrich Bullinger claimed, "We wish in no way to prescribe for all churches through these articles a single rule of faith. For we acknowledge no other rule of faith than Holy Scripture."[3] There is something about the dynamic of Reformed Christianity itself that demands multiple confessions. Instead of essential tenets, pluralism my constitute one of the "essential" features of Reformed Christianity. Jan Rohls notes "Because the Reformed tradition is so manifold, it

---

1. One example of an appeal to "essential tenets" without listing what these are is a question posed during ordination in the Presbyterian Church (U.S.A.): "Do you sincerely receive and adopt the essential tenets of the Reformed faith as expressed in the confessions of our church as authentic and reliable expositions of what Scripture leads us to believe and do, and will you be instructed and led by those confessions as you lead the people of God?" The Office of Theology and Worship, *Book of Occasional Services*, 57. The question is posed in identical form for the ordination of elders, deacons, and ministers of word and sacrament.

2. For a similar critique of a focus on "essential tenets," see Gerrish, "Introduction," 6.

3. Bullinger, *Conversations with the Confessions*, 9.

should be easier for Reformed churches to accept confessional pluralism in general, over against churches with a common doctrinal basis."[4] Yet, the "ease" of accepting confessional pluralism has often proven difficult. Much of the history of Reformed Christianity on both sides of the Atlantic can be traced to the search for a singular, authoritative confession. The Westminster Confession, for British and American Presbyterians, stands out particularly prominently, a statement that provided "the sole doctrinal standards"[5] in both of these branches of Reformed Christianity.

Despite the "chief authority" that the Westminster Standards offered among some strands of Reformed tradition for a period of time, attempts to craft a singular confession for Reformed Christians have routinely failed. Nothing emerged out of the Reformation period, and nothing since has been accepted by the churches tracing their lineage to Calvin, Zwingli and their heirs. In 1925, the World Alliance of Reformed Churches revisited the question of a common Reformed creed and eventually rejected it as necessary (aided by Karl Barth's warning to WARC that such a creed was impossible to conceive). Considering this history of an elusive quest for a common creed, Dirkie Smit remarks that an attempt at crafting a universal creed "would contradict just about every aspect of Reformed faith, piety and life."[6] The quest has failed, in other words, because there is something about the Reformed tradition that resists a common, binding confession.

Yet the persistent habit of writing and re-writing confessions continues in each generation of the Reformed family. This habit may indicate something about a Reformed understanding of the practice of confessions: that they are always partial and incomplete. As Margit Ernst writes, "Reformed creeds and confessions have only *provisional, temporary,* and *relative* authority and are therefore subject to revision and correction."[7] An inability to formulate "essentials" means that the church continually revisits what is (or is not) essential to the confession of faith. Such a habit would seem appropriate for a tradition whose slogan is often described as "reformed and always being reformed" by the Word of God. In this read, the incompleteness and indefiniteness of Reformed Christianity is its great strength: it prevents the faith from ossifying, it stands in question any human attempt to attribute authority to anything else than the sovereign God, it points to the necessity of each generation to claim the faith for itself, it points to the church's understanding of God's activity at each moment in history.

---

4. Rohls, "Reformed Theology," 39.
5. Rogers, *Presbyterian Creeds*, 140.
6. Smit, "Trends and Directions," 319.
7. Ernst, "We Believe," 89.

Reformed Themes and Habits?

Other attempts to describe a theological identity to Reformed Christianity focus less on a list of tenets and more on an overarching theme. The tendency here is not to enumerate what is most "essential," but to offer a pattern that gives some coherence to the diverse emphases within the tradition and to sketch some bounds to the tradition itself. Over the ages, several themes have emerged as prominent: election (or predestination), an emphasis on the sovereignty of God, a sustained polemic against idolatry, or an emphasis on the covenant between God and humanity/creation. What makes a theology "Reformed," in this account, is whether or not one of these themes is prominent. John Leith offers a twentieth-century defense of considering the Reformed tradition as grounded in an understanding of God's sovereignty: "A case can be made that the central theme of Calvinist theology . . . is the conviction that every human being has every moment to do with the *living* God."[8] What makes the tradition "Reformed" is its continued orientation toward God's sovereignty, glory, and power. In this view, what holds together Schleiermacher's "feeling of absolute dependence," Calvin's account of creation as the theater of God's glory and Barth's notion of a wholly Other God who loves in freedom is that each emphasizes that God is God, we are not God, and that all that is is directed toward God's majesty.

Orientation toward the covenant is also a prominent theme within Reformed Christianity: from Calvin's defense of infant baptism, which shows the Reformed churches' understanding that all members of the church are heirs to God's covenant (*Institutes* IV.16.5), to Barth's insistence that covenant is the internal basis of creation (*CD* III.1), to the Accra Confession's repeated refrain that God's covenant with creation is what compels Christians to resist economic injustice and ecological destruction (paras. 20, 22, 37). Other attempts at conceiving Reformed identity have focused on idolatry (as in some interpretations of Calvin) or election (as in some interpretations of Barth). To say that Reformed theology has emphasized these themes is widely shared among observers of the tradition. But, the question remains whether isolating any one of these themes constitutes a test of whether a theology is "Reformed" or not.

Many have criticized the tendency to isolate one theme as characteristic of the tradition. Some of them, moreover, are so broad that it is not clear that there is anything distinctively "Reformed" about them at all. Take Leith's observation that Reformed theology insists that "every human being has every moment to do with the *living* God" as an example. To claim

---

8. Leith, "Ethos of the Reformed Tradition," 5.

that this insight is distinctively Reformed is also to suggest that there are other traditions within Christianity that do not emphasize this theme. This corollary begs the question: what tradition doesn't emphasize our moment-by-moment encounter with God, that God really is God and we are not? We search traditions and theologies in vain to find interpretations of the human person that are independent of an encounter with the living God. Leith's insight, it seems to me, is more a characteristic of the Christian understanding of the person and God's sovereignty in general than it is a "distinctive" of Reformed Christianity. One risk of isolating a singular theme in Reformed Christianity is that it is construed so broadly that it hardly becomes a descriptor of a *particular* tradition.

Perhaps "covenant" is a better characterization of this elusive tradition. One might certainly argue that Reformed Christianity has emphasized this theme to a greater extent than other church bodies. In its conception of Christian moral responsibility in the world, for example, Roman Catholics have generally preferred conceptions of the "common good" to notions of covenant.[9] Anabaptist theology tends more toward the calling of the saints to embody a peaceable kingdom distinct from the world rather than a drive to transform the world from within in response to the covenant God has established with creation.[10] But the notion of covenant as somehow central to the Reformed tradition is also open to question. Despite its prominence, some have argued that covenant theology might limit the Reformed tradition instead of describing it fairly. Heleen Zorgdrager, for example, claims:

> Covenant theology is . . . a narrowing of the perspective of John Calvin. He actually developed a vibrant theology of participation and communion with Jesus Christ in the holy, all-encompassing and all-compassionate life of the triune God. Why should we start in Reformed theology from the idea of God and human beings as originally separated parties (which is the underlying idea of the covenant metaphor), and not begin with the primordial

---

9. See Mount, *Covenant, Community*, 1. This is not to say that Roman Catholicism does not employ language of covenant in its varied conceptions of the human person's relation to God and our relation to one another. Rather, the question is the degree of emphasis. In modern Catholic interpretations, including magisterial proclamations, "common good" language tends to be more prominent. Two twentieth century examples of this would include the Pastoral Letter on Catholic Social Teaching and the U.S. Economy, 1986 and the Vatican II document, *Gaudium et Spes*.

10. "I can, for instance, expect pacifism of a fellow believer who is committed to the same Lord, as I cannot expect it of other fellow citizens in a value-pluralistic nation." Yoder, *The Priestly Kingdom*, 110.

and—in Jesus Christ—restored *communion* between God and human beings?"[11]

Zorgdrager's point is well-taken. Covenant theology may not supply the common ground that undergirds Reformed reflection, and it might distort the understanding of the divine-human relationship in light of redemption in Jesus Christ. Zorgdrager opines that communion or Eucharistic theology might offer meaningful counterpoints within the tradition itself.

Some more conservative Reformed scholars have suggested that what makes theology "Reformed" is an emphasis on one (or more) of the Reformation "*solas*." Grace alone, faith alone, scripture alone. The late Fred Klooster has offered a rather straightforward claim about the "uniqueness" of Reformed theology: "The uniqueness of the Reformed churches, of the Reformed confessions and, subsequently, of Reformed theology is simply their allegiance to the Scriptural principle."[12] Klooster invokes Calvin's *Institutes* as "a manual for the reading of Scripture in contrast to the grandiose design of the summas"[13] and claims that the Scriptural principle concerns "the whole of Scripture," that Reformed theology speaks "where the Scriptures speak" and should be silent "where they are silent."[14] Indeed, Klooster cites Barth as one who, in the end, violates this essential mark of Reformed theology, because Barth understands the Bible as "witness to revelation, not itself revelation."[15] Klooster's argument about what makes theology "Reformed" is essentially a return to the Reformers' biblical hermeneutics. Of course there are exponents of this position on the contemporary scene. But to claim such a biblical hermeneutic as constituting what is "essentially" Reformed is highly questionable. For one, it may not be an accurate depiction of Reformed hermeneutics at all. Calvin's defense of money-lending, for example, displays far more sophistication than seeing the Bible as "revelation."[16] Second, it severely limits the ambit of "authentically" Reformed theologians. If biblical literalism may legitimately be claimed as a "child" of the Calvinist Reformation, so too can Protestant liberalism.[17] Indeed, the critical spirit of Calvin, his humanist scholarship, lives on in approaches to scripture that

---

11. Zorgdrager, "In Search," 169.
12. Klooster, "Uniqueness," 39.
13. Ibid., 41.
14. Ibid., 39.
15. Ibid., 47.
16. See Calvin's "Letter on Usury," in Janz, *Reformation Reader*, 219–22; see also Calvin's commentary on Exodus 22, *Commentaries on the Four Last Books of Moses*, 126–33.
17. See Elwood, *Calvin for Armchair Theologians*, 161–65.

go beyond what Barth himself suggested. Klooster's insistence on the Scriptural principle unnecessarily limits the Reformed family. Comparatively few contemporary Reformed theologians espouse the view of scripture that he claims lies at the heart of the tradition.

In light of the aforementioned difficulties, one final approach toward describing Reformed theology rests not on doctrine or a singular theme, but in discerning a pattern of "habits" or "traits" to a Reformed outlook. Leith, whose characterization of a Reformed ethos has already been noted, formulates a list of nine significant motifs that have shaped the tradition(s). In addition to the "majesty and praise of God" noted above, Leith cites the tradition's polemic against idolatry, the working out of God's purposes in history, an ethical life of holiness, a celebration of the life of the mind as divine service, preaching the Word of God, organizing the church for the care of souls, a disciplined life, and a stress on simplicity.[18] Instead of offering a list of essentials or isolating a singular theme, Leith's essay notes a broad pattern of traits throughout history. He makes a convincing case not for these traits as the exclusive property of the Reformed tradition, but their endurance across ages. In varied ways in diverse periods, these habits have abided.

B. A. Gerrish makes a similar argument, albeit with a different, shorter list. On his account, a Reformed habit of theology involves five elements: a tradition that is deferential to its forbears, critical of its forbears, open to truth wherever it may be found, practical in the sense that truth serves goodness, and evangelical in its orientation to the gospel. There is partial overlap here with Leith's account (with Gerrish's critical spirit finding an analogue in Leith's celebration of the mind) as well as a noting of traits that the other might have overlooked. (No equivalent of Gerrish's "evangelical" spirit seems to be present on Leith's account; no emphasis on preaching appears on Gerrish's.) Gerrish, too, makes a convincing argument. Indeed, one struggles to argue against either list. They are stated broadly enough that they might include many theologians and traditions (e.g., Calvin, Barth, Schleiermacher, Letty Russell) under one umbrella. An emphasis on "ethos" or "habits" might avoid the theological reductionism endemic to a focus on "essential tenets" or even an overarching Reformed "theme." The inherent pluralism of the tradition might best be expressed via an outlining of traits that both repeat themselves and shift over time. The question, of course, is what to include and what to leave out, as the enumeration of Reformed "habits" could conceivably be endless. (Where, for example, are the theological habits of "divine accommodation," "discernment of God's

---

18. Leith, "Ethos of the Reformed Tradition," 5–17.

presence in the natural world," the Reformation *solas*, or deliberation of the governance of societies in either list?) Might the endurance and shifting of certain Reformed habits over time also be crystallized in one of the classic theological loci? One way of accomplishing this would be to re-consider Reformed understandings of the Spirit. To that task I now turn.

The Holy Spirit in Reformed Thought: Theological Fragments and Considerations

Rarely has Reformed Christianity been described as a tradition of the Spirit.[19] The stereotype of the tradition is that it is too preoccupied with order, too suspicious of winds that quickly get carried away. Calvin was wary of enthusiasts, Westminster guarded against spiritual excess, Barth was suspicious of pietists. Each generation in the Reformed family, it seems, has been cautious of granting the Spirit too much ground. Pneumatology is the slipperiest of doctrines in the tradition, and as a result, often gets short shrift in the tradition.[20] The "incompleteness" of Barth's *Dogmatics* reflects, in part, his own recognition that he never was able to adequately address pneumatology. Yet pneumatology surfaces throughout Reformed history as a pivotal doctrine, and might even provide some "distinctive traits" to the tradition. In this regard, the tradition never really avoided pneumatology, even when it might have tried to. As one surveys the foundational documents of Reformed Christianity, some prominent themes emerge, and they help describe some of the ongoing vitality of the tradition.

Reformed theology has consistently provided parameters for considering the work of the Spirit. Early encounters with enthusiasts may have cast much of the tradition in the mode of testing the spirits to sense whether they are from God. Again, an exhaustive list of arenas for the work of the Spirit is impossible to maintain. Nonetheless, some areas of Christian life (and the life of creation) crop up routinely in early Reformed confessions

---

19. Several Reformed theologians, however, have been described as theologians of the Spirit, including Calvin and Schleiermacher. B.B. Warfield claims that "Calvin's greatest contribution to theological science lies in the rich development which he gives—and which he was the first to give—to the doctrine of the work of the Holy Spirit ... Above everything else he deserves, therefore, the great name of *the theologian of the Holy Spirit.*" *Calvin and Augustine*, 485–87. Barth asks about the possibility of a theology "predominantly and decisively of the Holy Spirit ... A theology of which Schleiermacher was scarcely conscious, but which might actually have been the legitimate concern dominating even his theological activity." Barth, *Theology of Schleiermacher*, 278.

20. One can read the entirety of Calvin's Book III of the *Institutes*, however, as pneumatology.

(and in Calvin) as specific sites of the Spirit's work. The intent, in my estimation, was not to limit the work of the Spirit to these specific arenas, but to note patterns in the Spirit's work as the church attempted to discern among the spirits. Six areas are worth special noting: the Holy Spirit's work in the inspiration and interpretation of scripture, the Spirit as uniting believers to Christ, the Spirit as the granter of faith, the Spirit's role in sanctification, the Spirit's presence in the sacraments, and the Spirit's presence throughout creation.

Perhaps the most cited work of the Spirit is her connection to scripture. In part, this may stem from the tradition's wariness against excessive spirits. Connecting Spirit to the Bible may represent the attempt to rein in enthusiasm. The book, in this sense, provides the window through which the Spirit blows. But the connection offers more than a window of restraint. Indeed, for Calvin, the book is glimpsed in light of the Spirit, who is both the author and interpreter of the Word. Holy Spirit "is the Author of the Scriptures: he cannot vary and differ from himself. Hence, he must ever remain just as he once revealed himself there" (*Institutes*, 1.9.2).[21] Here Calvin shows the double-valence of much subsequent Reformed thought: Spirit, as the author of Scripture means that the "book" is read in the context of the Spirit's work; and, because he must remain as he has revealed himself in scripture, the "book" provides the context for discerning Spirit's work. The result is both and expansive and restrictive view of the Spirit. Much subsequent controversy in Reformed life over the working of the Spirit might relate to which pole is being emphasized.

Much Reformed theology points to the pivotal role the Spirit plays in interpreting God's word in scripture. Reading scripture is not like reading any book. We read rightly when we are guided by God's spirit, who makes us readers and hearers of the Word. Hence, Westminster's affirmation that "The Spirit of God maketh the reading, but especially the preaching of the Word, an effectual means of enlightening, convincing, and humbling sinners, of drawing them out of themselves, and drawing them unto Christ."[22] Without the Spirit, the book risks becoming a dead letter. Calvin's metaphor of scripture providing spectacles that enable us to glimpse knowledge of God rests on an understanding of the Spirit's work. For him, it is the "secret testimony of the Spirit" (1.7.4) that provides the greatest justification of scripture's credibility. In this regard, Spirit speaks through the word in Scripture, making it a living word.

---

21. Calvin, *Institutes*. Hereafter, noted numerically by book, chapter and section.

22. "Larger Catechism," 7.265, 229. Hereafter noted numerically by confession and paragraph.

A second tendency among early Reformed theology is to describe Spirit as unifying the believer with Christ. If there is a mystical strand in Calvin's theology, this would surely be it: "The Holy Spirit is the bond by which Christ effectually unites us to himself" (3.1.1). One consequence of this view is that justification does not merely mean the reckoning of the believer as righteous, but the beginning of a transformation of the person, by grace. This emphasis might help explain some of the different nuances between Lutheran and Reformed understandings of the Reformation slogan "*simul iustus et peccator*." In Lutheranism, the slogan indicates the ongoing paradoxical existence of the believer in light of grace; in Reformed Christianity, the slogan tends toward a transformation of the believer, by grace, that remains ever-incomplete. Westminster echoes this strand in Calvin by locating the unifying work of the Spirit within the Christian church: "By the indwelling of the Holy Spirit all believers being vitally united to Christ, who is the Head, are thus united one to another in the Church, which is his body" (*Confessions*, 6.054). To be "in Christ" is also to be "in the Spirit" and a member of the Body. Spirit's indwelling results in a visible union with other believers, which is itself the outgrowth of the invisible-and-visible unifying of Christ with the church.

If union is the mystical strand in Reformed theologies of the Spirit, faith is the posture that confirms the working of Spirit in individual and corporate life. Calvin describes faith as "the principal work of the Holy Spirit" (3.1.4). His oft-cited definition of faith includes the memorable phrase of faith as "firm and certain knowledge of God's benevolence toward us . . . revealed to our minds and sealed upon our hearts through the Holy Spirit" (3.2.7). Here the work of the Spirit is *within* the person and community, transforming both by grace.[23]

In my reading of Calvin, faith is not a private matter between the individual and God, but witnessed in the gathered community as it hears Word proclaimed and celebrates the sacraments. One of the more notable emphases of Calvin's pneumatology is his connection of the Spirit to the sacraments. The work of the Spirit is what makes the sacraments efficacious: "The sacraments properly fulfill their office only when the Spirit, that inward teacher, comes to them, by whose power alone hearts are penetrated and affections moved and our souls opened for the sacraments to enter in"

---

23. Several Reformed confessions also attribute the gift of faith to the work of the Holy Spirit upon the heart of the human person. See Heidelberg Catechism, 4.065 and Westminster Confession, 6.078. Notably both confessions connect this "inner" work of the Spirit to "outward" communal rites, such as preaching the Word of God and the sacraments. As a result, the work of the Spirit is not a private, individual matter, but a bond of faith that draws believers together in the church.

(4.14.9). The Spirit "truly unites things separated in space," e.g., Christ's flesh and blood and our own (4.17.10). The life of faith is thus nourished in the company of others gathered around table, bath, and pulpit.

This gathering of community points to an additional trait of early Reformed understandings of the Spirit: that she did not only give birth to faith in the heart of believers, but ignited the ongoing transformation of Christian life under grace. Holy Spirit plays a prominent role in the sanctification of believers. Again, Calvin is illustrative: "He is called the 'Spirit of sanctification' [cf. 2 Thess 2:13; 1 Pet 1:2; Rom 1:4] because he not only quickens and nourishes us by a general power that is visible both in the human race and in the rest of the living creatures, but he is also the root and seed of heavenly life in us" (3.1.2). Many subsequent observers of the tradition have claimed that this emphasis in Reformed Christianity has led to its distinctive understanding of the law (in contradistinction from Lutheranism) and its generally hopeful regard of governmental institutions, of the possibility of holiness as a model in Christian life, and for the role of "saints" in the gradual transformation of society. Westminster claims the Spirit as "the only efficient agent in the application of redemption" and enumerates regeneration, conviction, moving to repentance, comfort, sanctification, and adoption as works of the Spirit (6.053), citing Spirit as the one who makes possible our ability to do good works (6.089).[24] By the Spirit, we are made ever anew.

Yet the most comprehensive note amid Reformed articulations of the Spirit is its intimation of the Spirit present in all creation. Just as Reformed Christianity has generally resisted privatized understandings of Holy Spirit, at its best it has also questioned articulations of the Spirit that claim it as restricted to the gathered communion of the faithful. Wherever we turn, wherever we journey, Holy Spirit is already at work, giving and sustaining life. This recognition is grounded in perhaps the earliest articulation of Holy Spirit as "Lord and Giver of Life" at Nicaea. Early in the *Institutes*, Calvin notes: "For it is the Spirit who, everywhere diffused, sustains all things, causes them to grow, and quickens them in heaven and in earth. Because he is circumscribed by no limits, he is excepted from the category of creatures; but in transfusing into all things his energy, and breathing into them essence, life, and movement, he is indeed plainly divine" (1.13.14). Holy Spirit is Spirit let loose in the world, unbounded, untamed, animating all things with the gift of life. The diversity of life itself is possible because of

---

24. The Confession of 1967 echoes similar strains as it points to the Spirit as initiator of "the new life in Christ" (9.21).

Holy Spirit's gift of life.[25] If we ask where the Spirit is active, the answer is *everywhere* in creation.

If this aspect of Reformed pneumatology has not always received extensive attention, it has been recovered of late. Jürgen Moltmann is indicative of this turn to creation in recent Reformed theology; for him, a theology of the Spirit is also creation-centered, allowing us to see the presence of God in all things. For Moltmann, the Spirit of God is "the power of creation and the wellspring of life . . . Every experience of a creation of the Spirit is hence also an experience of the Spirit itself. Every true experience of the self becomes also an experience of the divine spirit of life in the human being. Every lived moment can be lived in the inconceivable closeness of God in the Spirit."[26] There is no sphere of life where Spirit is not revealing itself; and, because life is pluriform, the responses to Holy Spirit will take on different hues and characteristics. Yet all are given life by the Spirit of God.

Reformed Christianity hardly has a uniform doctrine of the Spirit, but if one considers the historical arc of the tradition, some prominent traits emerge, including: the Spirit's role in the reading and writing of Scripture, its bond of faith and agency in providing union with Christ, its transformation of human and corporate life by means of the sacraments and the call to holiness, and its recognition of the Spirit let loose in the world, sustaining all things, drawing all into life. Reformed articulations of the Spirit are thus marked by striking particularity (connecting Spirit to Word and Sacrament) and unbounded by any particular (as Spirit is discerned in all life). If we take those traits to "heart" (to use an oft-repeating Reformed image in describing the work of the Spirit), one way of describing the diversity of Reformed theology itself is as a mark of the Spirit. The ever-elusive attempt to "describe" Reformed theology might be addressed by considering the tradition as a tradition of the Spirit.

Reformed Theology: A Tradition of the Spirit? Implications and Consequences

Perhaps a word of caution is in order here. I am not attempting to offer a new (or even an old) "definition" of Reformed theology. My work here is not to be confused with an attempt to confine, delimit, or constrain an incredibly vibrant, ongoing tradition. Instead, I am seeking to offer a doctrinal heuristic that might help the wider church sense some prominent patterns

---

25. The Presbyterian Brief Statement of Faith also echoes this strain: "We trust in God the Holy Spirit, everywhere the giver and renewer of life" (10.4).

26. Moltmann, *Spirit of Life*, 35.

in a very diverse tradition, without flattening the distinctive edges of the pluriform Reformed conversation. In that regard, I am trying to give some broad description to a varied tradition, but without resorting to a list of distinctive habits, traits, or claiming a particular Reformed ethos. Reformed theologies of the Spirit, I am claiming, offer one (but not the only) doctrinal lens for considering the tradition's staggering diversity, its refusal to subscribe to a singular creed, and its impetus toward personal, ecclesial, and societal transformation. One way of describing the tradition's ongoing vitality comes from its critical reflection on a central tenet of ecumenical Christian faith, confession of the Holy Spirit as Lord and Giver of Life. It is worth considering Reformed Christianity as a tradition of the Spirit because such consideration emphasizes: 1) the impetus toward personal, ecclesial and societal transformation; 2) the ever-provisional nature of confessions of faith; 3) the diversity of Reformed life, and the "unbounded" nature of the Spirit's reach; 4) its call to resist idolatry in all its forms; and 5) the bounded nature of the church's confession and its connection of the work of the Spirit to the reading of Scripture and the celebration of the sacraments. To these marks I now turn.

Reformed Christianity might be considered a tradition of the Spirit because it perennially emphasizes the transformation of individual and corporate life. Holy Spirit, as sanctifier of life, summons us to a life of holiness, a life not limited to individual morality or personal piety. Without this recognition, Calvin's conclusion to his *Institutes* (politics and government) seems puzzling and idiosyncratic. But if this conclusion is glimpsed in light of the Spirit's transforming, sanctifying work, it represents the outgrowth of a distinctive Reformed insistence about the Spirit who is not confined to the workings of the "heart" or the gathered community, but who makes possible the doing of good works, and the ordering of human life according to the law. Calvin's reflections on civil government have echoed throughout the ages, even among his Reformed detractors. But despite their diverse interpretations of the role of government, Reformed Christianity has generally resisted the call to opt out of politics altogether.

This emphasis on the ongoing, transformative work of the Holy Spirit in corporate life, however, has also given rise to abuses within the Reformed tradition. The conviction that earthly saints have a role in making society conform more nearly to the Reign of God coupled with an insistence that God is working out God's purposes in history has often led to crusading triumphalism. The "shining city on a hill" of Puritan New England, Reformed-Afrikaner notions of apartheid, and recent examples of American exceptionalism, all drink from some of the wells that have nourished Reformed Christianity. But in these cases, when joined with racism, nationalism, and intolerance, the wells become poisoned. And an emphasis on the transformative life made present in the Holy Spirit quickly becomes the very thing that smothers life, silencing peoples in the name of an onward march of progress. Each generation of the Reformed faith has had to grapple with demons of its own making, because the transformative impulse present in its tradition can often prove destructive.

But if the work of the Spirit also summons us to "unmask idolatries in Church and culture, to hear the voices of peoples long silenced, and to work with others for justice, freedom, and peace" ("Brief Statement of Faith," 10.4), then the pneumatological bent of the tradition recalls another perennial emphasis of Reformed Christianity: to resist idolatry. If the Spirit makes possible our response of "yes" to the life given by God, the Spirit also enables us to say "no" to whatever forces inhibit life and deal in death. Holy Spirit is also a Spirit of resistance, summoning us to resist the destructive and triumphalist strains of our own tradition. Kristine Culp names this dimension rather clearly: "To resist is a *call* to engagement, not a political program or polity. This call, moreover, assumes an underlying diagnosis of idolatry. At its best, Reformed thought offers a *call* to resist idolatry with confession and social-cultural-political engagement, not a *program for* political transformation."[27] Reclaiming Reformed Christianity as a tradition of the Spirit can help us diagnose when the impetus to reform becomes a self-righteous crusade, when images become idols.

Recognition of the Spirit may also highlight the Reformed tradition's insistence that all confessions of faith are provisional and partial. The Spirit, not our confession, is the sole Lord of life. Nearly every attempt to maintain a universally binding creed in the Reformed tradition has failed. And this failure is one strength of the tradition, as it stresses the ever-provisional, ever-recurring growth in the life of faith. Life in the Spirit is always incomplete, short of the eschaton. Faith is not captured in a creed, but witnessed in a Spirit who seals us in the heart (to paraphrase Calvin and some of the early Reformed confessions). Faith is continually re-awakened and re-made by the One who is faith's author. The Reformed inability to compose a "final" creed bears strong resonance with its understanding of Holy Spirit who nudges, ignites, and sustains the heart of faith. And yet the Reformed churches continually are at work composing, revising, and revisiting statements of faith in light to the Spirit who gives life. A confession, thus conceived, is a fragment of the church's response to the work of the Spirit, an ever-partial attempt to speak to that life.

---

27. Culp, "Always Reforming," 158.

This means that the church's confessions will always be diverse. The Spirit of the living God is let loose in creation, sustaining and giving life to all. On the one hand this means that the Reformed tradition is somewhat "unbounded." Neither the church's confession of faith, nor its attribution of the work of the Spirit can be restricted to codified statements. The confessions of the Reformed churches take on distinctive hues in different context. It is well-nigh impossible to harmonize the great diversity of Reformed confessions: Westminster, Barmen, Accra, Belhar. Each age, each context, addresses questions of faith anew. Each generation, in constructing statements of faith, asks in what ways it is being reformed by the Word of God. Each reciter of statements of faith voices the hope that the Spirit is moving through, addressing, and giving life to each context in which the faith is confessed. If Reformed history is any indication, this work will go on, and will elicit not one, but many, statements of faith.

If Reformed Christianity has emphasized the "unbounded" nature of the Spirit let loose in creation, it has also carefully delineated some bounds to discerning the Spirit's work. At the very beginning of the Reformed "movement" writers of confessions recognized that not every spirit let loose in the world is the Spirit of God. Suspicion of enthusiasts, wariness over confusing Holy Spirit with spirits of power, ambition, and chaos, permeate much of these early writings. Many subsequent Reformed confessions (with Barmen and Accra as prominent examples) can be read as guides to *discerning* the Spirit. For this reason, there is also a "bounded" nature of the church's confession, paralleling its attempts to trace some contours to the work of the Spirit in Christian life. In much of Reformed history, discernment of the Spirit is connected to Scripture and the sacraments. To discern Spirit at work in the world, the church looks to the Bible and sacraments. Does the claim of Spirit's work accord with the broad witness of Scripture and the gift of life offered in bath and table? Despite its manifold diversity in confessing the faith, Reformed Christianity has almost always outlined things that are to be *rejected* in confessing the faith. Indeed, many confessions are as notable for what they say "no" to (again, Barmen is illustrative), as for what they say "yes" to. Reformed Christianity has routinely been careful in marking the work of the Spirit. Sometimes this has meant it has moved rather slowly in recognizing Spirit at work in the world. But in its often plodding manner, the tradition has stressed the need to discern the spirits, and mark out the bounds of a faith that responds to a Spirit let loose in the world. In the end, one legitimate test of any confession is whether it gives life, or whether it inhibits life in its fullness.

Conclusion

Describing Reformed theology is a difficult task. How does one trace the contours of an exceedingly diverse (and rather prolific) tradition? Attempts at characterizing the tradition will doubtless continue. Such attempts seem to fall short, however, if they focus on a set of "essential" Reformed tenets that ultimately separate Reformed Christians from the wider church. It is more appropriate to try to establish broad patterns and habits in the Reformed ethos across time, recognizing that any enumeration of these patterns and habits will invariably be partial and incomplete. One way of giving shape to these varied patterns and habits is to consider Reformed Christianity a tradition of the Spirit. In a surprising way, what is in some ways an "underdeveloped" Reformed theme, might express some of the bounded-unbounded diversity of the tradition itself. This is obviously not the only way to characterize Reformed theology, but it is one that can give significant impetus to the ongoing task of confessing the faith in each generation, in each context. As Reformed Christians face the future, it might be worth revisiting and revising its confession of the Spirit as giver of life.

Bibliography

Barth, Karl. *The Theology of Schleiermacher.* Edited by Dietrich Ritschl and translated by Geoffrey W. Bromiley. Edinburgh: T. & T. Clark, 1982.

Bullinger, Heinrich. Cited in Small, Joseph D., ed. *Conversations with the Confessions: Dialogue in the Reformed Tradition.* Louisville: Geneva, 2005.

Calvin, John. "Commentary on Exodus 22." In *Commentaries on the Four Last Books of Moses*, Vol. 3, 126–33. Grand Rapids: Eerdmans, 1950.

———. *Institutes of the Christian Religion.* Edited by John T. McNeill. Philadelphia: Westminster, 1960.

———. "Letter on Usury." In *A Reformation Reader: Primary Texts with Introductions*, edited by Denis R. Janz, 219–22. Minneapolis: Fortress, 1999.

Culp, Kristine. "Always Reforming, Always Resisting." In *Feminist and Womanist Essays in Reformed Dogmatics*, edited by Amy Plantinga Pauw and Serene Jones, 158. Louisville: Westminster John Knox, 2006.

Elwood, Christopher. *Calvin for Armchair Theologians.* Louisville: Westminster John Knox, 2002.

Ernst, Margit. "We Believe the One Holy and Catholic Church . . . : Reformed Identity and the Unity of the Church." In *Reformed Theology: Identity and Ecumenicity*, edited by Wallace M. Alston Jr. and Michael Welker, 85–96. Grand Rapids: Eerdmans, 2003.

Gerrish, B. A. "Introduction: Doing Theology in the Reformed Tradition." In *Reformed Theology for the Third Christian Millennium: The 2001 Sprunt Lectures*, edited by B. A. Gerrish, 1–11. Louisville: Westminster John Knox, 2003.

Klooster, Fred H. "The Uniqueness of Reformed Theology: A Preliminary Attempt at Description." *Calvin Theological Journal* 14 (1979) 32–54.

Leith, John H. "The Ethos of the Reformed Tradition." In *Major Themes in the Reformed Tradition*, edited by Donald K. McKim, 5–18. Grand Rapids: Eerdmans, 1992.

Moltmann, Jürgen. *The Spirit of Life: A Universal Affirmation.* Translated by Margaret Kohl. Minneapolis: Fortress, 1992.

Mount, C. Eric. *Covenant, Community and the Common Good.* Cleveland: Pilgrim, 1999.

Presbyterian Church (U.S.A.). "The Larger Catechism of the Westminster Confession of Faith." In *The Constitution of the Presbyterian Church (U.S.A.) Part I: Book of Confessions.* Louisville: Presbyterian Church (U.S.A.), 1996.

Rohls, Jan. "Reformed Theology—Past and Future." In *Reformed Theology: Identity and Ecumenicity*, edited by Wallace M. Alston, Jr. and Michael Welker, 34–45. Grand Rapids: Eerdmans, 2003.

Rogers, Jack. *Presbyterian Creeds: A Guide to the Book of Confessions.* Louisville: Westminster John Knox, 1991.

Smit, Dirkie. "Trends and Directions in Reformed Theology." *Expository Times* 122 (2011) 313–26.

Warfield, B. B. *Calvin and Augustine.* Philadelphia: Presbyterian & Reformed, 1956.

Yoder, John Howard. *The Priestly Kingdom: Social Ethics as Gospel.* Notre Dame, IN: University of Notre Dame Press, 1984.

Zorgdrager, Heleen. "In Search of a Shared Theology: Reformed Theology between the Contextual and the Universal." *Reformed World* 61 (2011) 159–70.

2

Reformed Identity and Relevance in Zambian Context

Motifs, Challenges and Prospects

LAMECK BANDA

Introduction

"WHO AM I?" AND "Why do I exist?" Geographically, one would identify me as an African who resides in Zambia, one of the countries in the Southern-Central region of Africa. Socially and religiously, I may as well be recognized as a Christian who is a member of the Reformed family of Christian churches. I am further identified among the many companions who devote their lives to a serious reflection, articulation and contextualization of the Reformed faith[1] in their local settings. In a nutshell, I am identified as a Reformed Christian theologian who tries to make a contribution to the vast body of scholarly wisdom. In other words, I endeavor to live a faith "always being reformed" in a contemporary globalized and challenging world.

Therefore, one would presume that the questions "Who am I?" and "Why do I exist?" seek to highlight issues of identity and relevance of one's particular state of existence in a particular context. I suppose we hold the

---

1. In this article I use "Reformed faith" interchangeably with terms such as "Reformed identity," "Reformed tradition" or "Reformed theology." By this I refer to a theological tradition that emerged from the 16th century Reformation, particularly the theologies of Martin Luther (1483–1546), Huldrych Zwingli (1484–1531), Heinrich Bullinger (1504–1575) and John Calvin (1509–1564). "The main emphases of Reformed theology include the Scriptures as authority, Christ as the sole agent of salvation, and faith as the means of justification." McKim, *Westminster Dictionary*, 234.

same intent when we reflect on the theme, "*Always Being Reformed: Challenges, Issues and Prospects for Reformed Theologies Today*." On the one hand, as Reformed theologians we have the mandate to always retain our Reformed identity in our reflection and articulation of the Reformed faith. On the other hand, we are to let our faith be relevant to both the global context and our specific local contexts despite the alarming and overwhelming challenges that continue to arise. This thrust of reformed identity and relevance is summarized in the words of Shirley C. Guthrie:

> The Reformed confessional tradition points the way toward the discovery of an understanding of Christian faith and life that is (1) authentically and unreservedly Christian and *just for that reason* open to pluralistic conversation and community; and (2) truly relevant *just because* it openly and unapologetically seeks to make a distinctively biblical-Christian contribution to the quest for unity in diversity in our pluralistic church and society.[2]

Reformed faith seeks to both preserve the identity of authentic Christian faith and life and remain relevant in a pluralistic contemporary context. Reformed faith preserves its identity by adhering to and asserting specific fundamental tenets that include: the five historical "*solas*": *sola gratia, solus Christus, sola fide, sola Scriptura,* and *soli Deo gloria* with regards to salvation;[3] the *authority of scripture*; the *sovereignty of God*; the *Lordship of Jesus Christ*; the *sanctifying work of the Holy Spirit*; *justification by faith*;[4] priesthood of all believers; fellowship of the church; and stewardship. As Migliore contends, theological reflection and articulation is a "continuous [and strenuous] process of inquiry."[5] This entails that Reformed theological reflection preserves authentic Christian identity by continuously searching for the fullness of the truth of God made known in Jesus Christ on one hand. It is thus a continuous process of seeking, contending and wrestling for the truth as Jacob did all night long at Peniel as we read in Gen 32:22–32. Reformed theological reflection, on the other hand, is about being relevant in a specific setting by seeking to address the real issues that affect the church in particular and society as a whole. It never ceases to address challenges that press upon our faith and life, and those of our society. Through the enabling grace of God, it continuously searches for answers to the questions that arise from present-day contexts.

2. Guthrie, *Always Being Reformed*, 15.
3. Reeves, *Unquenchable Flame*, 106.
4. Hoekema, *Saved by Grace*, 172.
5. Migliore, *Faith Seeking Understanding*, 8.

The thesis of this chapter is concerned with what "always being reformed" means in a contemporary globalizing and challenging Zambian context. This piece of writing, therefore, aims at addressing the question of how adherents of the Reformed faith can always bridge the gap between self-identity and relevance in the Zambian context. In discussing the topic, the chapter underscores outstanding Reformed affirmations in relation to contextual issues that are cardinal in the Zambian context. The essay further draws attention to specific and prominent challenges that keep questioning the Reformed faith in Zambia. This treatise ends by assuring that Reformed faith can still be relevant to the Zambian context regardless of the alarming and overwhelming challenges.

Reformed Affirmations and Zambian Context

What do Reformed tenets imply in the Zambian context? In order to respond to the question at hand, there is need to delineate prominent affirmations in relation to the Zambian context.

To adhere to the authority of scripture is to affirm that *the Bible is the foundation for sufficient knowledge about God.* The Bible contains God's written Word which brings human beings into awareness of God, and God's salvation for humankind.[6] Burgess informs us that the "Holy Scriptures contain all that is necessary for our knowledge of God's holy and sovereign will, Jesus Christ the only Redeemer, our salvation, and our growth in grace."[7] The Bible is the yardstick for human discovery of God's Will which was revealed in the person and salvific work of Jesus Christ through the Holy Spirit. This will makes believers grow in faith, life and practice. This affirmation has implications for the Zambian context. There is a tendency in Zambia of falling into the trap of either neglecting the authority of scripture altogether and seeking other sources for help in times of need, or distorting a text from the Scriptures in order to suit personal desires and interests. For instance, one chooses to rely more on some prophecy from an 'anointed wo/man of God' than the voice of God as revealed in Scripture. Others use the Bible to justify exploitation and violence against weaker sexual partners on the basis of gender or class.[8] To the contrary, adhering to the authority of Scripture in Zambia implies paying attention to the voice of God and faithful interpretation of Scripture for total life-transformation.

---

6. Uprichard gives three important features of the Bible as: inspired, accurate and sufficient, 175–82.

7. Burgess, *Framework of Our Faith*, 66.

8. Gillham, "Combating Gender-Based Violence," 95.

To attach with great humility to the sovereignty of God is to affirm *God's freedom and power to love, redeem and share life with hostile, sinful and vulnerable humanity.* In God's freedom, God does not require any form of counsel to exist and act (Isa 40:25). This shows God's *aseity*: God's otherness and entire self-existence are not dependent upon anything else.[9] Thus, God exists and acts in freedom. However, God is free to exist and act in a way that is for the other: Freedom to love, redeem and share life with hostile, sinful and vulnerable humanity. In God's power, God demonstrates God's might and ability to perform for the well-being of human beings and non-human creatures. Nothing that exists in the universe has the ability to thwart God's plan and purposes. Hence, despite human hostility and sinfulness in Zambia, God stoops down to love and share life with sinful and vulnerable Zambians. Zambia as a nation is generally known to be historically peaceful. As Zambians we not only preach about this peace, but we also thank God for being gracious to us that since our independence in 1964 we continue to enjoy this amount of peace despite having more than seventy-three tribes who speak different languages altogether. This is amazing and takes the grace of God! However, at times we tend to be hostile to one another and take peace for granted. For example, recently we have experienced some forms of political violence, which are actually a source of concern. In such a situation Zambians need to exercise their freedom and power to uphold peace and unity through care, love and solidarity for mutual relationship and interdependence.

To adore the Lordship of Jesus Christ is to affirm *God's ability to liberate people from forces of evil, and the need for our total submission.* Jesus' incarnation was the act of God to identify Godself with the human race in the person of Jesus Christ. Equally, through the atoning work of Jesus Christ, God demonstrated God's way to liberate people from all that oppress them. Thus, in the incarnation God entered into solidarity with humankind with the sole purpose of liberating the human race from bondage through the atoning work of Jesus Christ. Burgess stresses this point by focusing on the significance of Jesus' two natures, divinity and humanity:

> If He was not divine, then His life, death, and resurrection did not complete God's saving action in the world. If He was not human and did not go through the same temptations and struggles we face, then His saving action would not be where the problem is, within the realm of our human affairs, and we have no ground for any relationship with Him.[10]

---

9. McKim, *Westminster Dictionary*, 115.
10. Burgess, *Framework of our Faith*, 29.

REFORMED IDENTITY AND RELEVANCE IN ZAMBIAN CONTEXT

In a Zambian context, certain people tend to be overwhelmed by threats from spiritual forces. There is fear of witchcraft,[11] especially in rural Zambia, where it is believed that one with magical powers and charms can take other people's lives or property. This scenario compels many people to seek protection from witchdoctors and herbalists. In the recent past, fear of Satanism[12] has taken a central stage. Many people are terrified to hear of certain people who are directly used by the devil to cause carnages on many Zambian roads and all sorts of misfortunes in families and society at large. This is one among many reasons why a number of people are seeking anointing oil from 'anointed men and women of God' to anoint their personal properties and themselves as a form of protection. The message in all these forms of worship and fear is that the Lordship of Jesus Christ assures us God's protection regardless of the seemingly powerful forces of evil. The affirmation of Jesus' Lordship provides hope of victory over powers of darkness because the incarnate Christ conquered these powers, sin and death through his sacrificial death on the cross and resurrection from the grave. Hence, believers in Zambia need not to fear forces of darkness, but render total submission to Christ in all situations that seem to threaten their lives.

To uplift the sanctifying work of the Holy Spirit is to affirm *God's ability to effect renewal and growth in individual believers*. As Burgess rightly puts it, the Holy Spirit is not an impersonal force as some people and churches perceive; God the Holy Spirit is the working agent of God the Father and God the Son in individuals, community and the world. In other words, the Holy Spirit is the Spirit of the triune God who participates in God's being as an act of mutual sharing of life and love among members of the Godhead.[13] Migliore affirms that the Holy Spirit is "the uniting love of the Trinity, the power of community in diversity, of mutual love and friendship."[14] God the Holy Spirit is at work to recreate life by effecting renewal and growth for mutual relationship with God and fellowship with fellow believers and service in the church and the world. A close look at the Zambian context reveals certain manipulations of the identity and work of the Holy Spirit. In

---

11. "Witchcraft" is the practice of using human powers in concert with demonic forces which is condemned in Exod 22:18; Deut 18:9–14; and Gal 5:19–20 as contrary to the worship of the true God. See McKim, *Westminster Dictionary*, 304. In my mother-language (Chewa), witchcraft is *Ufiti*, which can mean sorcery, the practice of witchcraft itself, or casting a spell on others like a computer virus. See Paas, *Dictionary*, 339.

12. McKim, *Westminster Dictionary*, 248, defines "*Satanism*" simply as the practice of worshiping Satan. My Chewa renderings of the term "Satanism" are *kupembedza ziwanda* (worshiping demons) or *mpingo wa satanic* (Satanist church). See Paas, *Dictionary*, 653.

13. Burgess, *Framework of Our Faith*, 47.

14. Migliore, *Faith Seeking Understanding*, 169.

certain circles of the Zambian context, the Holy Spirit is viewed merely as "a power" which one can use whenever in need of it or threatened by danger of some sort. In fact, in some cases you find people bestowing the Holy Spirit to others just as one is distributing candies or peanuts from one's pocket. This leads to a judgmental attitude where some individual Christians would perceive themselves as more filled with Holy Spirit than others. Such manipulations may not exist when true identity and work of the Holy Spirit is upheld. Hence, there is need for renewal and growth to take place because such manipulations are actually an indication of immaturity. Where there is maturity, mutual life flourishes and genuine love blossoms.

To declare the doctrine of justification by faith is to affirm *God's grace in Jesus Christ as the sole basis of salvation.* The emphasis here is that salvation does not come to us through human merit. Salvation is by God's gracious initiative through faith in that God declares us righteous on the sole basis of the righteousness of Jesus Christ as attested in Rom 1:17, 3:28, 5:1, and Gal 3:1–25.[15] An answer to question 33 in the Shorter Catechism further provides us with a clear thrust of justification:

> Justification is an act of God's free grace, wherein he pardoneth all our sins, and accepteth us as righteous in his sight, only for the righteousness of Christ imputed to us, and received by faith alone.[16]

Justification is the action undertaken by God as the supreme Judge who acquits us of our sins on the basis of Christ's righteousness. We reciprocate to this action by God in faith whereby we obediently accept it to be true and we commit ourselves to follow Christ. In Zambian reformed churches, there is now an emerging tendency of indirectly perceiving salvation as a human activity. You hear sentiments from church members like "I go to church so that I can be saved," "I give money in order that God can save me," "Let us serve in our committees so that we may enter heaven," "I sing for Jesus so that I can enter heaven," and so on. To some extent, these sentiments show levels of knowledge about how salvation is bestowed. In the end, this perception is taken as a norm and hence the truth about salvation as attested in scripture is overshadowed. Whatever the case may be, salvation still remains a divine gracious initiative and human beings receive it through faith. This calls for teaching of members in the church by ministers and theologians.

To echo ethical Christian living through priesthood of all believers, fellowship of the church and stewardship is to affirm *God's call for*

---

15. McKim, *Westminster Dictionary*, 152.
16. Presbyterian Church (U.S.A.), *Constitution*, 178.

participation in God's ministry, unity in the community of faith and Christian responsibility towards God's creation. God saves individuals for service in the church and world. Therefore, every believer has a duty to participate in God's ministry of preaching God's word, of interceding for others and of service through various offices. The church being the body of Christ under the headship of Jesus Christ, every believer should promote unity as modeled by the triune God (Eph 4:1–6). Furthermore, believers need to be responsible for God's creation through faithful stewardship that shuns extravagance and devastation, but seeks proper and responsible use of the gifts of God's creation. Reformed churches in Zambia believe they are part of the larger body of Christ, and that each member in these churches plays an active role in enhancing unity of purpose. This is clearly noticed in occasions where the Reformed churches unite with other mother bodies[17] for prayer in a situation of need, such as the tripartite elections[18] and the country's jubilee celebration.[19] They also come together to discuss burning and cross-cutting issues in the country like gender-based violence and national socio-economic policies. The challenge for Reformed churches in Zambia is how to deal with environmental issues like waste management, littering in many suburbs and charcoal burning in rural areas. It is a challenge because one wonders how the Reformed churches can on the one hand affirm their responsibility towards God's creation, and then fail to live that affirmation on the other hand. In a nutshell, this state of affairs still leaves a huge challenge over how adherents of the Reformed faith in Zambia can truly live in obedience to God's Word by working for the transformation of society through seeking justice for God's creation.

This brings us to the discussion on the specific challenges in Zambia that pose a threat to the Reformed faith. The real concern is on the survival of Reformed identity and its relevance in such an environment of pressing multi-faceted challenges.

---

17. By "mother bodies" I refer to Evangelical Fellowship of Zambia (comprising of churches mainly from the Pentecostal and charismatic tradition), Zambia Episcope Conference (comprising of churches mainly from the Catholic tradition), and Council of Churches in Zambia (embracing churches mainly from the Reformed and Presbyterian tradition).

18. Every five years Zambia holds tripartite elections which include Presidential (choosing a Republican Head of State), Parliamentary (choosing of Members of Parliament) and Local government (Choosing of Councilors as civic leaders) elections.

19. Zambia celebrated her fiftieth anniversary on October 24, 2014, under the theme, "Commemorating God's favour of fifty years of independence for continued peace, unity, democracy, patriotism and prosperity." Sadly, three days later the country lost the Republican President, Mr. Michael Chilufya Sata, who died in London after a long illness.

Pressing Challenges on the Reformed Faith in Zambia

Reformed faith in Zambia has of late been rocked with a number of pressing challenges. These challenges pose the question of identity of the Reformed faith and whether this is of any relevance on the Zambian scene. We therefore briefly discuss the challenges that pose a threat to the Reformed faith in Zambia.

The first challenge that poses a threat to the Reformed faith in Zambia is what I would call a *porous religious plurality*. The influx of many churches in Zambia, especially those with Pentecostal influence, was at its peak mainly during the transition from a one party state to multi-party politics. This religious plurality became prominent when the first Republican President, Dr. Kenneth David Kaunda's regime was removed from power through a ballot in 1991 and the subsequent declaration of Zambia as a Christian nation by Kaunda's successor, President Fredrick Titus Jacob Chiluba, the following year. It is interesting to note that most of the mainline churches like Reformed Church in Zambia, to which the author belongs, opposed sharply the declaration citing lack of wider consultation as one among the many reasons. The President actually leaned much on the Pentecostals in his consultation and hence received overwhelming support from Pentecostal and Charismatic traditions. The result of the declaration was the proliferation of tele-evangelists (e.g. Ernest Angley) who conducted a number of crusades and revival meetings.[20] These crusades were mostly organized by local Pentecostal pastors under the influence of the President. Since the time of the declaration of Zambia as a Christian nation, and subsequent inclusion of the declaration in the preamble of the republican draft constitution, many churches and religious groupings with divergent doctrines have mushroomed. Coupled with the weak regulatory framework on faith-based organizations in the nation, this plurality poses a great challenge to Reformed faith. The identity of the Reformed faith is slowly being questioned and in the end it is gradually being rendered irrelevant. One notable example is the author's experience in class[21] where a few students show levels of resentment of some doctrines simply because of their exposure to non-reformed teachings which may not be in conformity with the Reformed faith.

Related to porous religious plurality is the *escalation of prosperity gospel* as an overwhelming challenge to the Reformed faith. I have given a lengthy account of the genesis, growth and teaching of the prosperity

---

20. Gifford, *African Christianity*, 202–203.

21. The author is a lecturer in systematic theology at Justo Mwale University in Lusaka, Zambia.

gospel movement in an earlier article.[22] It was during the Post-war healing revivals that prosperity theology first came to prominence, and its teaching later became prominent in the so called "Word of Faith" movement and in the tele-evangelism of the 1980s. Later, in the 1990s and 2000s, it was adopted by influential leaders in the Charismatic movements and promoted by Christian missionaries throughout the world, leading to the establishment of mega-churches. Preachers of the prosperity gospel have influenced multitudes that are desperate to hear a promising message. The movement has commanded worldwide numerical growth partially due to the massive amounts of money the leaders are able to extract from the faithful. The influx of cash is visibly noticed in huge buildings, extensive ministries, and wide exposure on television. One interesting factor about the growth of this movement is that it is mainly significant among the poor and middle class of the "Third World," and also outside the mainstream churches. This is also why prosperity gospel is spreading rapidly across sub-Saharan African countries like Zambia. The basic teaching of this movement is that God desires Christians to be prosperous financially, physically, spiritually, and in all aspects of life. In order to obtain prosperity in health and wealth, faith is paramount. If God used the word to bring everything into existence, believers, too, have the potential, through faith, to bring good health and wealth into reality. To be sick and in debt only shows a lack of faith. Impoverished countries like Zambia often find this doctrine more appealing than that of the mainline churches. This leads to many believers practicing dual membership. For instance, on a Sunday one would attend a church service in the morning at a Reformed church and another in the afternoon at a church where s/he hears appealing messages and experiences the performance of miracles and/or deliverance. This scenario has made Reformed pastors respond by incorporating traits from prosperity gospel teachings in an attempt to stay relevant.

The third notable challenge on Reformed faith has to do with *environmental issues* such as piling of waste and breakage of sewer systems in cities, and charcoal burning in rural communities. Waste management has been a challenge whereby piles of garbage remain uncollected in most parts of urban Zambia. Coupled with waste management is the challenge of continuous breakages of sewer systems which not only cause environmental degradation, but also are health hazards. A very serious environmental problem in rural Zambia is charcoal burning. In fact, Zambia has been identified as one of the top countries in the world with the highest deforestation rates. Research indicates that Zambia, which has approximately fifty

22. Banda, "Dialoguing at 'Mphala,'" 67–70.

million hectares of forest, was losing huge hectares of forest reserve in a year mainly due to the practice of charcoal burning. It was recorded in one of Zambia's local newspapers where the United States Agency for International Development (USAID) urged Zambia to control deforestation. Dr. Anna Toness, the economic growth team leader at USAID showed worry over the rate at which Zambia was losing its forest. He indicated that the country is estimated to be losing at least three hundred thousand hectares of forest each year. For this reason, "Zambia risks depleting its forest cover in fifteen years if the current rate of deforestation is not controlled."[23] Deforestation has affected production of mushrooms, caterpillars and other wild fruits for human beings and animals. Furthermore, it has also affected trees that support rural communities through wood, food, fuel, feed, fiber or organic fertilizers, which are vital for the ecosystem of any given area. Although charcoal trading is a lucrative business and charcoal is one of the most accessible and affordable energy sources for the eighty percent of Zambia's households who have no access to electricity, charcoal burning has had adverse effects on Zambia's forests. Reformed theology, though keen on articulating the doctrine of creation, appears to be silent in addressing crucial concerns of environmental crises. Hence, the lingering question remains as to how the identity of Reformed faith can be relevant in the Zambian context where the environment and forest are at stake.

African Traditional Religion, particularly the influence of herbalists and witch-finders is another challenge to Reformed faith.[24] The belief in superstition and practice of witchcraft is deeply rooted in Zambian context, typical in most African societies. According to Bosch, in traditional African society evil and suffering are generally authored by a witch.[25] However, witches are not the only source and agents of diseases, evil and suffering. These vices also come from a category of malevolent ancestral spirits, people who died in wickedness and with a curse, and now they take that evil to those that are living. To remove the bad omen (and suffering) which is believed to have come from ancestral spirits, a religious ritual is performed whereby a sacrifice is offered in order to let the spirit rest in peace (what is known as "*kugoneka mzimu*" in my language). If it is suspected that diseases, evil and suffering are a result of witchcraft, an exercise of witch-hunting is undertaken. This exercise is performed by the witch-finder/hunter or

---

23. *The Post*, 8.

24. This challenge to the Reformed faith is mostly an extract from my PhD dissertation.

25. Bosch, *Problem of Evil in Africa*, 41.

kamcape.²⁶ Stewart and Strathern narrate that when a witch-finder comes to the village, s/he has all the men and women lined up before a headman, as for an inspection.²⁷ All the people are told to pass by the witch-finder, who catches their image ("spirit") in a small mirror and is said to be able to tell at once whether they are guilty of witchcraft. Those selected are told to yield up their "horns and medicine," and these are then collected at a cross-road outside the village for everyone to inspect. Each person is told to drink the *mucape* liquid (cleansing medicine), and they are then declared free from witchcraft. Anyone who drinks the medicine but afterwards returns to the ways of witchcraft dies a grisly death. The witch-finders also sell minor protective charms and medicine sewn in small cloth bags. The whole idea of these practices is to get rid of the suffering and pain which is brought about by witchcraft practices.²⁸ Currently, if you stroll in streets of most Zambian cities you will notice many herbalists selling their roots-medicine in small makeshift stores. Advertisements by herbalists in both electronic and print media go out in great numbers each day. They advertise their medicines for various purposes such as protection, healing, sexual enhancement and male organ enlargement, richness, etc. Since herbalists give impressions of the ability to solve all human problems, their ads are enticing to many people (Reformed believers included) who flock to them for aid of some sort. This is a challenge to Reformed faith in that God's sovereignty and ability to deal with human problems is undermined. Jesus' salvific power through death and resurrection is as well rendered irrelevant.

Related to the challenge of African Traditional Religion, is the *alarming threat from "Satanism."* Many people in urban Zambia associate any misfortune with the activities of Satanists. It is believed that Satanism is a powerful and evil religious organization or movement under the influence and control of Satan, whose members masquerade as 'demons' in order to control and inflict pain on and kill many people. Kroesbergen-Kamps states that Satanism became a popular description for a variety of occult practices in Zambia since the 1990s.²⁹ She further notes that the concept of "Satanism" in Zambia is clearly connected to older discourses on witchcraft. However, Satanism is believed to be more advanced than witchcraft. Although there are many testimonies that come from ex-Satanists who are now converted to Christianity, contrasting views grip many people in Zambia. On the one

26. *Kamcape* simply means the performer of cleansing of the evil practice; in this case, witchcraft.

27. Stewart & Strathern, *Witchcraft*, 61.

28. More details on witch-finding and punishment are discussed by Van Breugel, *Chewa Traditional Religion*, 218–24.

29. Kroesbergen-Kamps, "Dreams and Nightmares of Modernity," 105.

hand, those who hold a naturalistic and secularized worldview are unwilling to admit the existence of Satanism and relegate all talk of this concept to a category of mere superstition. They categorically declare that there is no clear evidence that this religious movement is actually active in Zambia.[30] On the other hand, those who hold a mystic and spiritualized worldview admit the existence of Satanism and take seriously the intense satanic involvement in human society.[31] They equally declare that Satanism is very real in that people are inflicted with pain and killed, and their property destroyed at the hand of Satanists. Whatever view one upholds with regards to Satanism, it would be naiveté and a portrayal of blindness to completely discard the alarming threat that emanates from stories of Satanism. Beliefs about Satanism are a threat to Reformed faith in that apart from the fear that it generates in people's minds, affirmation of God's sovereignty is at stake because God's power and ability to overcome all forms of evil is doubted. This becomes an overwhelming challenge in that Reformed relevance in such a mystical society is queried.

Zambia is rocked by a *tension between technological advancement and various forms of suffering* as another challenge to Reformed faith. The country, as the entire African continent, appears with two contrasting faces: a brighter and more promising face on the one hand, and a gloomier and more hopeless face on the other. Describing this scenario from the African Christological perspective Mwaura testifies:

> On the one hand, (Zambia) depicts a picture of faith, hope and dignity in the crucified Christ; on the other, one of despair, suffering, hopelessness and death. (Zambian) Christians as cross bearers live in their faith, believing that Christ is reflected in them in every aspect of their being, and as they face their daily struggles in an oppressive environment which they sometimes do not comprehend.[32]

It is because of this dual-faceted appearance in their existence that Zambians define their situation as that of suffering. This is an ambiguity which to some extent is characterized by elements of globalization.[33] Globalization is a dynamic and an ever-progressing phenomenon. Therefore, one would define globalization simply as what was particular is becoming universal, and what existed only locally and regionally is being presented

---

30. Ibid., 105.
31. Grudem, *Systematic Theology*, 420.
32. Mwaura, "Reflecting Christ Crucified," 97.
33. My article in *Insights*, 24–29, explains the dual-faced ambiguity of globalization in relation to African contextual theology.

globally.[34] Spinder makes it precise by stating that "one of the consequences of globalization is that time and space are as it were compressed: the world has become smaller and it is possible to engage in activities which can be followed somewhere else in the world, regardless of the distance from these activities."[35] It strengthens the tendency to conform and become uniform, to set aside local and regional perspectives under the influence of global political and economic order. Globalization appears to be dual-faced in Zambia. On the one hand, globalization promises positive strides which are full of progress and development. Global technological boom in forms of over-flourishing of communication gadgets like cell phones, computers, touch pads, internet, facebook, twitter and improved media; free market economy; Zambian democratic plural society; promotion of human rights; huge investments especially from Chinese multi-national companies; and many more advancements. This chapter, for instance, has enjoyed the benefits of globalization in that sending it to the editor and publishers has been made easier through a shortest possible time. In short, globalization has realized an advanced quality of life to a great extent. On the other hand, globalization depicts a gloomy face with overwhelming challenges such as overshadowing of the poor, marginalized and voiceless especially in the underprivileged communities of Zambia, suppression of local cultural identities leading to identity crises, an ever-widening gap between the rich and poor, and a growing generation gap. Others are urbanization and overpopulation which lead to vices such as crime, prostitution, and spread of HIV and AIDS epidemic, increased number of street kids, high unemployment levels and abject poverty. In short, globalization portrays this ambiguity which in itself intensifies suffering among Zambian people.

Analyzing the Zambian context of suffering, one may agree with the Peruvian theologian, Gustavo Gutiérrez, who describes suffering of the poor in terms of hunger and exploitation; insufficient health care; lack of proper and decent housing; lack of proper formal education; unemployment and minimum wage systems.[36] Suffering in this case is experienced by the poor who are vulnerable due to lack of basic essentials for human survival. In other terms, suffering is as a result of a multidimensional poverty: historical, socio-economic, dialectical, theological, and political realities.[37] Moltmann refers to the multifaceted nature of suffering as the

---

34. Here, I am indebted to Moltmann's viewpoint on globalization, "Destruction and Healing of the Earth," 189.

35. Spinder, *Faith and Reflection*, 14.

36. Gutierrez, *Truth Shall Make You Free*, 10.

37. Sobrino, *Spirituality of Liberation*, 159–60.

vicious circles of death, which is a reality in the Zambian society.[38] Suffering in Zambia is multifaceted and can be summarized by the devastating effects of political and socio-economic vices such as hunger, unclean and/or insufficient water, unemployment, poverty, diseases like HIV/AIDS with poor health care, malnutrition, insufficient medicine and health care units, unsatisfactory living conditions, the large numbers of orphans, widows and street children, high levels of illiteracy, low wages and deplorable working conditions, decreasing education standards, and an influx of refugees from war-torn countries which poses security concerns for the nation. Whatever the causes ascribed to suffering in Zambia, one thing for sure is that such a state of affairs remains a challenge to the identity of the Reformed faith. Reformed faith is expected to be relevant by way of tackling the issues that affect ordinary people on the ground. It needs to attend to people's needs so as to alleviate suffering among the Zambian populace other than casting theories in abstraction.

Despite the gloomy picture depicted by the magnitude challenges underscored above, Reformed faith faces exciting prospects in Zambia. Thus, the next section describes an expected role of Reformed faith to attain a brighter future, thereby becoming more relevant to the Zambian context.

Prospects of the Reformed Faith in Zambia

"Always being reformed" entails preserving the tenets of the Reformed faith in an ever-changing contemporary environment. It equally involves the longing to be of relevance in this milieu without losing our identity as Reformed believers. The Reformed tradition in the challenging Zambian context needs to maintain its identity and at the same time be relevant to that context. The future of the Reformed faith in Zambia, and indeed in the world at large, lies on how it influences its immediately changing environment while retaining its own identity.

To begin with, Reformed *stance on biblical truth* is a strong point for Reformed faith to make an impact in Zambia. As Rice confirms, "Scripture has always been central in the lives of Reformed Christians. They have rightly been called a people of the Book."[39] In other words, Reformed faith is uniquely identified as a tradition that constantly seeks to give a right and holistic interpretation of Scripture. In fact, in the many Reformed churches in Zambia, Scripture is so central that in almost all church occasions sharing from the Bible precedes all other activities. Scriptural truth in proclama-

---

38. Moltmann, *Crucified God*, 329–33.
39. Rice, *Reformed Spirituality*, 95.

tion and practice of the church is paramount in a changing and challenging Zambian context. This stance on biblical truth gives the Reformed faith an opportunity to be a true witness in an environment where many conflicting doctrines are emerging. Despite so many misleading teachings that Zambian citizens hear during various worship services, in media and religious conferences, there is still the burning desire for the truth. To illustrate the point, one of my colleagues and I were approached by some youths in a local congregation of the Reformed Church in Zambia with a request that we arrange for some teachings on the history and doctrines of the church. According to them, they had realized that they heard enough of strange teachings from different wo/men of God. Some of these teachings were so misleading that a number of youths had been swayed. This of course was an opportunity for my colleague and I to present the truth as attested in Scripture. From the request by the youths one can clearly see that Reformed teaching still remains an avenue for that yearning for the truth. In this case then, there is need for Reformed faith not to sway from its stance on biblical truth, but make itself relevant by filling the vacuum with the truth that people so desperately desire.

The second prospect is Reformed advocacy for a *concrete and holistic conceptualization of God*. Instead of presenting an unbalanced conceptualization of God which put God as transcendent on one extreme end and God as immanent on the other, Reformed faith gives a balanced projection of God. In fact, the emphasis is on the trinitarian projection of God. According to Moltmann God as triune "is not a solitary, unloved ruler in heaven who subjugates everything as earthly deposits do. This is a God in community, rich in relationships. After all, 'God is love.'"[40] God as triune seeks to establish a communal relationship with all creatures where harmony, care, love, solidarity and respect for one another are the driving virtues in that community. In the triune life mutual indwelling (or *perichoresis*) is the innermost mystery and the secret of the divine loving community. In other words, as Migliore asserts, "trinitarian theology holds together the affirmations of the transcendence of God over the creation and the immanence of God in creation."[41] The concrete and holistic conceptualization of God in the Reformed faith is a trinitarian view of God. On the one hand God's being is conceptualized as transcendent, while God is equally understood as immanent on the other. Therefore, this entails a balanced conceptualization of God which is essential in addressing challenges characterized by the Zambian context. Once Reformed faith unashamedly gives such a concrete

---

40. Moltmann, *Destruction and Healing of the Earth*, 175.
41. Migliore, *Faith Seeking Understanding*, 108.

and holistic projection of God from a trinitarian perspective in the Zambian context, people develop confidence in the sovereign and immanent God. They rekindle genuine adoration and obedience to the great and loving God and real respect, care and coexistence in a mutual communal relationship with one another. The trinitarian projection of God helps Zambians to build a real outlook of life in relationship with God, other people and the rest of the creation. Hence, this is an opportunity for Reformed faith to explain the egalitarian view of God which is revealed from the trinitarian understanding of God. Where many people are overwhelmed by threats from witchcraft and Satanism Reformed theology needs to assure them with the power and presence of the triune God. In this case, Reformed faith becomes relevant without losing its identity in a specific challenging Zambian context.

Consideration of ecological issues is a third strong point for the prospect of Reformed identity in Zambia. Reformed faith is keen in dealing with ecological issues by being inclusive in its theological undertaking. Furthermore, it pays attention to the effects of the ecological crisis. For example, Reformed faith recognizes the effects that would emanated from global warming. On these effects, Mugambi foretells that "Global warming that results from pollution will have great implications on the planet and will affect many aspects of our lives including food security, health and availability of clean and safe drinking water mostly through flooding and droughts."[42] Zambia is not an exception insofar as the effects of global warming are concerned. Already the seasons, especially summer or rainy season, are not as predictable as they have been in the past, and that affects planning for a planting season and food security. Hence, the planting of food crops may be rendered futile if there are floods or droughts. For this reason, Reformed faith has an opportunity in Zambia not only to identify itself with ecological concerns, but also to be relevant by being seen to address such concerns. Earlier on in the same article, Mugambi made a call that "humans have the choice to make the environment better than they find it, or to leave it worse than when they occupied or were born on it."[43] Reformed faith in Zambia can still echo the same call by urging the church in Zambia not to consider issues to do with climate change and its effect as just side issues to its divine calling. On the contrary, they need to take these issues as fundamental components of new challenges that they have to face in their quest for a better Zambia. Therefore, Reformed faith needs to encourage the church in Zambia to harness its potential in dealing with environmental issues through its stewardship as a call from God. The church in Zambia has the capacity, the will and

---

42. Mugambi, "Climate Change," 17.

43. Ibid., 16.

God's blessings at its disposal to handle issues of ecological concern. For this reason, Reformed faith can play a major role with its message of good stewardship for non-human creatures and the environment as a whole.

Another prospective point for Reformed identity in Zambia is to address *gender*[44] *issues*, particularly Gender-Based Violence (GBV), which has taken a central stage in Zambia today. GBV refers to any harm perpetrated against a person's will on the basis of gender.[45] It includes any act of verbal or physical force, coercion or life-threatening deprivation, directed at an individual woman or girl that causes physical or psychological harm, humiliation or arbitrary deprivation of liberty and that perpetuates female subordination. It is based on an unequal power among men, women, boys and girls. Women and girls are often the targets because of social norms and beliefs that perpetuate their perceived second-class social status. In a nutshell, Gender-Based Violence includes various forms such as physical, sexual and psychological abuse of women and girls in the home, in communities, and in schools. Gender-based violence in Zambia has recently been a source of concern. Many women have either ended up being mutilated or killed by the male folk due to GBV. Reformed faith can take this scenario as an area not only for academic reflection, but also for action to address the vice from its on perspective. By doing so, it would not only show that it is equally concerned, but also it would make itself relevant to one of the real issues that affect the Zambia society.

The fifth prospect of Reformed identity in Zambia is its nature as a *beacon of hope in suffering*.[46] God promises hope of flourishing in the entire creation. Humankind participates in the realization of the promised hope for newness and fullness of life through the empowering work of the Holy Spirit. In God's providence, God works through humankind to fulfill God's purposes for the entire creation.[47] In this sense, human participation and engagement in the practical activities that seek to enhance the fullness of life is actually God's work through the Holy Spirit in human beings. The emphasis for this participation should be a response to what God has already done (and continues to do) and a commitment to enhance the wholeness of life

---

44. By "gender" we refer to the socially ascribed differences between males and females.

45. On this definition and all the insights and explanations on Gender-Based Violence that follow, I am indebted to the article posted on http://www.sciencedirect.com/science/article/pii/.

46. I extract most of this information from my PhD dissertation.

47. Reformed identity as a beacon of hope encompasses the cosmic and ecological significance which entails cosmic and ecological transformation in the present life and the eschatological future as we read in Rom 8:18–27.

on earth. This calls for a holistic approach in dealing with suffering in Zambia. Such a holistic approach is multifaceted and becomes a real beacon of hope in suffering. For the Zambian context, such a holistic approach ought to involve and address a number of aspects that affect life: i.e. human rights violations, poverty and wealth, gender inequalities, gender-based violence, children's and women's sexual abuse, political and social injustices, ecological crisis and injustice, spiritual transformation, and renewal of cosmos. In order for this hope of the fullness of life to be realized, there is also need for commitment on the part of Zambians to work for the betterment of the country. This requires Reformed theology to inculcate a work-culture that aims at realization of the new and better life in the present. It needs to stress that hope in suffering comes about with a transformed mindset: a right attitude and practical efforts that bring about that hope. This also demands a transformation of human will which is aligned to God's will, and works towards enhancing mutual relationship in society. In concrete terms, there is need to realize that Zambians have a part to play to achieve hope in suffering. They are called to be obedient by doing and accomplishing God's will here on earth, and working against injustice and exploitation at all levels.

Last but not least, Reformed identity in the Zambian context can truly be relevant when it embraces the virtue of *sensitivity to a changing world*. As stated earlier, globalization presents a dual-faced ambiguity, and life generally is dynamic. Zambian context is not immune to the challenges and changes that happen on the global scene. Therefore, for Reformed identity to survive and be relevant in such a challenging and dynamic environment, it needs to consider and embrace "a multi-faceted framework" which adheres to a set of guidelines. In an article on the ambiguity of globalization, I suggest some guidelines which can still be considered if Reformed faith is to be sensitive to a changing world.[48]

The first guideline, as pointed earlier, is that Reformed faith has to continue to *consider the centrality of scripture* by maintaining the biblical soundness. This means keeping the scriptural base and tone ablaze by reflecting the trueness of the gospel of God's own self-disclosure in Jesus Christ as attested in Scripture. Secondly, Reformed faith needs to *be sensitive to the needs and problems of the locals* in a specific Zambian context. Since theology is influenced by the life-experiences of the local people of a particular context in time and space, Reformed theology has to pay attention to such life-experiences. Thirdly, Reformed faith has to *be realistic about the experiences of the Zambian context*. Instead of exaggeration about the intensity of the needs and problems of the Zambian milieu, Reformed theological

---

48. Banda, "Ambiguity of Globalization," 28–29.

enterprise needs to adopt a sensitive and realistic approach. Fourthly, Reformed faith needs to *study the global social, cultural, economic, ecological, political and even religious mega trends* and how they influence Zambia as a nation. Reformed identity in Zambia needs to conversant with what is going on in the world and how these events are impacting the Zambian community. Furthermore, Reformed faith needs to *allow the global realities to influence the locals*. By this we mean Reformed identity in Zambia needs to be willing to assimilate global changes and also be ready to be transformed by the same. Another guideline to embrace is that Reformed faith in Zambia needs to *be ecumenical-minded*. This calls for interaction with other Christian traditions and religious groupings to enrich, evaluate, cross-examine, dialogue, ventilate and share with each other issues of common concern such as HIV/AIDS. There is also need for Reformed faith in Zambia to *co-ordinate reformed identity with Zambian identity*. Here, the emphasis is on leaving enough and genuine room for interaction and dialogue between reformed heritage with the Zambian cultural locale. Reformed faith in Zambia has to *assimilate the interdisciplinary, interfaith and holistic approach* as well. Reformed theology as a discipline needs to listen to and involve other non-Christian religious groupings in Zambia and non-theological disciplines such as sociology, economics, accounts, law, philosophy, psychology, political science, and many others. Lastly, Reformed theologians in Zambia need to *work closely with expatriate theologians*. In as much as Zambian Reformed theologians need to take a lead in undertaking theological reflection in Zambia, expatriate theologians can as well contribute by providing their own expertise.

Conclusion

In trying to contribute to the theme under discussion, *"Always Being Reformed: Challenges, Issues and Prospects for Reformed Theologies Today"* this chapter has focused on the thesis of what "always being reformed" means in a contemporary globalized and challenging Zambian context. It has thus dealt with what it implies to preserve the identity of an authentic Christian Reformed faith, and remain relevant in a pluralistic contemporary Zambian context. This has to do with the question of how adherents to the Reformed faith can always bridge the gap between self-identity and relevance in Zambia. I have underscored that Reformed faith confidently leans on and asserts specific affirmations which define its identity within the Christian family and are paramount with regard to the Zambian context. In order to clearly comprehend and appropriately respond to the Zambian context, the article further draws our attention to heart-breaking challenges that keep on questioning the Reformed identity in that setting. This is to help us understand that if Reformed faith has to retain its identity and be relevant in the Zambian milieu, it cannot afford to neglect such overwhelming challenges. The treatise further assures that despite the alarming and overwhelming challenges, Reformed faith can still be relevant in Zambia. In this sense, prospects for the Reformed faith in Zambia lie in relation to a number of themes: e.g. strong stance on biblical truth, concrete and holistic conceptualization of God, consideration of ecological and gender issues (such as Gender-Based Violence), a promising identity as a beacon of hope in suffering, and its sensitivity to a changing world. The article concludes by affirming that for Reformed identity to survive and be relevant in a challenging environment like Zambia, it needs to consider and embrace "a multi-faceted framework" which adheres to and provides specific guidelines. The impact of Reformed faith in Zambia can only be felt when it desires to be relevant by addressing specific Zambian contextual issues and challenges.

Bibliography

Banda, Lameck. "The Ambiguity of Globalization: A Pressing Challenge for African Contextual Theology." *Insights: The Faculty Journal of Austin Seminary* 122 (2007) 24–29.

———. "Dialoguing at 'Mphala': A Conversation on Faith Between John Calvin and Proponents of the Prosperity Gospel." In *In Search of Health and Wealth: The Prosperity Gospel in African, Reformed Perspective*, edited by Hermen Kroesbergen, 63–77. Wellington: Christian Literature Fund, 2013.

———. "Hope in Suffering: An African Interpretation of Jesus' Resurrection." PhD diss., University of the Free State, Bloemfontein, 2010.

Bosch, David J. "The Problem of Evil in Africa: A Survey of African Views on Witchcraft and of the Response of the Christian Church." In *Like a Roaring Lion: Essays on the Bible, the Church and Demonic Powers*, edited by Pieter de Villiers, 38–62. Pretoria: UNISA, 1987.

Burgess, Harold W. *The Framework of our Faith: The Basics of Knowing Christ*. Anderson, IN: Warner, 2005.

Gifford, Paul. *African Christianity: Its Public Role*. Bloomington: Indiana University Press, 1998.

Gillham, Simon. "Combating Gender-Based Violence: The Bible's Teaching on Gender Complementarity." In *Men in the Pulpit, Women in the Pew? Addressing Gender Inequality in Africa*, edited by Jurgens Hendriks et al., 93–103. Stellenbosch: EFSA Institute, 2012.

Grudem, Wayne. *Systematic Theology: An Introduction to Biblical Doctrine*. Grand Rapids: Zondervan, 1994.

Guthrie, Shirley C. *Always Being Reformed: Faith for a Fragmented World*. Louisville: Westminster John Knox, 1996.

Gutiérrez, Gustavo. *The Truth Shall Make You Free: Confrontations*. Translated by Matthew J. O'Connell. Maryknoll, NY: Orbis, 1990.

Hoekema, Anthony A. *Saved by Grace*. Grand Rapids: Eerdmans, 1989.

Kroesbergen, Hermen, ed. *In Search of Health and Wealth: The Prosperity Gospel in African, Reformed Perspective*. Wellington: Christian Literature Fund, 2013.

Kroesbergen-Kamps, Johanneke. "Dreams and Nightmares of Modernity: Accusations and Testimonies of Satanism in Zambia." In *In Search of Health and Wealth: The Prosperity Gospel in African, Reformed Perspective*, edited by Hermen Kroesbergen, 100–112. Wellington: Christian Literature Fund, 2013.

McKim, Donald K. *Westminster Dictionary of Theological Terms*. Louisville: Westminster John Knox, 1996.

Migliore, Daniel L. *Faith Seeking Understanding: An Introduction to Christian Theology*. Grand Rapids: Eerdmans, 1991.

Moltmann, Jürgen. *The Crucified God: The Cross of Christ as the Foundation and Criticism of Christian Theology*. Translated by R. A. Wilson and John Bowden. London: SCM, 1974.

———. "The Destruction and Healing of the Earth: Ecology and Theology." In *God and Globalization*. Vol. 2, *The Spirit and the Modern Authorities*, edited by Max L. Stackhouse and Don S. Browning, 166–90. Theology for the Twenty-first Century. London: Trinity, 2001.

Mugambi, Jesse N. K. "Climate Change and Care for Creation." Paper presented at the International Symposium of the All-Africa Conference of Churches, Nairobi, Kenya, 2013.

Mwaura, Philomena N. 2000. "Reflecting Christ Crucified among Africa's Cross Bearers." *Mission Studies* 17 (2000) 97–102.

Paas, S. *Dictionary/Mtanthauziramawu: Chichewa/Chinyanja—English, English—Chichewa/Chinyanja*. Kachere Series 31. Zomba: Kachere, 2009.

Presbyterian Church (U.S.A.) *The Constitution of the Presbyterian Church (U.S.A.): The Book of Confessions*, Part 1. Louisville: The Office of the General Assembly, 1999.

Reeves, Michael. *The Unquenchable Flame: Discovering the Heart of the Reformation*. Nashville: B & H Academic, 2009.

Rice, Howard L. *Reformed Spirituality: An Introduction for Believers*. Louisville: Westminster John Knox, 1991.

Sobrino, Jon. *Spirituality of Liberation: Toward Political Holiness*. Robert R. Barr. Maryknoll, NY: Orbis, 1988.

Spinder, H. *Faith and Reflection: The Place of Theological Education in 21st Century Mission*. Utrecht: ICCO/Kerk in Actie, Mission Department of PCN, 2011.

Stewart, Pamela J., and Andrew Strathern. *Witchcraft, Sorcery, Rumors, and Gossip*. New Departures in Anthropology. Cambridge: Cambridge University Press, 2004.

Uprichard, R. E. H. *What Presbyterians Believe*. Antrim: The Oaks, 2011.

"USAID Urges Zambia to Control Deforestation." *The Post,* July 11, 2013, 8.

Van Breugel, J. W. M. *Chewa Traditional Religion*. Blantyre: CLAIM, 2001.

3

Semper Reformanda as a Confession of Crisis

Jason A. Goroncy

This essay takes three aims: (i) to map in brief the theo-historical genesis of the *semper reformanda* aphorism; (ii) to consider that idea vis-à-vis the Reformed habit of confessing Jesus Christ; and (iii) to suggest one area where the witness of many Reformed communities today *might* call for urgent attention in the spirit of the *semper*.

Semper reformanda: Some Theo-Historical Particulars

There are, at the outset, a number of ways that the tradition has conceived the notion of *semper reformanda*. I will here note just six:

1. While there is general consensus that the *idea* of *semper reformanda* is not foreign to the ethos and instincts of the sixteenth century reformers, the *etymological history* of the *reformanda* sayings is somewhat disputed. Some have argued that their origins emerged from developments towards the close of the Dutch *Nadere Reformatie*, a claim bolstered by drawing attention to passages from Jacobus Koelman (who himself attributed the idea to his teacher Johannes Hoornbeeck) and from Koelman's friend Jodocus van Lodensteyn. In 1678, Koelman, when describing the designation "Reformed," rehearsed ideas that he had published in 1673; namely, that "we must come to be called Reforming, and not only Reformed, so that we always must be Reforming if we want to be Reformed and be worthy of that name, because that is what we are attempting."[1] The notion also appears in van Lodensteyn's *Beschouwinge van Zion* [*Contemplation of Zion*], first published in 1674, where the relevant passage reads:

---

1. Koelman, cited in Bush, "Calvin and the Reformanda Sayings," 287.

> Such [a] person of understanding [i.e., one who was busy working toward restoration] would not have called the Reformed Church *reformata*, or reformed, but *reformanda*, or being reformed. What a pure church would that become that was always thus occupied? How precise in truth? How holy in practice?[2]

Evident here is a way of thinking about *reformanda* in terms of repairing "the ruins of the Church,"[3] as John Calvin would plead with Edward VI of England, the concern here being with the ecclesia's repentance rather than its inventiveness. Here, *reformanda* encapsulates a vision for restoring the purity of the church deformed by theology and practice back to some more fitting state. This interpretation of the *reformata/reformanda* aphorisms appears, in fact, more than a century before Koelman and van Lodensteyn in the work of the Italian reformer Girolamo Zanchi (Jerome Zanchius)—in, for example, his 1562 correspondence to Theodore Beza,[4] and in his treatise *De Reformatione Ecclesiarum* based on verses from Isaiah 1. Concerning the latter, and after recalling that the work of reform *is God's*—i.e., is that action undertaken by God at a time and via a method of God's choosing—Zanchi proceeds to describe the mode of God's "most pure and most sincere" (*purissima et sincerissima*) reform as one of judgment, of the turning of God's hand against God's elect, of smelting away the dross and removing all the alloy (Isa1.25). "Everything," he writes, "that is not according to the word of God [*secundus Verbum Dei*] is alloy."[5] The "first in needing to be Reformed," Zanchi argues, is the Pope "who has first place in the church of Rome," and then, in addition, "everything else"—worship (*religio, cultus*), faith (*fidem*) and morals (*mores*), among other things, must be restored/reformed (*reformanda*) *sicut ab initio*, "as they were at first,"[6] until everything is "perspicuum" (transparent, clear). Only then can the church be truly called "reformed" (*reformata*): "A church that claims it is reformed (*reformata*), while retaining anything of papism," is not in truth "a city of faith." So understood, the *ecclesia reformata*, was not, according to Zanchi, impossible in principle, although it was not easily obtained and

---

2. Van Lodensteyn, cited in Bush, "Calvin and the Reformanda Sayings," 286. According to Bush, this is "the earliest documentable source" of the *reformanda* sayings. Ibid., 288. Others, such as W. A. Visser't Hooft, attribute the origins of the formulation, *ecclesia reformanda quia reformata*, to Gisbert Voetius (1589–1676). See Nebelsick, "Ecclesia Reformata Semper Reformanda," 59.

3. Calvin, *Commentary on Isaiah*, 240.

4. Zanchi, "Zanchi a Bèze," 60.

5. Zanchi, "De Reformatione Ecclesiarum," bd. 3, col. 714. Here I draw from Bush, "Calvin and the Reformanda Sayings," 291–97.

6. Ibid., 714.

would require constant vigilance. For Calvin, on the other hand, in whose writings the *reformanda* sayings themselves are absent, the *idea* is present not as a goal to be acquired (as it was for Zanchi) but as the description of an *ongoing process* of unshackling the church from liturgical, pastoral, and theological abuse, a process that could, to be sure, achieve an acceptable and maintainable measure. As abuse ridden and as deformed "among the ruins of Papism" as the church was, Calvin still hoped that it could be rebuilt.[7]

2. This sense of reform as an *ongoing process*, as *semper*, as "a permanent condition of the Church's health,"[8] appears in a number of early sources: The Edict of Nantes in 1598, for example, signifies the National Synods of the French Reformed Church evidencing a "strong commitment to continuous reformation."[9] Also, according to Theodor Mahlmann, the Lutheran theologian Friedrich Balduin argued, in 1610, that reform was an unremitting posture for the church to adopt,[10] a position repeated among the Reformed in a plethora of revisions of seventeenth-century confessions of faith. A few decades later, in 1644, John Milton, in his eloquent tract *Areopagitica*, argued that "God is decreeing to begin some new and great period in his church, even to the reforming of reformation itself."[11] The Westminster divines, in their *Directory of Public Worship* (1645), also spoke of God's call for "further reformation."[12]

The spirit of the *semper* in the *reformanda* aphorisms was not always met with welcome, however, even among the Reformed. For instance, the Synod of Privas (1612)—called amid bitter political struggles, division among nobles and among churches, and the rise to power within the church of bureaucratic hardliners such as Daniel Chamier—witnessed the practical end to a commitment to confessional development on the basis that such would in fact promote further destabilization and challenge to those who found themselves empowered on the winning side of debates. Unlike, for example, the Scots Confession (1560) which made plain that any church confession was strictly subordinate to Holy Scripture—that "interpretation or opinion of any theologian, Kirk, or council" which is found to be "contrary to the plain Word of God" is to be corrected by such and that such was expected to be a continual process undertaken by a listening church whose

---

7. Calvin, *Ioannis Calvini Opera*, 15:335.
8. Forsyth, "Cross as the Final Seat," 589.
9. Armstrong, "Semper Reformanda," 119.
10. See Mahlmann, "Refomation," 416-27; Mahlmann, "Ecclesia Semper Reformanda," 57-77. I am indebted here to Theissen, "Witness and Service," 226.
11. Milton, "Areopagitica," 167.
12. Thompson, *Liturgies of the Western Church*, 356.

fidelity was never to be directed to the Confession itself—the Confession which was the fruit of the Synod of Privas, and which all pastors—Huguenot and other—were required to sign, "effectively closed off the possibility of any further substantial change to the confession; hence, for all intents and purposes, it brought to an end the previous commitment to the concept of *semper reformanda*."[13] The oath begins as follows: "I, the undersigned, do receive and approve the entire contents of the Confession of Faith of the Reformed churches of this Kingdom, do promise to persevere in it to the very end, and not to believe nor teach anything which does not conform to it." Measures which on the surface appear to be concerned to promote unity and conciliation are, on closer inspection, "only part of a hard-line position that tends more toward exclusivity than inclusiveness."[14] So Brian Armstrong, reflecting on this period, describes "an official reversal of position regarding 'continuing reformation'":

> For the first fifty or more years the Huguenots considered it important to revise the confession in the light of other confessional positions and new insight into, and understanding of, Scriptural teaching. The hope was to forge an atmosphere of inclusiveness in the Reformed world. At the beginning of the seventeenth century, under the pressure of external threat to an established church and under the scholastic methodology and precision that emerged in the face of this new polemical orientation, there was a gradual but steady move to affirm that their confessional position was the only true and acceptable interpretation of God's truth. So it became an atmosphere in which definitive charges of heresy could be made and applied.[15]

Such betrays a spirit not too unlike that which has for many yielded the Westminster Confession, from 1690 onwards, as "a doctrinal test for ministers and office bearers."[16] Clearly, the understanding among the majority of Reformed churches in the earlier centuries of the Reformed movements of *reformanda* as restoration towards the church's former or yet-to-come purity discovers a markedly different accent in ensuing centuries when the *reformanda* sayings "flowered and mutated in the hothouse of historical, theological, and devotional writing into an entire genus of aphorisms that are given entirely different interpretations."[17] This development has

13. Armstrong, "Semper Reformanda," 136.
14. Ibid., 137.
15. Ibid., 138.
16. Burleigh, *Church History of Scotland*, 155.
17. Bush, "Calvin and the Reformanda Sayings," 288.

witnessed most of its growth since Karl Barth's 1947 essay "Die Botschaft von der Freien Gnade Gottes," and his lecture given the following year on "Das christliche Verständnis der Offenbarung."[18]

3. The *reformanda* aphorisms themselves function as something of a confession that the church is in need of reform and that it can in no way reform itself. True reform would happen, Calvin averred, when people "look for the good which they desire from none but God," confide in God's power, trust in God's goodness, depend on God's truth, and turn wholeheartedly to God, resting on God with full hope, and by necessity resorting to God.[19] Reformation, in other words, is not, in the final analysis, in-house repair work, as it were, but an action of *God* (*Deus ipsa*) who in the grace of love's judgment calls the church to renewed obedience and continuing reformation through the "unchangeable and highest standard given in the Scriptures."[20]

4. In the hands [sic] of God,

> Scripture . . . builds the church up by breaking the church open, and therefore in large measure by breaking the church down . . . Scripture is as much a de-stabilizing feature of the life of the church as it is a factor in its cohesion and continuity . . . Through Scripture the church is constantly exposed to interruption. Being the hearing church is . . . the church's readiness "that its whole life should be assailed, convulsed, revolutionized and reshaped."[21]

The Word, together with his undivided counterpart the Holy Spirit, reveals, puts to death, makes alive, and leads. This is God's way of reforming the church, and is "at once the miracle and the tribulation of the Church, for the Church is condemned by that which establishes it, and is broken in pieces upon its foundations."[22] Again, Barth:

> In order to be able to come about at all, in order to be born again as a Christian church, Reformed doctrine needs the free, sharp draught of the knowledge of the Word of God from the Scripture and the Spirit, "born" with the natural violence of a volcanic outbreak, from the one-time unity of the Reformed church.

---

18. See Barth, *Die Botschaft*, 19; Barth, *Texte zur Barmer*, 156. The "Das christliche Verständnis der Offenbarung" lecture was republished as "The Christian Understanding of Revelation" in Barth, *Against the Stream*, 203–40.
19. Calvin, "Necessity of Reforming," 187.
20. Barth, *Word of God and Theology*, 216. Cf. Barth, *CD* II/2, 806.
21. John Webster, *Holy Scripture*, 46–47. Webster here cites from Barth, *CD* I/2, 804.
22. Barth, *Epistle to the Romans*, 341.

Reformed *"through the Word of God"*: This is the original and proper meaning of the name we carry.²³

Any reform of the church's doctrine or worship or governance, just as everything else under heaven, is subject to interrogation with "the exact standard of the Word of God."²⁴ At its best, the Reformed project has encouraged the church to keep returning to Holy Scripture in order to discern its vocation described in light of the Word proclaimed therein. This has often involved hearing the command to repent of the godless banality and trivialization of its worship and to recover its nutrition in the Spirit's gifts of Bible, font, and table; to reject self-veneration and be given over to service of the Word fleshed out in the living documents of congregations and thereby confess the eternal and living Word who breaks himself open to God's people in new times and in new places.

5. Relatedly, while *reformatorische Theologie* is to be considered a "theology of permanent reformation," this does not indicate a habit of "endless cycle of idea and action, endless invention, [and] endless experiment"²⁵ for its own sake. *Ecclesia semper reformanda* is not *ecclesia semper varianda*. We might here recall Calvin's final address to the Company of Pastors in Geneva wherein Calvin cautioned that while the pastors should continue the work of reforming the church's worship, they should (at least according to Jean Pinant) modify nothing about Geneva's additional ecclesial arrangements:²⁶ "I pray you make no change, no innovation. People often ask for novelties. Not that I desire for my own sake out of ambition that what I have established should remain, and that people should retain it without wishing for something better, but because all changes are dangerous and sometimes hurtful."²⁷ Clearly, if Calvin is to be among our guides here, the idea of *semper reformanda* is not one that can simply be taken up by way of justifying the efforts of those calling for ecclesial modernization, a charge that Calvin himself had to ward off: "We are accused of rash and impious innovation, for having ventured to propose any change at all in the former state of the Church."²⁸

---

23. Barth, *Word of God and Theology*, 220–21.
24. Calvin, "Necessity of Reforming," 187.
25. Eliot, "Choruses from 'The Rock,'" 147.
26. See Calvin, *Ioannis Calvini Opera*, 21:167.
27. Ibid. 21:893–94. Also in Calvin, *Letters, Part 4*, 376.
28. Calvin, "Necessity of Reforming," 185. Working in the sensitivity of Calvin's wake but less anxious about unconstrained ideas than is the French lawyer, Michael Jinkins considers the notion of *semper reformanda* precisely in terms of "innovation," defined as "the capacity to draw from the experience of ancient Christian communities and to adapt these lessons to new situations," and as the "capacity to adapt and change

6. To regard *semper reformanda* as a description of the church's perpetual posture during this time between the times is to regard it as a mode of witness (*signa*) to God's eschatological promise, as "an event that keeps church and theology breathless with suspense, an event that infuses church and theology with the breath of life, a story that is constantly making history, an event that cannot be concluded in this world, a process that will come to fulfillment and to rest only in the Parousia of Christ."[29] To this note we shall return.

Semper reformanda: Confessing Christ

The Dutch missiologist Hendrik Kraemer attested that "Strictly speaking, one ought to say that the Church is always in a state of crisis and that its greatest shortcoming is that it is only occasionally aware of it. The Church," he continued, "ought always to be aware of its condition of crisis on account of the abiding tension between its essential nature and its empirical condition."[30] This deeply Reformed instinct provides a fruitful platform for our thinking further about the notion of *semper reformanda* vis-à-vis the Reformed habit of confessing Christ, the subject to which we now turn.

Confession as response

Because the birth, witness, and end of the Christian community finds its decisive ground, content, and orientation in the life of one begotten of the Virgin Mary, crucified under Pontius Pilate, and raised from the tomb of Joseph of Arimathea, the most responsible Christian theology grants priority to the question of *who* over that of *how*, and always seeks to answer the latter in terms of the former. We might understand Reformed confessions too as being foremost not about articulating a set of theological formulae—still less about justifying the church's existence![31]—but rather about taking up the particular invitation[32] to participate in a movement of response, and

---

to new conditions in new environments and to do so in ways that remain appropriate to who we are called to be as a community of followers of Jesus Christ." Jinkins, *Church Transforming*, 105.

29. Moltmann, "Theologia Reformata," 121.
30. Kraemer, *Christian Message*, 24–25.
31. On which see Käsemann, *Perspectives on Paul*, 120–21.
32. See Matt 16:15; Mark 8:29; Luke 9:20.

that principally to two very specific, and related, questions—"Who is Jesus Christ today?" and "What is he doing in the world?"[33]

Christians ought to abandon the temptation to build uncritically and unrepentantly on foundations laid yesterday, must refuse to live today on the interest amassed from yesterday's capital, and instead take up a perpetual posture of beginning anew at the beginning, of "freely granting the free God room to dispose at will over everything that [human beings] may already have known, produced, and achieved," and to submit to God's care, judgment, and disposing of history's continuance.[34] This is not a call to discard that which the community has heard before, to of necessity substitute past hearings with new ones, or to build on foundations of our own making. It is, rather, a call to risk taking seriously the transcendent Word who breaks afresh into our state of affairs in continuously new ways, and who calls for the hard work of discernment and interpretation upon the horizon of the present. Far from treating the Reformed tradition akin to a museum piece visited occasionally with reverence but disregarded or flouted in normal time, the call *semper reformanda* is a summons to the church catholic to be what Alasdair MacIntyre names a "living tradition," the virtuous bearer of a "continuous" and "socially embodied argument" about what it is and about the goods that constitute its life.[35]

Responding to the Word

However else we may wish to define the Christian community, it is a community distinguished by its being *addressed by* and its *making public of* this Word who is gospel. As Barth asserts, "What always makes [the church] the church, what distinguishes it from any other fellowship of faith and spirit and distinctive orientation and sacrament, is the vital link between this very specific hearing and making heard, the Word which it receives and passes on."[36] The church, in other words, is a community continually brought into being by and for God's audacious speech-claim from which its concrete existence hangs and about which it is compelled to speak. The latter is the church's principal theological task—to examine its public confession in light of what it has heard (principally in Scripture but not only there), to enquire as to the extent that the address that takes place in Christian preaching is congruous with the revelation that engendered the prophetic

---

33. See Bonhoeffer, *Berlin*, 303; Bonhoeffer, *Christology*, 43–67.
34. Barth, *Evangelical Theology*, 166.
35. MacIntyre, *After Virtue*, 222.
36. Barth, *Göttingen Dogmatics*, 24.

and apostolic kerygma. To ask, in other words, about the extent to which its speech, made where it is heard in the "inevitable ambivalence and ambiguity" of its creaturely existence,[37] is identical with *the Word of God*; the extent to which its speech is *Christian* speech. The necessity of the dogmatic task is not fashioned by piety or by the sincere desire for ecclesial renovation but is demanded only by the possibility of service to the divine speech, by the predicate that "God has spoken, speaks now and will again speak." And its purpose, as Barth contends, is that "in this realization this transcendent happening should become immanent within the Church's proclamation, and that proclamation itself should be what in virtue of the promise (the promise which has to be continually apprehended by the Church, in faith and in the obedience of faith) it already is—the Word of God."[38]

God's first summons to a teaching community, therefore, is "to hear, that is, to listen to Jesus Christ as attested in Holy Scripture."[39] The provisionality and sinfulness of the church means that its hearing of and participation in God's address is always imperfect and uncertain. It therefore carries the skepticism of faith towards everything it speaks and produces, aware that its responsiveness is always a less-than-perfect correspondence to the divine speech that elicits it. Such hearing indubitably in no way guarantees that the community will not slip into idolatry—"from obedience into disobedience, from the doing of the Word of God into the doing of human will or fancy"[40]—but it does signify that the community's principal and continuous task is to hear, to respond to, and to come under the judgment of the divine address.

Responding in tempore et in loco

The church is not unique among creaturely societies in its need to make decisions, without a spirit of rigidity or exclusiveness, about the paths on which it should walk in the world. Such decisions are often fraught with conflict and complexity but, as Dag Hammarskjöld reminded a gathering at the Royal Albert Hall in London in 1953, "No institution can become effective unless it is forced to wrestle with the problems, the conflicts, and the tribulations of real life."[41] It is the church's dangerous claim, however, that its judgments and confessions—its own unique wrestlings—are not

37. Jüngel, *Christ, Justice and Peace*, 70.
38. Barth, *CD* I/2, 800.
39. Ibid., 802. Cf. ibid., 797, 812.
40. Ibid., 802. See also ibid., 807–8.
41. Cordier and Foote, *Public Papers*, 203.

made entirely *ex creatio* but represent a community under the lordship of the Holy Spirit who goads response *to* the Word *in* the array of socio-historical contexts in which hearing is effected. A community's responsible witness, therefore, calls for something more (and certainly no less!) than simply for its best minds to be at work, and something more than simply repeating what it has heard and spoken in times past, even though responsible listening will not show disdain to either resource. This means, among other things, that responses to the Word *in tempore et in loco* from communities at once ecumenical, catholic, and historical will "not support any compulsion towards homogeneity which subjects all churches to the same self-understanding and expects an identical orientation in doctrine and life."[42] We can expect, therefore, that faith's confession will be characterized by continuity[43] *and* departure, both of which are fruit of the hearing of the one Word of God, hearing which admits a plurality "as wide as that already found in the biblical witness."[44]

Another way of conceiving this idea is to think about confession *as commentary*. As the community hears the Word, it remains inadequate to simply repeat biblical texts. It can point to such texts, but it must also speak in its own words and so with the accent of its own time. Confession, of course, is much more difficult than parroting, and the risks of misspeaking and of speaking out of turn are manifestly heightened. But there can be no other way for the community made new in the event of hearing and speaking, the event which rescues the church from being a museum. Conceived otherwise, freedom threatens metamorphosis into confessionalism, and the gospel into an ideology; moves which, for the Reformed at least, are oxymoronic because their project is not concerned to defend shibboleths, or to erect systems, or to police boundaries of interpretation, but, in a spirit of self-criticism (apart from which its work would be a "nonsense (or worse)"[45]) and of faith, to call the world's one catholic community back to its ground and *raison d'être* in the insubordinate Word of God.

---

42. Weinrich, "Openness and Worldliness," 4.

43. Continuity here does not imply something static, as if past hearings become dogmas that are then either apotheosized or replaced entirely by a new authority. Rather, as Michael Polanyi has argued in *The Tacit Dimension*, knowing is always embodied, always relies on personal commitments—dogmas can never be wholly discarded or examined in abstraction from previously-formed judgments, but are *lived in* and *reshaped* by the reality with which we engage and in which history is neither lost nor determinative.

44. Weinrich, "Openness and Worldliness," 5.

45. Williams, *Resurrection*, 53.

While it is faith's claim that "the Word of God and the *kairos* of its proclamation are inseparable,"[46] confessions conceived *in tempore et in loco* can only ever hope to claim to be interim approximations of an unappealable truth. Due attention to contextually-determined and hermeneutically-responsible confession is never considered to place the Reformed at a disadvantage, however, but is rather understood as an aspect of responsibility given by God. Evident here is a confession about God's livingness, about the sovereignty and freedom of divine revelation, about the contemporaneity of the hermeneutical community's ancient and eschatological faith, and about the belief that God's Word creates the context and the context becomes the *kairos* of risk from which the community must not retreat and out of which it must bear witness, part of the content of which will be a confession about the provisionality of its own speech vis-à-vis God. It is the sheer fact of God's livingness that also leads the confessing community to reject all moves to deify past articulations of the faith. To cite Barth at length:

> The "given" things in history that were laid before the feet of our forefathers were not the objects of a loving and devotional reverence but rather the objects of serious and critical examination. The conservative principle with which they, too, naturally operated, was crisscrossed and broken by them precisely through its opposite, such that their beginnings show only a very fragmentary loyalty toward the past, and actually show a broad, smooth, unsparing break with it . . . There is . . . strictly speaking, no Reformed tradition outside the one timeless tradition, namely, that of the appeal to the open Bible and the Spirit which speaks out of the spirits. In a very well-thought-out manner, our Fathers did *not* leave behind for us *any Augustana* which authentically interprets the Word of God, never mind a Formula of Concord. They have not left behind *any* "Symbolic books" which later, like those of the Lutherans, would come to have a whiff of having been "inspired." Instead, they have only left us *confessions*, of which more than one begins or ends with the open caution of better teaching in the future . . . Our task *could*, therefore, consist of a careful revision of the theology of the Geneva or the Heidelberg Catechism, or of the *Canons of Dort*, but it *could* also . . . consist of the setting up of a new confession, a *Helvetica tertia*, just as the founders allowed themselves to replace the prior by a posterior. Both possibilities are equally tenable in the Reformed church.[47]

---

46. Moltmann, "Theologia Reformata," 123.
47. Barth, *Word of God and Theology*, 207–9.

If, where, and when the community deems that such revisions are required, such will most responsibly take place, as I have already intimated, *in* the most respectful conference with the ancient catholic faith—with that which has been heard and confessed before, *semper, ubique, ab omnibus*, always, everywhere, and by all believers—and *with* the significant risk that a listening and speaking faith demands in the world. The Theological Declaration of Barmen, for example, properly makes plain that the call upon "pardoned sinners" is not to form ecclesiastical bubbles which isolate and insulate them from the "sinful world," but rather to "testify in the midst" (Barmen III) of such while resisting every temptation to "become a propaganda weapon of a political movement" or "a society for the propagation of views about the next world."[48] The "free, grateful service to [God's] creatures" (Barmen II), in other words, is undertaken by a community profoundly aware of its own worldliness, and intensely on guard against any hint of "artificial opposition to the 'world.'"[49]

With Michael Weinrich, we might identify three possible ways for the church to understand its own worldliness vis-à-vis the world: The first concerns the church tending towards "self-dissolution . . . into the secular 'world,'" properly appropriating "the self-understanding of the 'world' as its own," acknowledging the maturity of the "world" and establishing with such "genuine agreement of the Gospel" so that the church "attains complete solidarity with the 'non-religious' world precisely where freedom is promoted." By so doing, the church advocates for freedom—wherever it is sought and no matter how secularized its expression—on the basis of the Gospel, whereby "helping the 'world' which is trapped in the problem of self-explanation, discover the necessary blessing of a total meaning which the church is to preserve from all ideological petrifications in which the freedom that has been gained will inevitably be squandered."[50]

A second possibility points in the reverse direction: By "mourning the spreading secularization as the specific danger for a society that is endangering itself," the church "expects a conversion of the 'world' to the authoritative orientations as they are now to be found only within" its own bounds.[51] While Rome and Constantinople might be tempted to advocate for such a position, Protestantism must not.

Rather than advancing some kind of *via media*, a third prospect advances a route whose way of understanding the church–world relationship

---

48. Conway, *Nazi Persecution of the Churches*, 84.
49. Weinrich, "Openness and Worldliness," 8.
50. Ibid., 8–9.
51. Ibid., 9.

does not assume opposition between them. Instead, the church is here considered in principle to be part of the world, inconceivable apart from it and sharing with it creation's distress, groans replete with hope, and the suffering and abysmal alienation associated with God's hiddenness. The church is "not called to demonstrate the realization of allegedly steadfast principles and maintainable values but to the continually new search to live the humanity of human beings in solidarity with the world and its needs."[52] It does, however, see "the 'world' which it shares with all other people in a particular light"[53]—a light which testifies that neither it nor the world are self-explanatory; that witnesses to God's reconciliation of the world to himself in Christ (2 Cor 5:19); which offers an explanation of the "world" which the "world" can never accept on its own terms and which contradicts the world's inescapable distress because it sees and hears in Jesus Christ God's promise that humanity is no longer bounded by "the nothingness with which death threatens us."[54] And because the church "trusts this promise it has to witness to the 'world' in word and deed that it is not the distress that is the true motor of all worldly events. Rather," Weinrich continues, "in the midst of the doubt and distress it confesses that the 'world' has not been abandoned to itself but has an opposite that is turned toward it, which has combined itself with the destiny of the 'world' in a simply salvific way so that in all its distress the 'world' can create courage and hope out of that."[55] At the same time, it "shares with the 'world' the unavoidable embarrassment of not being able to prove its particular interpretation of reality as either generally evident or at all compelling."[56]

The Christ who comes "clothed with his gospel"[57] impedes the idolatrous pretensions of religious habits and exposes them for what they are, admonishing and announcing to the church that insofar as it exists as a visible institution it exists as and among every other sinful entity in the world, with no claims of privilege upon God or upon God's movements and activities in the world. So Weinrich:

> It is certainly not given to the church ... to demonstrate convincingly to the "world" that it speaks of more than the strange self-prescription of a Baron von Münchhausen, who pulled himself out of the quagmire by his own hair. The church is and remains

---

52. Ibid., 21.
53. Ibid., 9.
54. Ibid., 14.
55. Ibid.
56. Ibid., 9–10.
57. Calvin, *Institutes*, III.ii.6.

part of this "world." The church is not called to romp about in the "Beyond." The "Beyond" becomes accessible to the church only when it is recognized in the here and now, i.e. if it reveals itself, whereby this revelation cannot become simply subjected to the conditions of this world. Revelation does not authorize demonstrations; it corresponds to confession and witness. The "*missio*" of the church is realized in that—it is to confess and to witness to the special turning of God to the world. And thus in this respect everything that the church can do and not do is, at bottom, never something that arises out of itself. The church is not the earthly agent of God but his worldly *witness* (Acts 1:8). The Protestant Church is a worldly church in that it knows that it does not possess God's Word, does not manage it and does not distribute it more or less generously. The church itself has to hear the Word continually anew, always has to seek it anew like manna in the desert. That is the fundamental meaning of *semper reformanda*. This does not produce any triumphalism of possession and salvation, no pleasure in religion and no guarantee of durability.[58]

Weinrich's use of the word "witness" here recalls that the community travels not without significant commendation, however. It is, after all, the community of God's election. In such is its freedom from all particularity of express forms, including cultural ones. Moreover, the divine election recalls that the earthly-historical body of Christ is constituted by the same event that is the content of the community's proclamation activities—the Word of God "visibly and concretely actualised."[59] One important implication of this is noted by the Dutch missiologist Christiaan Hoekendijk:

> We should be aware of a temptation to take the Church itself too seriously, to invite the Church to see itself as well-established, as God's secure bridgehead in the world, to think of itself as a *beatus possidens* [a blessed possessor] which, having what others do not have, distributes its possession to others, until a new company of *possidentes* is formed. We reach here a crucial issue. It is common to think of evangelism, to think of the apostolate, as a function of the Church. *Credo ecclesiam apostolicam* is often interpreted as: "I believe in the Church, which has an apostolic function." Would it not be truer to make a complete turn-over here, and to say that this means: I believe in the Church, which is a function of the Apostolate, that is, an instrument of God's

---

58. Weinrich, "Openness and Worldliness," 14–15.
59. Barth, *CD* III/2, 616.

redemptive action in this world. Or to put it in terms we used here, the Church is (nothing more, but also nothing less!) a means in God's hands to establish shalom in this world. It is taken into the triumphal procession of the glorified Son of Man and on its way it discovers that it walks amid the tokens of the coming Kingdom.[60]

Hoekendijk is correct, moreover, to aver that "Church-centric missionary thinking is bound to go astray, because it revolves around an illegitimate centre."[61] That the church, as "a function of the Apostolate," is reconceived and reformed anew only by the interruptive movements of Word and Spirit is a central insight of the Reformed, both in the sixteenth century and in the radical witness of the dialectical theology of the twentieth century—*Ecclesia reformata semper reformanda secundum verbum Dei*.

That *reformanda* is coupled with *semper* is, partly, a confession that the confessorial community witnesses amidst present concrete conflicts and challenges and is not frenzied to repristinate debates of earlier centuries. It is the community, in other words, elected to exercise a responsibility to hear and to witness to Christ *in tempore et in loco*. This singular call is bifurcated by efforts to defend static definitions of particular ecclesial traditions, efforts often motivated by modern quests for identity but which, when apotheosized, raise significant barriers for the witness of a community which is ecumenical and catholic. Put otherwise, such endeavors denote that the community has little theological sense of its own time and eschatological way; i.e., the sense that it always confesses more than it has been or than it can be. Such concerns, moreover, can signify an effort to "make a name for ourselves" (Gen 11:4), and may also betray a misjudged conviction that fidelity to and participation in the movement of divine election calls for seeking salvation via the restoration of one's tradition (of which Scripture and the interpretation thereof is a part) and its particular social embodiments. Such would signify a community witnessing to itself rather than to God's soteriological achievement in Jesus Christ, a witness truly of interest to the "world."

Moreover, as we shall have reason to further develop below, the community confesses Jesus Christ only ever as "a pilgrim people, always on the way towards a promised goal" *but never there*, always aware of the temptation to trust in golden calves along the way but pressed to make plain that that which it believes "was from the beginning," is the "word of life" which it has heard with its own ears and seen with its own eyes and touched with

---

60. Hoekendijk, "Call to Evangelism," 170.
61. Hoekendijk, *Church Inside Out*, 38.

its own hands (1 John 1:1). This ecclesiology of journey is powerfully articulated in The Basis of Union for the Uniting Church in Australia, most explicitly in Paragraph 3. Through that "most fundamental Paragraph in the whole Basis of Union,"[62] the Uniting Church confesses that "the faith and unity of the Holy Catholic and Apostolic Church"[63] is not a "series of human aspirations"[64] but is built upon and emerges out of a life and history given to it by God, namely Jesus' own life and history. This gift—who he is and what God does in him—is the content of the community's confession and witness; acts which, because of the nature and scope of God's claim upon all creation in Christ, extend to the entire cosmos. The ecumenical body of Christ is called by God to witness to God's will for all creation which is life with creation's catholic Lord in whom, through whom, and for whom all things exist, hold together, and come into God's promised shalom (Col 1:16–17, 20). This is to recall, among other things, that God's pilgrim people live both *by* and *towards* promise. It is also to confess that here among all the communities of the world is one which would stray into utter disorientation were it not for One who "feeds the Church with Word and Sacraments," and for the gift of the Spirit given "in order that it may not lose the way."[65] It is to offer no claim that it represents God in the world, nor that God has entrusted God's work to it *in toto*, nor that it in any way mediates between God and the world. Rather, it bears witness to the fact that the content of God's good news is the mediatorship that God himself provides in Jesus Christ.

Confession as eschatological event

Insofar as it properly belongs under the rubric of the third article, the church is a movement open to God's future, a movement without sense apart from eschatology. As Michael Owen has observed, "The meaning of Jesus Christ is not exhausted in ecclesiastical realities, but is to be fully expounded only in terms of the universal eschatological reconciliation and renewal. The Church's function is to serve that. Its nature is to be described in terms of its participation in the process and anticipation of the end of it."[66] Its branches might extend to the present, but its roots exist in the future it mediates to the world, and so its life is "shot through and through with tension and

---

62. McCaughey, *Commentary*, 19.
63. Uniting Church in Australia, *Basis of Union*, §3.
64. McCaughey, *Commentary*, 19.
65. Uniting Church in Australia, *Basis of Union*, §3.
66. Owen, *Back to Basics*, 82.

SEMPER REFORMANDA AS A CONFESSION OF CRISIS

crisis."[67] Consequently, the church must ever be aware of its own provisionality, its transitoriness, and its imperfection, disregard for which threatens to turn a movement of the Spirit's work into a series of idolatrous sects whose resources will, with little doubt, in turn be exhausted by efforts at self-preservation. This reality informs the content of the community's witness regarding the radical discontinuity between Jesus and the world, that belonging to Jesus disrupts all other modes of belonging.

To confess, therefore, is to choose a way of being which is both continuous and discontinuous with one's history, a way that confesses with saints past but also confesses *as if for the first time*. This is not to abandon or to disregard the past (for that too is God's gift) but it is to confess that creation is not oriented to return to it, that creation is being pulled forward by the Spirit of the Father into the promises of life with him who was crucified before the foundation of the world. He who promises to be present as Emmanuel is ever the coming one who eludes our capture, and whose being-with-us is characterized by an invitation to follow, to seek, and to love. To confess, in other words, remains an act of hope, faith's broadcast of the true time, and love's joyous announcement that the church's sociohistorical form will never correspond entirely to its destiny.

The temptation to capture revelation as some fixed given, as "a thing," is precisely what the formula *ecclesia reformata semper reformanda* seeks to safeguard against. The formula is itself a confession that the church is never more or less than a creature of an ever-new event of God's disruptive achievement in Jesus Christ, a *"happening"*[68] which cannot be fixed to a date on this world's calendar but is, as Rudolf Bultmann has argued, "always present (in proclamation)," always that which "demands our decision," always "in actuality . . . a beginning for us, whether we want it to be or not." The "omnitemporal event" of Christ marks the end of secular time.[69] To hear the Word of God thus is to hear "a word which is addressed to me, as *kerygma*, as a proclamation" which, precisely because it is God's act, precludes verification.[70] This puts a nail in the coffin of both evangelical fundamentalism (with its attempts to locate certainty in a fixed dogma or set of writings, the Protestant equivalent to Rome's inerrant magisterium) and of liberal historicism (with its efforts to deify human experience), and

---

67. MacKinnon, *Church of God*, 99.

68. Barth, *Table Talk*, 26.

69. Barth and Bultmann, *Letters*, 94; Bultmann, *Das Verkündigte Wort*, 237–38. See also Bultmann, *Jesus Christ and Mythology*, 78–79; Bultmann, *New Testament and Mythology*, 144.

70. Bultmann, *Jesus Christ and Mythology*, 71. See Käsemann, "Die Anfänge christlicher Theologie."

brings about both an existential and epistemological crisis while at the same time functioning as a critique of any suggestion that the present possession of the Spirit represents history's *telos*.

The event of Christ pronounces a judgment against attempts to universalize the concrete relation between God and human persons, or those efforts to offer neutral and observable comment. "God is not a given entity" but remains radically transcendent, *sui generis* in action, and resistant to objectification."[71] As J. Louis Martyn avers, God's event in Jesus Christ "is not visible, demonstrable, or provable in the categories and with the means of perception native to 'everyday' existence . . . The inbreak of the new creation is itself revelation, apocalypse." Faith alone knows, although can never grasp, this transfiguration of the vista of history, the aftermath of which is bifocal vision, the facility to see "both the evil age and the new creation simultaneously."[72] Little wonder, therefore, that to read the Bible is to risk the loss of "spiritual stiffness and a pious know-all manner," is "always a preparation for emergency."[73]

To gather our thoughts: The call *ecclesia reformata semper reformanda secundum verbum Dei* is a call, like that advanced to Kierkegaard's Abraham, to the risky work of staking one's entire being upon what one believes one has heard from the coming God, a word ready to fall only on today's soil, and which eludes all efforts of capture. It is a call to stake all upon the claim that "the nerve centre of the design and the firm ground which gives us confidence concerning our own destiny"[74] is solely the promise made to "those who see its logical absurdity"—that "Christ *must* reign."[75] So Barmen's attestation that "in the midst of a sinful world, with its faith as with its obedience, with its message as with its order," the church is "solely [Christ's] property," living and wanting to live "solely from his comfort and from his direction in the expectation of his appearance" (Barmen III). For a community to embody the spirit of *semper reformanda secundum verbum Dei* is, at least, to construct its life and doctrine "in the light of its future goal." Eschatology, therefore, "should not be its end, but its beginning."[76] It is to herald the righteousness of the coming God—the indivisible relationship between eschatology and ethics, of hope vis-à-vis the imminence of judgment, the characterization of which is not only the freedom of being-as-responsible

---

71. Bultmann, *Faith and Understanding*, 45.
72. Martyn, *Galatians*, 104.
73. Sauter, *Protestant Theology at the Crossroads*, 14, 59, 64.
74. Käsemann, "Subject of Primitive," 135.
75. Käsemann, "Apologia for Primitive," 195.
76. Moltmann, *Theology of Hope*, 16.

but also the burden of (apparent) recklessness and dispossession, the subject to which we now turn.

Confession as dispossession

In *Gemeinsames Leben* (*Life Together*), Dietrich Bonhoeffer suggests that one can "never know in advance how God's image should appear in others." God's "free and sovereign" activity always manifests itself, he says, not only in forms "completely new and unique," but also in forms that appear to us to be "strange" and "even ungodly." Of this we ought not to be surprised, for God patterns persons in the likeness of one who himself "certainly looked strange and ungodly,"[77] actions which may indicate something of the shape of how the Creator's activity operates in other ways too. Ever elusive, ever free, ever strange, the Word is heard and seen (or not seen and heard) in unlikely places (e.g., Isa 53:4; Matt 25, 27:4, 22; Luke 23:38–41; John 4:39).

Such recalls that the Bible does not provide a universal ethic that bypasses the particular demands placed upon those who seek to leave behind all claims to power and entitlement and to follow Jesus in community. Such persons are distinguished by their association with one who keeps odd company, who calls persons to peculiarity, who continually corrects our range of view regarding the world's true nature, and who forms a people constituted by and for a love so radically other-person-centered that they refuse to imagine life apart from blessing those who are opposed to them. It is a people who do life together "in the midst of the traffic and turmoil and conflict of the world"[78] in such a way that they are entirely uninvested in their own self-preservation. It is a community entirely hopeful that it "should find orientation and consolation in the promise that it will remain a true community of witness as long as it remains a community of true witness."[79] It is a community that has also, in many places, been taken out of slavery and now enjoys the inducements of other worldly lords. It is equally a community that, in some of those same places, now finds itself disregarded by those same lords and residing among its own ruins in the exile of God's liberating promise to be "aliens and strangers" (1 Pet 2:11). It is, paradoxically, the most worldly of communities, called and given over by the Word for a vocation entirely in this world but finally dependent on resources from outwith it. It is a community that lives faithfully with the receding horizon of postponed dreams and made free thereby to throw itself entirely into

---

77. Bonhoeffer, *Life Together*, 95.
78. Stringfellow, *Private and Public Faith*, 19.
79. Schwöbel, "Creature of the Word," 154.

the embarrassing service of Jesus, and that not for God's sake but solely for the sake of the world. It is a community that risks the refusal to participate in the politics of violence and in the economies of human indignity. It is a community that manifests God's orientation for every part of creation. It is a community that ventures out "beyond the security of objective certainties, [and] worldly possessions, [and] finite aspirations and society's approval." It is a community seeking to alienate itself from any notion that displays inane optimism about the church *in se*. It is a community that risks even its life with God so that it might "become contemporary with Christ."[80] It is a community that has the occupation of its hope precisely in the shattering of human certitude and in the call to witness to the claim that one "can exist authentically only in the surrender of certainty and by the grace of God."[81] It is a community, therefore, that is always learning how to fail, always discovering and unveiling its uneven record, always losing the taste for "ecclesiastical earnestness" which can only ever truncate the truth and which will sooner or later lead to heresy.[82]

I suggested earlier that the community's principal and ongoing task is to hear God's address. "But," as Barth reminds us, "it must listen in such a way that its whole life is put in question. It must listen in a readiness that its whole life should be assailed, convulsed, revolutionised and reshaped." Its continual return to this "startingpoint" in faithfulness, gratitude, and with regard for all that it has hitherto received from the hand of the Lord, means that it is "radically prepared for the fact that to-day, to-morrow and the day after the whole of its treasure will again have to be enlightened and illuminated, assessed and weighed by the Word of God."[83] In view here is a community for whom the event of divine self-exposure *to* destruction "for the sake of history's deliverance *from* destruction"[84] is determinative for its own life, and provides the pattern for its own witness in this time between times. In view here is a community which recognizes as Lord one uninsulated "against the catastrophe and boundless sorrow which would be creation's devastation and time's annihilation,"[85] one who risks losing history in its entirety through the dereliction of the beloved Son in whom "all things hold together" (Col 1:17). Such a community recognizes that its participation in the *missio dei* is always accompanied by repentance and transfiguration, by

80. Rae, *Kierkegaard and Theology*, 180.
81. Barth and Bultmann, *Letters*, 92.
82. Barth, *CD* I/2, 808; cf. Ernst, *Multiple Echo*, 221.
83. Barth, *CD* I/2, 804. See also 809–10.
84. Lewis, *Between Cross and Resurrection*, 298.
85. Ibid., 298.

an awareness that it itself is a community under judgment, "a community perceptibly in process of transformation away from exclusivity and uncriticised patterns of power."[86] It is a community delighting in the freedom of existing for others only.[87] Consequently, its witness is "*always* a witness of resistance to the *status quo* in politics, economics, and all society. It is a witness of resurrection from death," a reminder that the event *par excellence* of the new creation—namely, the resurrection of the dead Jesus—generates a movement and ethic undetermined by that which is passing away and determined by what is to come. This is to "constantly risk death—through execution, exile, imprisonment, persecution, defamation, or harassment— at the behest of the rulers of this age. Yet those who do not resist the rulers of the present darkness are consigned to a moral death, the death of their humanness. That, of all the ways of dying, is the most ignominious."[88]

The confessing community is called to lose faith in present arrangements, to be entirely undaunted by "what the world calls possible," and to trust instead in the completely irresponsible impossibilities which "exist first on God's lips" and in God's imagination.[89] As the community journeys the infrequently-trodden path away from the centers of imperial power and towards the embarrassing outskirts of Jerusalem and its public scorn it is given the kind of freedom to be the light of the world and the city on the hill of which its Lord speaks, the kind of freedom characteristic of the Holy Spirit unconstrained by the "protective guardianship" of the *status quo* of establishment. Such journeys are never free of cost; neither is the political and ecclesiastical dead hand of authoritarianism that would tame the Spirit in the name of "orthodoxy" free of such. Like the dogmatic task itself, the quest for existence before and in God requires that the subjects learn "some sort of dispossession, the constant rediscovery and critique of the myth of the self as owner of its perceptions and positions." The truth, as Rowan Williams reminds us, "requires loss, self-displacement, a never-ending 'adjustment,'" a move "away from the illusions of rivalry,"[90] and the sacramental practice of "relinquishing the fantasy that the work of Christ is 'resigned' into our hands."[91] As Williams would reflect elsewhere:

> If we had to choose between a Church tolerably confident of what it has to say and seeking only for effective means of saying

---

86. Williams, *Mission and Christology*, 10.
87. Bonhoeffer, *Letters and Papers*, 56.
88. Stringfellow, *Instead of Death*, 101.
89. Brueggemann, *Commentary on Jeremiah*, 269.
90. Williams, "Between Politics," 17.
91. Williams, *Mission and Christology*, 20.

it, and a Church constantly engaged in an internal dialogue and critique of itself, an exploration to discover what is central to its being, I should say that it is the latter which is the more authentic—a Church which understands that part of what it is *offering* to humanity is the possibility of living in such a mode. What the Church "has to say" is never a simple verbal message: it is an invitation to entrust your life to a certain vision of the possibilities of humanity in union with God. And to entrust yourself in this way is to put your thinking and experience, your reactions and your initiatives daily into question, under the judgment of the central creative memory of Jesus Christ, present in his Spirit to his community.[92]

The missiological implications are obvious—the good news is shared with the explicit awareness of its strangeness to us, of its being entirely unbound to our understanding. To preach the gospel, therefore, is to experience a profound letting go, an unmastering, dispossession. It is to experience oneself as the unstable bearer of a live question.

Hans Küng reminds us that "the phrase '*ecclesia semper reformanda*' is not just a slogan for times of especial difficulty," but a description of the character of a community *en route*, of pilgrims "journeying through the midst of time."[93] Such a community-in-diaspora is always betraying its "exodus culture," is always willing to travel "away from the old institutions"[94] and fixed abodes. It lives an "eschatological existence," thrust into "an unprecedented history" of free people and into a "continuous risky adventure with always hazardous improvisations." Insofar as this is true, its life manifests the act of God's creation liberated from the oppression of worlds too tamed and is called into an open and risk-charged history with unbridled horizons. Only a people who are open toward *this* future are "up to date," take a realistic position among all the facts, and deserve to be called "sanguine."[95]

God's "wandering people"[96] are no continuing city and have no lasting possession, "no finality in [their] institutional life."[97] They are those for

---

92. Williams, "Women and the Ministry," 12.

93. Küng, *Church*, 130–31. Barth introduced the phrase *ecclesia semper reformanda* to Küng in Basel in 1959. See Küng, *My Struggle for Freedom*, 167–68.

94. Hoekendijk, *Church Inside Out*, 158. We must be careful not to say that the diaspora community *must* always travel "away from the old institutions" lest we fix the form of the church in advance. Barth's caution against radical*ism* applies here. See Barth, *Romans*, 529; cf. Tillich, *Protestant Era*, 162.

95. Hoekendijk, *Church Inside Out*, 161–63.

96. A phrase borrowed from Käsemann, *Wandering People of God*.

97. McCaughey, *Commentary*, 21.

whom the paradox articulated in the *theologia crucis* is inescapable—the *verbum crucis* which alone makes life intelligible, and which "should give us pause when we are tempted to go a-whoring after those delicately balanced systems of philosophical theology that academic teachers offer us from time to time."[98] People on pilgrimage travel light, are awake to the truth that their strength lies in the knowledge that they are, in principle, weak; that they are not "called for [their] own sake or to develop a particular splendour which all too quickly tempts [them] toward a problematic self-consciousness." A pilgrim people live without "any special authorization or qualifications" that can be summoned up over against the world in order to obtain "a special self-consciousness." A pilgrim people is not "an institution of salvation" which has "at its disposal means of grace that it can simply distribute."[99] Rather, as Ben Myers has noted, it is:

> the most vulnerable of all communities, roaming through the world with no place of its own, suspended over the abyss of nonbeing, upheld solely by a Word that calls it continually into being. It is a church whose identity lies outside itself, whose institutional continuity is not a possession but an eschatological promise . . . Without a time, without a place. The church of Jesus Christ is the most fragile of all institutions, since its own constitution (so to speak) strictly prohibits any attempt to win for itself institutional security and continuity . . . [T]o confess is to venture the risk of obedience. To confess is to stand exposed before the strangeness of the one who calls.[100]

To confess is to put "safety last,"[101] to take up the sole vocation of the Word of God wherein there is neither norm nor ideal nor principle from which preconceived speech can be derived. To confess is to abandon all presumption of God's mind, to disown all commandeering of privilege in God's economy, to patiently abstain from claiming precognition of the judgment of God's Word, to continually risk the judgment of God's Word, to esteem the autonomy and freedom of God's will, to risk declaring in word and deed the grace who encounters us (1 John 1:1).

---

98. MacKinnon, *Church of God*, 95.
99. Weinrich, "Openness and Worldliness," 2.
100. Myers, "In His Own Strange Way," 40, 41.
101. Hoekendijk, *Church Inside Out*, 148–66.

Semper reformanda: The Possibility of Witness and the Collapse of the (Constantinian) Status Quo[102]

That the church in the West may be witnessing the collapse of the Constantinian arrangement in which the Reformed have so deeply invested occasions the opportunity to reconsider its relationship vis-à-vis the State, a reconsideration demanded moreover by the gospel's eschatological character. Certainly, a community marked by a determination to be sustained by God's Word alone will be a community that risks dismantling the old alliances between throne (or parliament) and altar. It will become an "unreliable ally" (Barth) for every political system because to be church is to be engaged in ongoing renegotiation about practices and their fittingness to the Gospel in unreliable circumstances. It will be a community, therefore, which discourages all "stupid allegiance to political authority as if that were service to the church and, *a fortiori*, to God,"[103] and therefore a community that risks radical dissent from all current arrangements, Constantinian or otherwise. Such dissent is an indication not only that the stakes are high, but also that human achievement has, as Davis McCaughey reminds us, a "transitory character" about it. "The great weakness of all ideologies," he writes, "is that they are utopian and self-righteous," a reality about which dissenters on both the right and the left appear to be most aware.[104] Here rises the question concerning the fallenness of principalities and powers, fallenness which is conjunctive with but not dependent upon or derivative of humanity's renunciation of life in the sheer gift of God's Word who is not bound to any "system" and who acts to undo the scandal that recalcitrance has fashioned, to announce his sole lordship over all things uninitiated by the threat of death, and to renew creation's vocation in freedom and service.

Without minimizing some of Christendom's remarkable achievements, it seems to me judicious that the ecclesial and theological traditions forged under its assumptions, atmosphere, and protection undergo critical judgment vis-à-vis the Word of God; i.e., Jesus Christ. John de Gruchy rightly challenges Reformed communities, especially those who have aligned themselves with the dominant political powers, to break free from "the 'Constantinian captivity' which has been part of the legacy of the Reformed tradition since the sixteenth Century." This does not mean, he avers, "adopting a politically neutral stance or eschewing the responsible use of power." Indeed, a project like the Reformed's is, after all, essentially *public*

---

102. The phrase "Constantinian status quo" comes from Stringfellow, *Conscience and Obedience*, 48.

103. Ibid., 49.

104. McCaughey, *Tradition and Dissent*, 33.

and acutely concerned for the public commons. "The question is not," therefore, "whether the church is going to use political influence, but how, on behalf of whom, and from what perspective it is going to do so. Is it going to be used 'to preserve the social prestige which comes from its ties to the groups in power or to free itself from the prestige with a break from these groups and with genuine service to the oppressed'?"[105] The question testifies to the church's kenotic trajectory, a trajectory that is open to the world and is for the world, a for-ness that occasions imperatives and opportunities that it dare not desert lest it abandon that eminently gospel note that God does not will that the world go to the dogs—*Nulla salus extra mundum*, "There is no salvation outside the world."[106]

I have written elsewhere[107] in support of the church's positive contribution to civic life, a contribution that acknowledges the State as a power ordained by God, and that affirms public service and even the dignity of political office which, though habitually debased, can remain an expression of God's gift and calling. Certainly, I have no qualms with the Reformed instinct to perceive *both* the law *and* the gospel as expressions of divine grace. I do believe, however, that realities about the State and the Church are not simply transferable, that there are responsibilities of government that are incompatible with service of Jesus Christ, that the Christian community, unlike the State, is, for example, called to operate "without human force and by God's Word alone,"[108] and, with de Gruchy, that "creative infidelity and sterile fidelity ultimately amount to the same thing—a failure to hear the liberating and life-giving Word in relation to our own historical context."[109] There is a conflict to be named here, a conflict that alone makes both history and the Christian life intelligible, and that if avoided empties the Word of God of its free and gracious character, creating a crisis incomparable with any whose origins lie in this world, and that thrusts the church into a new situation before God's seat of judgment. It is a crisis especially for those who hanker after a secure life, a kind of *sturmfreies Gebiet* ["invulnerable area"] in the world—whether it be in the form of ecclesiastical establishment, or of philosophical, constitutional and/or institutional guarantees such as threaten to sabotage the community's prophetic and apostolic character by blasphemously envisioning it as an "embodiment of an ultimate security."

---

105. De Gruchy, "Toward a Reformed Theology," 107–8. Here de Gruchy cites Gutiérrez, *Theology of Liberation*, 266–67.

106. Schillebeeckx, *Church*, 12.

107. Goroncy, "Church and Civil Society," 195–210.

108. The Augsburg Confession, 28.

109. De Gruchy, *Liberating Reformed Theology*, 73.

Such a move only encourages "a ground for boasting rather than an opportunity for presence" and a status at pains to ensure "a counterfeit security rather than a way of assuring that there shall be no withdrawal from the actualities of human life."[110] More scandalously, such a flight to security signals "a withdrawal from accepting the peril and the promise of the Incarnation"; namely, the call to live "an exposed life" before God, one "stripped of the kind of security that tradition, whether ecclesiological or institutional, easily bestows."[111]

Such exposure characterizes equally the epistemic precariousness and necessary incompleteness of faith's orientation, a situation that invites people of faith to grasp towards what—or, more properly, towards him whom—they seek to know. Faith lives not on abstract principles but *in*, *dependent upon*, and *oriented towards* the *mysterium Christi* in which we are deprived of the "sort of security that we tend uncritically to associate with a dependence for which we claim ultimacy." Here, as Donald MacKinnon avers,

> We are left asking questions in a process of interrogation that is partly, though not entirely, self-interrogation, to which we see no easy end; but this may be as it is because the mysteries that set our inquiring in motion have their authority over us, thus continually to disturb our minds, only because they do touch what is ultimate, which is at once within and yet wholly beyond our comprehension.[112]

Such ceaseless vacillation, the irresolution between finding and fashioning, calls for a mode of unremitting receptivity to, dependence upon, and reformation by the Word—*Ecclesia reformata semper reformanda secundum verbum Dei*—witness to whom, in the inconspicuous reality of God's self-giving, is the *raison d'être* for this most idiosyncratic of communities. For such a community to compromise or abandon fidelity to this vocation is to invite "mistrust, repudiation, [and] contempt even if it seeks to justify that infidelity by reference to historical necessity or even pastoral opportunity."[113]

Against the "unyielding commitment" of "ecclesiological fundamentalism"[114] that, apprehensive at the prospect of institutional death and radical alteration, gropes for "a return to a seemingly unequivocal set of credal standards," practices, or causes which, it is hoped, might "justify"

---

110. MacKinnon, *Stripping of the Altars*, 26, 28.
111. Ibid., 33, 34.
112. MacKinnon and Lampe, *Resurrection*, 85.
113. MacKinnon, "Christology and Protest," 186–87.
114. MacKinnon, *Stripping of the Altars*, 9, 23, 60.

its position vis-à-vis the world, the church is given "only one identity that teleologically enshrouds its entire existence from birth to death"[115]—namely, the Word of God by which it is birthed through the waters of baptism and by which it is oriented through the proclamation activities of table and pulpit where the *ecclesia via media* hears the Word afresh and is commissioned for its strange service in the world, service fulfilled precisely by being true to its own self as the creature of the living Word and thereby confronting the world, its principalities and powers, with the truth concerning its own nature and destiny. Only when the church is "the church"—i.e., a people who embrace life in the world under the judgment of the divine Word—might the world be given a vision of an alternative way of being that recognizes the necessity for repentance and that looks forward to the *kairos* of the Word's coming again.

---

115. Jinkins, *Church Faces Death*, 110n55.

Bibliography

Armstrong, Brian G. "*Semper Reformanda*: The Case of the French Reformed Church, 1559–1620." In *Later Calvinism: International Perspectives*, edited by W. Fred Graham, 119–40. Kirksville: Sixteenth Century Journal, 1994.

Barth, Karl. *Against the Stream: Shorter Post-War Writings 1946–52*. London: SCM, 1954.

———. *Die Botschaft von der freien Gnade Gottes*. Theologische Studien 23. Zürich: Zollikon Evangelischer Verlag, 1947.

———. *Church Dogmatics*. Translated by G. T. Thomson et al. Edinburgh: T. & T. Clark, 1936–77.

———. *The Epistle to the Romans*. Oxford: Oxford University Press, 1968.

———. *Evangelical Theology: An Introduction*. Translated by Grover Foley. 1963. Reprinted, Grand Rapids: Eerdmans, 1979.

———. *The Göttingen Dogmatics: Instruction in the Christian Religion*. Translated by Geoffrey W. Bromiley. Grand Rapids: Eerdmans, 1991.

———. *Texte zur Barmer Theologischen Erklärung: Mit einer Einleitung von Eberhard Jüngel und einem Editionsbericht*. Edited by Martin Rohkrämer. Zürich: TVZ, 2004.

———. *The Word of God and Theology*. Translated by Amy Marga. New York: T. & T. Clark, 2011.

Barth, Karl, and Rudolf Bultmann. *Letters 1922–1966*. Translated by Geoffrey W. Bromiley. Grand Rapids: Eerdmans, 1981.

Bonhoeffer, Dietrich. *Berlin: 1932–1933*. Translated by Isabel Best and David Higgins. Minneapolis: Fortress, 2009.

———. *Christology*. Translated by John Bowden. London: Collins, 1966.

———. *Letters and Papers from Prison*, edited by Eberhard Bethge, et al. Translated by Isabel Best, et al. Minneapolis: Fortress, 2010.

———. *Life Together; Prayerbook of the Bible*. Edited by Geffrey B. Kelly. Translated by Daniel W. Bloesch and James H. Burtness. Dietrich Bonhoeffer Works 5. Minneapolis: Fortress, 1996.

Brueggemann, Walter. *A Commentary on Jeremiah: Exile and Homecoming*. 2nd ed. Grand Rapids: Eerdmans, 1998.

Bultmann, Rudolf Karl. *Faith and Understanding*. Edited by Robert W. Funk. Translated by Louise Pettibone Smith. Philadelphia: Fortress, 1987.

———. *Jesus Christ and Mythology*. New York: Scribner, 1958.

———. *New Testament and Mythology and Other Basic Writings*. Translated by Schubert M. Ogden. Philadelphia: Fortress, 1984.

———. *Das Verkündigte Wort: Predigten, Andachten, Ansprachen 1906–1941*. Edited by Erich Grässer and Martin Evang. Tübingen: Mohr/Siebeck, 1984.

Burleigh, John H. S. *A Church History of Scotland*. London: Oxford University Press, 1960.

Bush, Michael. "Calvin and the Reformanda Sayings." In *Calvinus Sacrarum Literarum Interpres: Papers of the International Congress on Calvin Research*, edited by Herman J. Selderhuis, 287. Reformed Historical Theology 5. Göttingen: Vandenhoeck & Ruprecht, 2008.

Calvin, John. *Commentary on the Book of the Prophet Isaiah, Volumes 1 and 4*. Translated by William Pringle. Grand Rapids: Baker, 2003.

———. *Institutes of the Christian Religion*. Edited by John T. McNeill. Translated by Ford Lewis Battles. Philadelphia: Westminster, 1977.

———. *Ioannis Calvini Opera Quae Supersunt Omnia*, edited by Guilielmus Baum, et al., 15:335. Berlin: Schwetschke, 1863–1900.

———. *Letters, Part 4, 1559–1564*. Edited by Jules Bonnet. Translated by Marcus Robert Gilcrist. Grand Rapids: Baker, 1983.

———. "The Necessity of Reforming the Church." In *Calvin: Theological Treatises*, edited by J. K. S. Reid, 187. London: SCM, 1954.

Conway, John S. *The Nazi Persecution of the Churches, 1933–1945*. Vancouver, BC: Regent College Publishing, 1968.

De Gruchy, John W. *Liberating Reformed Theology: A South African Contribution to an Ecumenical Debate*. Grand Rapids: Eerdmans, 1991.

———. "Toward a Reformed Theology of Liberation: A Retrieval of Reformed Symbols in the Struggle for Justice." In *Toward the Future of Reformed Theology: Tasks, Topics, Traditions*, edited by David Willis and Michael Welker, 103–19. Grand Rapids: Eerdmans, 1999.

Eliot, T. S. "Choruses from 'The Rock'—1934." In *Collected Poems, 1909–1962*, 147. New York: Harcourt, Brace & World, 1963.

Ernst, Cornelius. *Multiple Echo: Explorations in Theology*. Edited by Fergus Kerr and Timothy Radcliffe. London: Darton, Longman & Todd, 1979.

Forsyth, P. T. "The Cross as the Final Seat of Authority." *Contemporary Review* 76 (1899) 589–609.

Goroncy, Jason A. "Church and Civil Society in the Reformed Tradition: An Old Relationship and a New Communion." *Reformed World* 61 (2011) 195–210.

Gutiérrez, Gustavo. *A Theology of Liberation: History, Politics, and Salvation*. Translated by Sister Caridad Inda and John Eagleson. Maryknoll, NY: Orbis, 1988.

Hoekendijk, Johannes Christiaan. "The Call to Evangelism." *International Review of Missions* 39 (1950) 167–75.

———. *The Church Inside Out*. Translated by Isaac C. Rottenberg. London: SCM, 1967.

Jinkins, Michael. *The Church Faces Death: Ecclesiology in a Post-Modern Context*. Oxford: Oxford University Press, 1999.

———. *The Church Transforming: What's Next for the Reformed Project?* Louisville: Westminster John Knox, 2012.

Jüngel, Eberhard. *Christ, Justice and Peace: Toward a Theology of the State*. Translated by D. Bruce Hamill and Alan J. Torrance. Edinburgh: T. & T. Clark, 1992.

Käsemann, Ernst. "Die Anfänge Christlicher Theologie." In *Exegetische Versuche und Besinnungen*, 82–104. Göttingen: Vandenhoeck & Ruprecht, 1965.

———. "An Apologia for Primitive Christian Apocalyptic." In *Essays on New Testament Themes*, 169–95. Translated by W. J. Montague. Studies in Biblical Theology 1/41. London: SCM, 1964.

———. *My Struggle for Freedom: Memoirs*. Translated by John Bowden. London: Continuum, 2004.

———. "On the Subject of Primitive Christian Apocalyptic." In *New Testament Questions of Today*, 108–37. Translated by W. J. Montague. London: SCM, 1969.

———. *Perspectives on Paul*. Translated by Margaret Kohl. Philadelphia: Fortress, 1971.

———. *The Wandering People of God: An Investigation of the Letter to the Hebrews*. Translated by Roy A. Harrisville and Irving L. Sandberg. 1984. Reprinted, Eugene, OR: Wipf & Stock, 2002.

Koelman, Jacobus. *De Pointen van Nodige Reformatie, Ontrent de Kerk, en Kerkelijke, en Belijders der Gereformeerde Kerke van Nederlandt*. Vlissingen: Abraham van Laaren and Willem de Wilde, 1678.

Kraemer, Hendrik. *The Christian Message in a Non-Christian World*. London: International Missionary Council, 1938.

Küng, Hans. *The Church*. Translated by Ray Ockenden and Rosaleen Ockenden. London: Burns & Oates, 1992.

Lewis, Alan E. *Between Cross and Resurrection: A Theology of Holy Saturday*. Grand Rapids: Eerdmans, 2001.

MacIntyre, Alasdair. *After Virtue*. 2nd ed. Notre Dame: University of Notre Dame Press, 1984.

MacKinnon, Donald M. "Christology and Protest." In *Trevor Huddleston: Essays on His Life and Work*, edited by Deborah Duncan Honoré, 186–87. Oxford: Oxford University Press, 1988.

———. *The Church of God*. Westminster: Dacre, 1940.

———. *The Stripping of the Altars: The Gore Memorial Lecture Delivered on 5 November 1968 in Westminister Abbey, and Other Papers and Essays on Related Topics*. London: Collins, 1969.

MacKinnon Donald M., and Geoffrey W. H. Lampe. *The Resurrection: A Dialogue Arising from Broadcasts*. Edited by William Purcell. London: Mowbray, 1966.

Mahlmann, Theodor. "Ecclesia Semper Reformanda: Eine Historische Aufklärung." In *Theologie und Kirchenleitung: Festschrift für Peter Steinacker zum 60. Geburtstag*, edited by Hermann Deuser, et al., 57–77. Marburg: Elwert, 2003.

———. "Reformation." In *Historisches Wörterbuch der Philosophie* 8 (1992) 416–27.

Martyn, J. Louis. *Galatians*. Anchor Bible 33A. New York: Doubleday, 1997.

McCaughey, J. Davis. *Commentary on the Basis of Union of the Uniting Church in Australia*. Melbourne: Uniting Church Press, 1980.

———. *Tradition and Dissent*. Carlton South: Melbourne University Press, 1997.

Milton, John. "Areopagitica: A Speech for the Liberty of Unlicens'd Printing, to the Parliament of England." In *The Works of John Milton, Historical, Political and Miscellaneous*. London: Millar, 1753.

Moltmann, Jürgen. "Theologia Reformata et Semper Reformanda." In *Toward the Future of Reformed Theology: Tasks, Topics, Traditions*, edited by David Willis and Michael Welker, 121. Grand Rapids: Eerdmans, 1999.

———. *Theology of Hope: On the Ground and the Implications of a Christian Eschatology*. Translated by James W. Leitch. New York: Harper & Row, 1967.

Myers, Benjamin. "'In His Own Strange Way': Indigenous Australians and the Church's Confession." *Uniting Church Studies* 16 (2010) 40, 41.

Nebelsick, Harold P. "'Ecclesia Reformata Semper Reformanda.'" *Reformed Liturgy and Music* 18 (1984) 59–63.

Polanyi, Michael. *The Tacit Dimension*. Terry Lectures. Garden City, NY: Doubleday, 1966.

Public Papers of the Secretaries-General of the United Nations, Volume 2: Dag Hammarskjöld 1953–1956, edited by Andrew W. Cordier and Wilder Foote. New York: Columbia University Press, 1972.

Owen, Michael. *Back to Basics: Studies on the Basis of Union of the Uniting Church in Australia*. Melbourne: Uniting Church Press, 1996.

Rae, Murray. *Kierkegaard and Theology*. London: T. & T. Clark, 2010.

Sauter, Gerhard. *Protestant Theology at the Crossroads: How to Face the Crucial Tasks for Theology in the Twenty-First Century.* Grand Rapids: Eerdmans, 2007.

Schillebeeckx, Edward. *Church: The Human Story of God.* New York: Crossroad, 1990.

Schwöbel, Christoph. "The Creature of the Word: Recovering the Ecclesiology of the Reformers." In *On Being the Church: Essays on Christian Community*, edited by Colin E. Gunton and Daniel W. Hardy, 110–55. Edinburgh: T. & T. Clark, 1989.

Stringfellow, William. *Conscience and Obedience: The Politics of Romans 13 and Revelation 13 in Light of the Second Coming.* 1977. Reprinted, Eugene, OR: Wipf & Stock, 2004.

———. *Instead of Death.* 1976. Reprinted, Eugene, OR: Wipf & Stock, 2004.

———. *A Private and Public Faith.* 1962. Reprinted, Eugene, OR: Wipf & Stock, 1999.

Theissen, Henning. "Witness and Service to the World: Discovering Protestant Church Renewal in Europe." *Neue Zeitschrift für Systematische Theologie und Religionsphilosophie* 53 (2011) 225–36.

Thompson, Bard. *Liturgies of the Western Church.* Cleveland: Meridian, 1961.

Tillich, Paul. *The Protestant Era.* Translated by James Luther Adams. Chicago: University of Chicago Press, 1948.

Uniting Church in Australia. *The Basis of Union.* Melbourne: Uniting Church Press, 1992.

Weinrich, Michael. "The Openness and Worldliness of the Church." In *Reformed and Ecumenical: On Being Reformed in Ecumenical Encounters*, edited by Christine Lienemann-Perrin et al., 1–23. Amsterdam: Rodopi, 2000.

Williams, Rowan. "Between Politics and Metaphysics: Reflections in the Wake of Gillian Rose." *Modern Theology* 11 (1995) 3–22.

———. *Mission and Christology: J. C. Jones Memorial Lecture.* Brynmawr: Welsh Members Council, Church Mission Society, 1994.

———. *Resurrection: Interpreting the Easter Gospel.* London: Darton, Longman & Todd, 1982.

———. "Women and the Ministry: A Case for Theological Seriousness." In *Feminine in the Church*, edited by Monica Furlong, 11–27. London: SPCK, 1984.

Van Lodensteyn, Jodocus. *Beschouwinge van Zion: Ofte, Aandagten en Opmerkingen Over den Tegenwoordigen Toestand Van't Gereformeerde Christen Volk.* Utrecht: Clerek, 1674.

Webster, John. *Holy Scripture: A Dogmatic Sketch.* Current Issues in Theology 1. Cambridge: Cambridge University Press, 2003.

Zanchi, Girolamo. "Zanchi a Bèze [Strasbourg—février 1562]." In *Théodore de Bèze: Correspondance Tome IV, 1562-1563*, edited by Hippolyte Aubert, 60. Geneva: Droz, 1965.

———. "De Reformatione Ecclesiarum." In *Omnium Operum Theologicorum* 3, col. 714. Geneva: Crispin, 1619.

PART 2

Reformed Theology and Religious Diversity

4

Barth and Thatamanil
Two Theologians against Religion

MARTHA MOORE-KEISH

> "We begin with the proposition that religion is *faithlessness*; religion is a concern—one must say, in fact, *the* concern—of *godless* man."[1] —KARL BARTH

> "What might it mean for theology to think beyond and after 'religion'?"[2] —JOHN THATAMANIL

ONE OF THE MOST pressing questions in contemporary theology is this: how does one understand and practice one's own particular faith commitment in the midst of religious diversity? This issue has attracted an increasing amount of attention from Christian theologians over the course of the twentieth and early twenty-first centuries. In this essay, I will explore how the category "religion" itself complicates the effort to live faithfully amid multiple religious traditions. I will do this by engaging the work of two theologians, both of Protestant traditions: twentieth-century Swiss theologian Karl Barth and contemporary Indian-American theologian John Thatamanil.

---

1. Barth, *On Religion*, 55. This volume is Green's translation of and commentary on Barth's *Church Dogmatics* I/2, par. 17. All references to par. 17 of Barth's *Church Dogmatics* in this essay will come from Green's translation, unless otherwise noted.

2. Thatamanil, "Comparative Theology."

Background

Initially, the question was prompted by those engaged in mission and evangelism, who reflected on what and whether true knowledge of the God of Jesus Christ was available through the writings and practices of non-Christians. This field of study is generally called "theology of religion," meaning theological reflection on the existence of multiple human religion/s, particularly in relation to the Christian gospel. This era (roughly 1920s-1960s) also witnessed a growing question about whether and how salvation might be available to people who were not explicitly "Christian." One important turning point in this development for Christians around the world was the Second Vatican Council (1962–65), when for the first time the Roman Catholic Church acknowledged "rays of truth" in religious traditions other than Christianity. Beginning in the 1970s, theologians such as Alan Race and John Hick began to issue a strong challenge to the presumption that the Christian religion offered the only true way to God, and the now-familiar typology of exclusivism, inclusivism, and pluralism emerged to describe the three major "theologies of religious pluralism" (TRP). In more recent years, however, this typology itself has been challenged on a number of grounds: 1) because it is too simple, obscuring genuine differences among theological approaches, and 2) because it centers on the question of "salvation" as the guiding question, asking whether non-Christians can be "saved," while this category itself is not universally shared, nor the only significant question that might be asked about a religious tradition.[3]

Since the 1990s, increasing (but still small) numbers of theologians have been engaging explicitly in "comparative theology," reflecting theologically not only *about* religious diversity, but *with* theological resources of other religious traditions. As Francis Clooney describes it, "comparative theology is a manner of learning that takes seriously diversity and tradition, openness and truth, allowing neither to decide the meaning of our religious situation without recourse to the other."[4] Comparative theologians such as Clooney, Robert Neville, and John Thatamanil typically maintain strong commitments to a "home" tradition, but also take seriously the normative claims of at least one other religious tradition, learning "across religious

---

3. Mark Heim's work is particularly relevant here, both in *Salvations* and in *The Depth of the Riches*.

4. Clooney, *Comparative Theology*, 8. There was an earlier movement called "comparative theology" in the eighteenth–nineteenth centuries, as described and critiqued by Clooney himself on 30–40, and by Tomoku Masuzawa in *the Invention of World Religions*, 72–104. The contemporary movement of comparative theology, however, is not a direct descendent of this earlier discipline, though comparative theologians like Clooney are attentive to its positive intentions as well as its pitfalls.

borders"—and in the process, challenging the very notion that these borders are impermeable, or the traditions incommensurable.

In the midst of the burgeoning interest in thinking theologically about and with religious "others," the theology of Karl Barth has usually been considered less than helpful. As the opening quote shows, early in the *Church Dogmatics,* Barth issued a stinging indictment of all human religion as "faithlessness," and Christianity alone as the "true religion," because Christianity alone has received the revelation of God in Jesus Christ. This claim has caused many theologians, such as Paul Knitter, to label Barth an "exclusivist", that is, one who believes that Christians alone know God truly and are thus able to be "saved."[5] In his own writing, Barth demonstrated little direct knowledge of or interest in religions other than Christianity (with the exception of Judaism, and a notable footnote regarding Pure Land Buddhism in *CD* I/2).

One vignette displays clearly Barth's negative judgment regarding other religions. In a personal reflection written shortly after Barth's death, South Asian theologian D.T. Niles recalls with affection his first meeting with Barth, in 1935. In the course of that conversation, they talked about Christian communities in Asia living in the midst of people of other "faiths." Barth declared, "Other religions are just unbelief." Niles asked Barth how he knew that Hinduism was unbelief without ever having met a Hindu person. Barth answered "A priori." Niles just smiled and silently shook his head.[6]

Based on his blanket judgment on religion, it would appear that Barth has little to contribute to theologies of religious pluralism, and to comparative theology, other than a forceful "Nein!" In the past few years, however, some intrepid Barth scholars have suggested otherwise, re-engaging the Swiss Reformed theologian on the question of religion and religious pluralism with some provocative conclusions. J.A. DiNoia, Garrett Green, and Tom Greggs, for instance, have all offered careful readings of Barth's critique of religion. They all point out that Barth's primary concern was not other religious traditions, but Christianity itself, and the way that the modern concept of "religion" had come to dominate theological reflection. DiNoia insists that, contrary to popular understanding, Barth's judgment on religion is "emphatically not one that is pronounced upon the world of non-Christian religions by Christianity nor by its representatives. Nor

---

5. Knitter, *Introducing Theologies.*

6. Niles, "Karl Barth," 10–11. Though Barth's response here regards "Hinduism," as we will see, his primary target of religious critique is actually Christianity. His apparently dismissive response "a priori" will turn out to be an important contribution to comparative theology.

is it an empirical judgment."⁷ It is above all a critique of Christian piety, not a condemnation of others. Green likewise rejects the common interpretation of Barth as an enemy of the study of religion. In a bold move, he even advocates for Barth to be included in the "religious studies canon," precisely because of his "insider" status, as an incisive theorist of religion who is unapologetically grounded in a religious community.⁸ Most recently, Greggs has drawn from both Barth's and Bonhoeffer's critiques of religion to construct a "theology of religions against religion."⁹ According to a growing number of Christian theologians, then, Barth's critique of religion can contribute to a theology of religions that says more than "Christianity—true; the rest—false."

We live at the brink of a tantalizing convergence. For the very years that have witnessed a resurgence of interest in Barth's critique of religion have also seen mounting critiques of "religion" among religious studies scholars themselves. That is, theologians and religious studies scholars alike have voiced growing unease with the category "religion," as an invention of the nineteenth century that may obscure as much as it illuminates.¹⁰ It is this growing critique of "religion" that prompted comparative theologian John Thatamanil in a recent essay to ask the question posed at the beginning of this essay: "What might it mean for theology to think beyond and after 'religion'?"

As I noted at the outset, a major question for contemporary theology is this: how is one to think about and practice one's own faith commitment in the midst of religious diversity? But this question becomes yet more complicated when the very category of "religion" is troubled. Does the category of "religious diversity" create problems, distorting our vision, or worse, leading us quite away from God? *In this essay, I will focus on the critique of religion itself as the springboard for conversation between Barth and Thatamanil, two theologians who provide tools for doing theology in the midst of religious diversity even as they challenge the category of "religion" itself.* For each theologian, I will summarize his critique of religion, analyze the fundamental "sin" of religion that he identifies, as well as the implications for the

---

7. DiNoia, "Religion and the Religions," 250.

8. Green, "Introduction," 28.

9. Greggs, *Theology against Religion*. Other recent engagements of Barth and religion include Boulton, *God Against Religion*, esp. chapter 1; Chestnutt, *Challenging the Stereotype*; Chung, "Karl Barth's Theology"; Chung, "Karl Barth and Inter-Religious"; Krötke, "New Impetus," 29–42; responses by Anderson (43–46) and John P. Burgess (47–50), and rejoinder by Krotke (51–54); and Thompson, "Religious Diversity," 3–24.

10. For one notable example, see Masuzawa, *Invention of World Religions*, referenced above. Other references cited in the discussion of Thatamanil's essay below.

enterprise of theology. In the end, I will suggest ways in which I think these two theologians against religion can helpfully challenge one another, providing critical questions for other comparative theologians—particularly those of us working in confessional Christian traditions.

Barth on Religion

Barth offers his analysis and critique of religion clearly in par. 17 of his *Church Dogmatics* I/2.[11] The thesis statement of the entire paragraph, which he then develops over the course of the ensuing 90 pages, is this:

> God's revelation in the outpouring of the Holy Spirit is the judging, but also reconciling, presence of God in the world of human religion—that is, in the realm of attempts by man to justify and sanctify himself before a willfully and arbitrarily devised image of God. The church is the site of the true religion to the extent that through grace it lives by grace.[12]

Barth explicates this densely packed statement in three parts, which correspond to a thesis-antithesis-synthesis argument.[13] In the first part of 17.1, he acknowledges that God's revelation in Jesus Christ comes to real human beings, and thus takes the form of a human religion. "Viewed from this aspect," he says, "what we call revelation necessarily appears as something particular in the general field that one calls religion—as 'Christianity' or 'Christian religion'—one predicate of a subject that can have other predicates as well, one species in a genus to which other species belong as well. There are, after all, apart from and alongside Christianity, also Judaism and Islam, Buddhism and Shintoism, animistic and totemistic, ascetic, mystical, and prophetic religions of all kinds."[14] Since the work of the Holy Spirit involves real human beings, it enters the realm of real human religion. Furthermore, Barth acknowledges, all human cultures seem to have a universal sense of the ultimate, as a mysterious power that rivals their own. Christianity, then, is one form of human religion among others, because the Holy Spirit works with real human beings.

---

11. His critique of religion can also be found in his famous *Der Römerbrief*, first published in 1919, re-written for a second edition in 1922, and first published in English as *Epistle to the Romans*.

12. Barth, *On Religion*, 33.

13. As observed, for instance, by Geoff Thompson, "Religious Diversity," 7.

14. Barth, *On Religion*, 34.

Swiftly then follows the second part of his argument, the antithesis, for which Barth is so famous: "religion is *faithlessness [Unglaube]*; religion is a concern—one must say, in fact, *the* concern—of *godless* man."[15] Why so harsh, Herr Barth? It is important to understand here that "faithlessness," *Unglaube*, is not primarily false belief, but lack of trust in God's promises. Barth is not condemning a particular set of propositional misunderstandings, but a fundamental mis-orientation of the human in relation to God. His chief concern is that the category "religion," which names the human effort to know God, has come to take precedence over revelation, which names God's act of coming to humanity. The order of these terms in Christian theology from the mid-seventeenth to the early twentieth centuries became precisely reversed: "religion is an independent known quantity over against revelation, and religion is not to be understood from the point of view of revelation, but rather revelation from that of religion."[16] He has in mind a series of Protestant theologians, both conservative and liberal, who gradually accepted the proposition that Christian theology is simply "science of religion," or in other words, a systematic reflection on human efforts to know God.

Barth goes on to develop this critique (antithesis) by way of two observations about how revelation operates in scripture. First, "revelation is God's self-offering and self-presentation."[17] That is, when God speaks or appears to human beings in scripture, such revelation is utterly new, not based on human efforts to know God, but solely on God's own self-revelation. "Revelation does not hook up with the already present and operative religion of man but rather contradicts it . . . In the same way, faith cannot hook up with false faith but must contradict it—sublimate it—as faithlessness, as an act of contradiction."[18] He has in mind here examples such as Moses and burning bush, and Paul on the road to Damascus. As cases like these demonstrate, human religious commitment, far from providing helpful groundwork for receiving God's revelatory action, is judged and contradicted by God's self-revelation.

Second, "revelation, as God's self-offering and self-presentation is the act by which, out of grace and by means of grace, he reconciles man with himself."[19] In other words, human beings do not and cannot accomplish

15. Ibid., 55. Green translates *Unglaube* as "faithlessness" rather than "unfaith" (as in the original English translation) in order to suggest the primary meaning as lack of trust in God's promises.
16. Ibid., 45.
17. Ibid., 57.
18. Ibid., 59.
19. Ibid., 64.

their own reconciliation; only God can do that. And (by grace) that is precisely what God does in Jesus Christ. At this point it becomes clear (if it has not become clear already) that what drives Barth's critique of religion is a commitment to Luther's logic of justification by grace through faith, with the corresponding affirmation of *simul iustus et peccator*. We are justified not on the basis of anything that we do (not even our most impressive religious strivings), but precisely *as sinners*. Barth minces no words: "As a radical teaching about God, it is at the same time God's radical help, which comes to us as those who are unrighteous and unholy, and as such damned and lost."[20]

The third part of his argument, the synthesis, at last brings hope: though religion in and of itself is "faithlessness," it can become true in the same way that a sinner is justified: by grace. "No religion *is* true," says Barth. "A religion can only *become* true . . . And this happens in precisely the same way that man is justified: only from without . . . Like the justified man, the true religion is a creature of *grace*."[21] By God's grace, religion can be "sublimated" (*Aufhebung*), taken up into Christ by the Spirit and made a vehicle for revelation.[22] Religion then can be "true," as Barth said in his original thesis, to the extent that through grace it lives by grace.

Religion itself, in Barth's description, is the manifestation of human sin, which is essentially idolatry. He agrees with the critique of Feuerbach, that religion in general and Christianity in particular is simply the projection of human longing or human values onto God. We seek God, and in so doing, we make our own efforts into gods, seeking salvation in our actions, our desires. Note, however, that he is not rendering this judgment on the basis of the study of religious beliefs or practices; it is a theological judgment that emerges from faith in Jesus Christ who alone justifies people, solely by grace.[23] He is first and foremost concerned about theologians who take "religion" as a starting point, rather than starting with God's act of reconciliation in Jesus Christ. It is for this reason that he condemns religion as faithlessness.

The solution to this problem, according to Barth, is to turn to revelation, which comes to the realm of human activity from outside, not from within. In Jesus Christ, God has actually come to humanity, reconciled

20. Ibid.
21. Ibid., 85.
22. See Green, "Translator's Preface," viii–ix for his helpful discussion of the decision to translate *Aufhebung* as "sublimation" rather than "abolition," as in the original English translation of *CD* I/2 by G. T. Thomson.
23. This is what Barth meant when he responded to D. T. Niles that he judged other religions to be "unbelief" *a priori*.

humanity to God's own being—so this is no hypothetical possibility, but an actuality in which we should place our trust. Theology, then, is the "humble enterprise" of reflecting on proclamation, which is based on scripture, which is based on Jesus Christ. It is an investigation of how best to speak of God, always based *not* on human religion, but *only* on revelation.

Thus does Barth critique religion, analyze the sin implicit therein, and propose an understanding of theology that is not captive to religion. I turn now to John Thatamanil, who offers his own critique of "religion," even as he seeks a way of doing theology that is attentive to the diversity of religious traditions in the world.

Thatamanil on Religion

In his essay "Comparative Theology after 'Religion,'" Thatamanil challenges the boundaries that have been described between Christianity and "other religious traditions." He wonders, "why do Christian theologians, by and large, remain unwilling to enter into a substantive engagement with the normative claims and aims of other traditions?"[24] Part of the reason, he argues, is that Christian theologians have delimited their conversation partners by defining a typology of "religions," in which those who belong to other religious traditions (particularly the "Eastern religions") are defined as external "others," to be studied objectively, but not engaged as normative conversation partners. This development emerged particularly over the course of the 19th century, and can be seen clearly, for instance, in the work of Hegel, in his *Lectures on the Philosophy of Religion*. In response to the groundbreaking discovery of a common origin of Indian and European languages, which challenged the notion that Europe was a separate and superior culture, Hegel developed an evolutionary typology of religions that allowed Western theologians to view "other religions" as more primitive, and thus not significant for normative theological reflection.[25]

Hegel is just one prominent thinker among many in the nineteenth century who contributed to the invention of the term "religion" as a way to map and control differences among various peoples of the world. Thatamanil summarizes neatly the conclusions of several recent scholars who have pointed out the negative consequences of "religion" as a concept that purports to name a universal, essential aspect of human nature:

24. Thatamanil, "Comparative Theology," 240.

25. Thatamanil relies in his essay particularly on the work of Mandair, whose several essays include "Repetition of Past Imperialisms," and "What if *Religio* Remained Untranslatable?"

- The category "religion" has come to be used universally, "applied to peoples and traditions that did not themselves order their lives by appeal to these notions prior to the colonial project."
- "These Western habits of thought are problematic because these distinctions are hardly intelligible for 'other cultural complexes.' Moreover, once these distinctions are securely in place and taken for granted, it is easy to characterize traditions that do not recognize and abide by our distinctions as 'fundamentalist' in character."
- "By a complex set of colonial mechanisms . . . colonized peoples were constrained to think of themselves as religious and as members of particular religions."
- "Learning to think by way of the category 'religion' has given rise to the very idea of singular religious identity."
- "The notion of singular religious identity, in circular fashion, is generated by and in turn generates the idea that religions are neatly separated by clearly demarcated and impermeable borders."
- "A relatively fixed set of traditions is accorded the status of 'world religions.' Arriving at that status requires candidate traditions to take on markers of identity that define Christianity as a prototypical world religion, including most especially a written sacred scripture."[26]

"Religion," then, is a humanly (and colonially) constructed category that imposes universalizing homogeneity on "others," disregarding genuine difference and laying the groundwork for hierarchy and domination. As Thatamanil points out, religion, like "race," serves to "manage and contain proximity."[27]

Thatamanil does not use the theological category "sin" here, perhaps because it would distract from his central argument, or perhaps because it is fraught with its own theological problems. I continue to find it a helpful term, however, to name the flaw, the fault, the wound in human nature that generates our destructive behavior towards ourselves, each other, and the world at large. In Thatamanil's description of "religion," the sin he identifies is above all the urge to dominate, to control. It manifests itself in the colonial enterprise, which invents accounts of universal essential human nature so that those judged to be superior can justifiably manage those who are less evolved. Thatamanil seeks to confess this sin of the past, so that we may not fall prey to it in our theological future.

26. Thatamanil, "Comparative Theology," 242–43.
27. Ibid., 244.

What is the solution to this problem? How may we renounce this sin of universalizing essentialism, and all its ways? Thatamanil points out that traditions are not, and have never been, pure homogeneous wholes, but are now and have always been multiple, both within and without. That is, what we tend to label "religions" are in fact "always already hybrid and polyphonic."[28] How then is a theologian who wishes to take seriously the normative claims of "other religious traditions" to proceed? By confessing at the outset that theology is reflection on "the inherent creative multiplicity of tradition(s), a multiplicity that already bears within it the mark of tradition's encounters with difference."[29] On this basis, he challenges Christian theologians to take seriously the normative claims and aims of other traditions.

Thatamanil goes on in his essay to explore how the Madhyamika Buddhist philosophy of Nagarjuna, with its theory of dependent co-arising, can help Christian theology better analyze and address the human predicament. Here Thatamanil displays his full commitment as a comparative theologian, to the task of engaging the normative claims of those long regarded as "others," for the purpose of challenging and rethinking his own assumptions. For my purposes, however, it is his critique of "religion" and his understanding of theology that provide the most interesting points of comparison with the thinking of Barth.

Mutual Suspicion

To be sure, while these two theologians share a concern about "religion," each would have deep suspicions about the theological project and approach of the other. Barth, for instance, would worry about Thatamanil's statement regarding Nagarjuna's philosophy, "I find the figure of the nondual more adequate to experience than recourse to talk about the wholly Other."[30] Thatamanil here is rejecting an essentialist understanding of identity (either individual or corporate), and learning from Nagarjuna's teaching that the self is a product of "dependent co-arising." The world is not composed of separate essential entities; rather, "everything is empty of self-existence."[31] Barth's eyebrows would go up, however, not at the idea of nonduality or emptiness, but at the appeal to the term "experience." Human *experience* here seems to be the criterion by which to judge the adequacy of a theological construction. Barth would likely ask Thatamanil: how does this move

28. Ibid., 252.
29. Ibid.
30. Ibid., 253.
31. Ibid., 255.

avoid projection, judging a theological statement on the basis of our own personal experience, and thereby making God into our image? How does an appeal to human experience, without qualification, constitute a helpful basis on which to assess theological decisions? Don't we need something beyond our own self-interested perspectives to break in and enable us to see truth?

Thatamanil, in turn, would (and does) have serious questions about Barth. Barth's turn to "revelation" as a solution to the problem of "religion" can too easily nourish oppressive claims by those who have received such revelation. Christianity is made incommensurable with other religions, in Barth's view, not because of its human origins but because it is taken up ("sublimated") and transformed by God's grace in Jesus Christ. But this too easily perpetuates two problems: the presumed superiority of Christian religion and its bounded nature. Thatamanil would likely ask Barth: how do you avoid such a reified notion of Christianity, and how is the move of "sublimation" not a covert power play on the part of Christian authorities?

Points of Convergence

Granting these serious questions, there remain intriguing parallels between these two theologians and their critiques of religion. First, they share a concern about "religion" as a modern category deeply connected to human efforts to control and claim power. Barth raises this concern in his analysis of the theological shift that took "religion" rather than "revelation" as the starting point of theology. The discovery of "religion" as a social category was an important recognition of the seventeenth and eighteenth centuries, according to Barth, and theologians rightly paid attention to this emerging realm of the human sciences. But he continues,

> It is one thing to be open to the concerns, or even to the demonic power, of a particular age and something else to make its concerns one's own, to surrender to its demonic power. The latter is what theology must not do but what it began to do in the seventeenth century and did openly in the eighteenth. It fell prey to the absolutism by which the man of that age made himself the centre, measure, and end of all things.[32]

In other words, Barth claims that the turn to the study of religion was part of the modern preoccupation with human activity, to the exclusion of what God has done in Christ. And this preoccupation has had the effect of exalting humanity over God.

---

32. Barth, "On Religion," 48.

Thatamanil likewise criticizes the modern rise of "religion" for its power to distort human experience:

> the coercive power of the category, by constituting traditions as spaces of homogeneity, erases what should be obvious to any clear-eyed observer: religious traditions are internally marked by the widest and wildest kinds of difference . . . But perhaps the most subtle and consequential work accomplished by the category "religion" . . . is the way in which the category generates . . . the clear demarcation between the religions themselves, between internal and external, between self and other.[33]

By focusing on the invented category "religion," scholars have evaded multiplicity within traditions, as well as their fluidity. This in turn has bolstered the colonial enterprise of ranking and then controlling peoples perceived as "other." Both theologians, then, view the modern development of religion with grave concern for its alliance and support of human power schemes.

Related to their shared concern about the distorting power of the modern category of religion is their shared ethical concern about Christian self-promotion. Barth even asserts, in terms remarkably close to Thatamanil, that the fascination with "religion" as a common human phenomenon with a universal "essence" has led scholars to conclude, wrongly, that Christianity itself is the most superior form of human religion.[34] Thatamanil himself goes even further, raising concerns not only about false claims of Christian superiority, but claims by certain Christian theologians to speak for all. His critique of postliberal theologians makes this clear:

> Accounts of Christian theology that regard theology as an exercise in faithfulness to the deep grammar of Christian practice or keeping faith with the singular biblical metanarrative inoculate theology from having to engage all those who stand outside the tradition, all those who are othered. Those others are to be repulsed as threats, and dissenters are but heretics.[35]

For both theologians, "religion" can serve, and has served, not just human power in general, but Christian political power in particular, both within and beyond those who self-identify as Christians.

Finally, Barth and Thatamanil share a vision of theology as an enterprise that is spry, mobile, self-critical and accountable to something beyond

---

33. Thatamanil, "Comparative Theology," 248.
34. See Barth, "On Religion," 54, as well as Green's commentary, "Introduction," 16.
35. Thatamanil, "Comparative Theology," 250.

itself. For Barth, theology is a fourth-order discourse, the "humble enterprise" of reflecting on proclamation, which is based on scripture, which is based on Jesus Christ. It is therefore inherently aware of its limits, open to correction from outside, and at the same time "the free investigation of truth," "free for its own inexhaustible object."[36] For Thatamanil, theology that attends to difference within and among traditions is "carnivalesque," "messy, agonistic, creative . . . multiple"—thus a dynamic exploration not bound by predetermined categories, but ever willing to reconsider its presuppositions. Though they differ in their descriptions of what constitutes human freedom, both theologians speak compellingly of theology as an enterprise that is free, not bound by the constraints of distorting human categories of thought. And both regard theology as a task that requires others (God and humans) to interrupt our self-contained discourse in order to be truly free.

Fruitful Interchange

These points of convergence regarding the dangers of human "religion" suggest that these two theologians may actually have a fruitful interchange, sharing ethical concerns about Christian imperialism and the need for both freedom and accountability, and each alerting the other to significant pitfalls in the work of comparative theology.

Barth raises an important challenge to Thatamanil about the basis of his judgment that a certain theological construction is true. While Thatamanil calls for attention to multiplicity both within and among traditions, always eager to hear from the voices of those named "other," he, like every theologian, finally makes judgments about which theological constructions are more adequate than others. And how does he make this judgment? On the basis of what seems most adequate to lived experience.[37] Of course, lived experience is always the context in which a theologian works, and Thatamanil is keenly aware of the particularity as well as the multiplicity of that experience. He does not appeal to "experience" as universal, or pure,

---

36. Barth, "On Religion," 47. Wolf Krötke's comment here is apt: "Barth's negative pronouncements concerning religion and the religions are the obverse of an eminently positive theological intention. And this intention is to serve, in both the church and indeed the world in general, the *freedom for encounter with God*—God who in the power of the Spirit is not bound by any ecclesiastical boundaries, and even less by any theology." Krötke, "New Impetus," 32.

37. See, e.g., the appeal to "what should be obvious to any clear-eyed observer" (250) and his judgment that nonduality is "more adequate to experience than recourse to talk about the wholly other" (253).

and he remains ever open to being challenged. Yet "experience" seems to function as his theological norm. Barth's question about this move remains bracing: is our experience finally all we have as an anchor in the midst of multiplicity?

Thatamanil's challenge to Barth, meanwhile, is equally bracing. If Christianity alone is the "true religion"—by the grace of God and because of God's work of reconciliation in Christ—how can this fail to be oppressive? In Thatamanil's view, such an unflinching commitment to a single theological norm is suspicious, because it inevitably leads to a division between insiders and outsiders, orthodoxy and heresy, and thus the silencing of voices of dissent. If Barth continually calls for faithfulness to a "single biblical metanarrative" of God's act of reconciling the world in Christ Jesus, how does allegiance to such a single focus keep from regarding all others as threats, or heretics?

This conversation itself can serve comparative theology well, calling those of us who seek to work in this field to be honest about our operative theological norms, for better and for worse. From their very different historical settings and theological starting points, Barth and Thatamanil together set out a vision of theology that is playful, free—and resolutely not captive to human religion.

Bibliography

Barth, Karl. *On Religion: The Revelation of God as the Sublimation of Religion*. Translated and introduced by Garrett Green. London: T. & T. Clark, 2006.
Boulton, Matthew Myer. *God against Religion: Rethinking Christian Theology through Worship*. Grand Rapids: Eerdmans, 2008.
Chestnutt, Glenn. *Challenging the Stereotype: The Theology of Karl Barth as a Resource for Inter-religious Encounter in a European Context*. Religions and Discourse 48. New York: Lang, 2010.
Chung, Paul S. "Karl Barth's Theology of Reconciliation in Dialogue with a Theology of Religions." *Mission Studies: Journal of the International Association for Mission Studies* 25 (2008) 211–28.
―――. "Karl Barth and Inter-Religious Dialogue: An Attempt to Bring Karl Barth to Dialogue with Religious Pluralism." *Asia Journal of Theology* 15 (2001) 232–46.
Clooney, Francis. *Comparative Theology: Deep Learning across Religious Borders*. Hoboken, NJ: Wiley-Blackwell, 2010.
DiNoia, J. A. "Religion and the Religions." In *The Cambridge Companion to Karl Barth*, edited by John Webster, 250. Cambridge Companions to Religion. Cambridge: Cambridge University Press, 2000.
Gonçalves, Paulo. "Religious 'Worlds' and Their Alien Invaders." In *Difference in Philosophy of Religion*, edited by Philip Goodchild, 115–34. Burlington, VT: Ashgate, 2003.

Green, Garrett. "Introduction: Barth as Theorist of Religion." In Karl Barth, *On Religion: The Revelation of God as the Sublimation of Religion*, 1–29. Translated and introduced by Garrett Green. London: T. & T. Clark, 2006.

———. "Translator's Preface." In Karl Barth, *On Religion: The Revelation of God as the Sublimation of Religion*, vii–xi. Translated and introduced by Garrett Green. London: T. & T. Clark, 2006.

Greggs, Tom. *Theology against Religion: Constructive Dialogues with Bonhoeffer and Barth*. London: T. & T. Clark, 2011.

Heim, S. Mark. *The Depth of the Riches: A Trinitarian Theology of Religious Ends*. Grand Rapids: Eerdmans, 2000.

———. *Salvations: Truth and Difference in Religion*. Faith Meets Faith. Mary-knoll, NY: Orbis, 1995.

Knitter, Paul F. *Introducing Theologies of Religions*. Maryknoll, NY: Orbis, 2002.

Krötke, Wolf. "A New Impetus to the Theology of Religions from Karl Barth's Thought." *Cultural Encounters: A Journal for the Theology of Culture* 7 (2011) 29–54.

Mandair, Arvind. "The Repetition of Past Imperialisms: Hegel, Historical Difference, and the Theorization of Indic Religions." *History of Religions* 44 (2005) 277–99.

———. "What if *Religio* Remained Untranslatable?" In *Difference in Philosophy of Religion*, edited by Philip Goodchild, 87–100. Burlington, VT: Ashgate, 2003.

Masuzawa, Tomoku. *The Invention of World Religions: Or, How European Universalism Was Preserved in the Language of Pluralism*. Chicago: University of Chicago Press, 2005.

Niles, D. T. "Karl Barth—A Personal Memory." *South East Asian Journal of Theology* 11 (1969) 10–11.

Thatamanil, John. "Comparative Theology after 'Religion.'" In *Planetary Loves: Spivak, Postcoloniality, and Theology*, edited by Stephen D. Moore and Mayra Rivera, 238–57. Transdisciplinary Theological Colloquia. New York: Fordham University Press, 2011.

Thompson, Geoff. "Religious Diversity, Christian Doctrine, and Karl Barth." *International Journal of Systematic Theology* 8 (2006) 3–24.

5

"What Is Jesus Doing among the Spirits?"
Questions from a Mission Studies Scholar to Grassroots Caribbean Charismatic Evangélicos[1]

(Theological Implications of the Religious Interplay and Exchange between the Caribbean World of the Spirits and Charismatic Caribbean Protestants and Pentecostals)

CARLOS F. CARDOZA-ORLANDI

Introduction

I AM GRATEFUL FOR this opportunity to be included among this group of international Reformed colleagues addressing the question of the future of Reformed theology. As the reader will discover below, my Christian formation, both personal and academic, has been shaped by the Presbyterian

---

1. Charismatic *Evangélico(a)* is the term used by Latin American and Spanish Caribbean people to distinguish themselves from Roman Catholics. An *evangélico* (a) is usually a person who belongs to a Protestant or Pentecostal community, (b) reads and lives the Scriptures, (c) keeps a relatively strong counter-culture position in social and religious issues, (d) nurtures a spiritual discipline of prayer, Bible study, and reflection—a pious discipline—(e) tries to be compassionate, and (f) guides her/his life by spiritual experiences attributed to the Holy Spirit. More recent studies show that *evangélicos(as)*, if poor, develop new economic practices that contribute to a more stable household, and if middle class, have an inclination towards gaining some level of economic prosperity which results in a more tolerant attitude towards religious and social diversity. The charismatic dimension of the terms refers to a sacramental aptitude to the mystery of the Spirit grounded in both the gifts and the fruits of the Holy Spirit. The charismatic dimension is deeply influenced by Pentecostal traditions.

tradition in Puerto Rico and in the United States. I am grateful to God for this phase of my Christian journey.

This essay is part of my work on a topic that I hold dear to my heart: What does it mean to be a Caribbean Christian? Particularly, in this essay I explore inter-religious dynamics and Christian identity in the context of Afro-Caribbean religious cosmology. More specifically, this is the first essay where I begin to explore issues of Caribbean and charismatic Protestant identity (*identidad caribeña carismática evangélica*) and its interplay with Caribbean primal and cosmological worldviews and rituals, as expressed in Spiritism and *Lukumí* religions. I am drawn to connect Christian identity with two categories: (1) biography or *testimony* and (2) Christology. Hence, in this essay I am wrestling with the question, *what is Jesus doing among the Spirits?*

The essay has the following outline. First, I provide the reader with my scholarly journey in my field of world Christianity and mission studies. Here I provide the theological framework of my work and what follows in the essay. Second, I give the reader a short biography regarding my engagement with people who practice Spiritism and *Lukumí* religion to see the theological questions I raise in the third section. Finally, I offer some conclusions which basically point to further research as I develop a missiology for Caribbean Christian identity in the Caribbean religious cosmology.

I find that the Reformed dictum, *Ecclesia semper reformanda*, captures the process needed in Latina/o and Caribbean Christian communities as we gain insight and perspective into our Christian identity and our particular gift to the world church.

My Mission Studies Framework/Template for Theological Reflection

As a scholar of world Christianity and mission studies, my methodology is grounded in mission practice, historical inquiry, and theological reflection. My scholarly and practical work has been a journey, taking me in different and often perceived opposite directions. Yet, it has been a journey where I have grown in my faith and vocation as a theological educator. I have also gained insight and perspective in my academic grounding. Today, I can identify three different stages/categories that shape my mission studies framework.

1. I first focused on the action and theological reflection of *transmission*—the active engagement in communicating the gospel of Jesus

Christ to others—Christians and non-Christians. The emphasis has been on "the communication of the gospel *to others—those considered the subjects of mission.*"

2. As I continued my mission studies work and discovered the demographic transformation of the Christian religion, I added a second focus to my work, the *reception/appropriation* of the gospel in different communities—the contextualization and/or inculturation of the gospel among those who received a contextualized gospel. In relation to point #1 above, the emphasis shifted towards "the communication of the gospel *by others—those once considered the objects of mission.*" As I explored the relationship between these foci points—transmission and reception—I discovered the double nature of the Christian community: we are both subjects—transmitters—and objects—receptors—of God's mission in the world.[2] But I also discovered the agency of receptors—receptors are also subjects of the contextualization of the gospel—and the reversed role of transmitters. Transmitters are also objects of God's missionary activity. As a mission studies scholar with training in history, I continue to explore the complex dynamics between the transmission, reception, and appropriation of the gospel in and under different contextual dynamics.

3. As I dig into these complex dynamics, I discovered what Peter Phan calls the *participatory* method in world Christianity and mission studies.[3] This method grounds missiological practice and reflection in *testimony*[4]—the biographical engagement in the complex dynamics of transmission, reception, and appropriation.

In the participatory method I also discovered an inner dimension of communication: *Testimony* flows from the personal experience to a collective expression of the faith. *Testimony* is always under scrutiny by the faith community. Hence, the participatory method, the biographical or the *testimony* initiates a communication of the gospel that flows from within, yet it is embodied and historical in the collective experience of the Christian community.

---

2. For a detailed analysis of these foci, see my *Mission*.
3. Phan, "Doing Theology."
4. Phan uses the term *myth* to describe the agency of common people. By using the term he leaves open the source of the *myth*—it comes from all religions and cosmologies. I prefer to use testimony since it is closer to my own charismatic *evangélico* tradition.

"WHAT IS JESUS DOING AMONG THE SPIRITS?"

I do not see these stages/categories in a linear progressive development. I see then as overlapping spheres—not even concentric—colliding, yet attracting each other.

As I worked with the above stages/categories, it became clear to me that I needed a framework, a template, to integrate my mission studies categories. In my search, I have discovered pedagogical sources, metaphors of location, and theological rubrics to feed my vocation as a theological educator. In the field of pedagogy, bell hooks' reflections on theory and practice shape my teaching and writing. In her book *Teaching to Transgress: Education as the Practice of Freedom*, she states,

> When our lived experience of theorizing is fundamentally linked to processes of self-discovery, of collective liberation, no gap exists between theory and practice. Indeed, what such experience makes more evident is the bond between the two—that ultimately reciprocal process wherein one enables the other.[5]

She strongly persuaded me to understand that

> [A]ny theory that cannot be shared in everyday conversation cannot be used to educate the public."[6]

I am committed to be a scholar of world Christianity and mission studies grounded in everyday life experience and conversations.

The metaphors of location that shape my theoretical framework/template are the metaphors of "living at the borders" and "living at the seashore." As both a "Latino" in the United States and a Caribbean by heart and soul, both metaphors suggest a different location from whence to observe, participate and reflect on religious experiences. They also serve as a prism to refract and disperse experiences into my theological spectrum.[7] These metaphors remind me of where and how to locate myself as a mission studies scholar participating in the religious experience of transmitting, receiving and appropriating the gospel of Jesus Christ. Moreover, these metaphors lead me to a space of intersections and cross-fertilizations in my inter-religious encounters with the religious traditions of my contexts. In fact, these metaphors are coherent with the complex cross-cultural and inter-religious history of Latin America and the Caribbean. As Anne Fadiman suggests, "the action most worth of watching is not at the center of things, but where edges meet." She continues, "[T]here are interesting fictions and

---

5. hooks, *Teaching to Transgress*, 61.
6. Ibid., 64.
7. I discuss these metaphors in Cardoza-Orlandi, "Mission at the Borders," and "Rediscovering Caribbean."

incongruities in these places, and often, if you stand at the point of tangency, you can see both sides better than if you were in the middle of either one."[8]

In my essay, "Mission at the Borders," I identified 5 theological rubrics or guidelines that provide substance to a "border" or "seashore" mission studies approach. These theological rubrics or guidelines are both testimonial and missional. They are testimonial because they show my personal faith journey through a critical and scholarly lens in the field of mission studies and missional because they mirror a collective Caribbean and Latina/o Christian commitment to the communication of the gospel of Jesus Christ. These theological rubrics or guidelines recognize:

- that missiology and Christian identity are mutually shaped and dependent: my Christian identity informs my mission imperative just as my mission theology and practice is a prism of my Christian identity;
- that sound mission theology and practice cannot be monolithic or rigid; it needs to be open to the wind of the Spirit as we are guided beyond the mission categories that define who should or should not be evangelized/missionized;
- that theologies and practices of mission need to address with courage and integrity the difficult issues of Christianity's encounter with popular religions and religiosity. Theologies and mission practices for the twenty-first century cannot disregard these religious experiences and their social reality as superstitious, sub-cultural, marginal or demonic without a thorough engagement and theological sensibility;
- the need to develop a stronger missiological base to recognize and critically engage the continuous religious traffic and negotiations in the life of many in our communities and congregations, particularly among the marginalized and the poor;
- the need to address the challenge of people of other faiths, not only in the non-western world, but in the North American context as well. We are challenged to find the complex affinities between our faith and other faiths, as well as the distinctions and peculiarities of each. This task will help us discern and develop a missiology in the context of religious diversity.[9]

Summarizing, my mission studies framework/template holds my vocation as a theological educator. My work is guided by a passion to explore the dynamics of transmission, reception, and appropriation of the Christian gospel. I struggle to be faithful to my pedagogical conviction that personal and collective liberation requires a different social location—at the edges rather than at the center—and a participatory action with the people, their

8. Fadiman, *Spirit Catches You*, vii.
9. Cardoza-Orlandi, "Mission at the Borders," 25–27.

experiences and contexts. Lastly, my theological rubrics show a commitment I have to re-discover the gospel of Jesus Christ in the lived experience of God's creation, particularly in my Caribbean and Latino/a contexts.

There is one more important scholarly and biographical note that I would like to share with the reader. In my Christian formation, the Reformed tradition, particularly the Presbyterian tradition from and in the United States, has shaped my Christian vocational life. I was born and raised a Presbyterian in Puerto Rico. Both of my parents were leaders in the local Presbyterian church and in the presbytery. My early years as a Christian were shaped by a deep passion for the Christian Scriptures and an acute awareness of my sinful condition—two important Reformed principles.

In continuity with my Reformed Christian roots, I did my graduate work at Princeton Theological Seminary and for 16 years I served as a faculty member at Columbia Theological Seminary, a theological school affiliated with the Presbyterian Church (U.S.A.). I taught courses to many students whose ministry was going to be within the Presbyterian Church (U.S.A.) or affiliated with the Reformed traditions. Two of my favorite theologians from the global South are the late Rubem Alves and the late Kwame Bediako. Their work is deeply Reformed and contextual. Both of them exemplify the Reformed traditions of Brazil and Ghana, respectively. More recently, the work of Bible scholar and theologian Musa Dube has helped me wrestle with questions of biblical hermeneutics and African traditional religions, and particularly the African Initiative Churches. Her work, with an indentifiable Reformed angle and a profound depth of biblical scholarship, has provided theological and religious criteria to continue my theological exploration in the Caribbean religious cosmology and Protestant charismatic Christian identity.

A Brief Background

I have been involved in informal and formal inter-faith dialogue with followers of *Lukumí* religion (*Regla de Ocha, Santería*) and Caribbean Spiritists for more than 18 years. These religious traditions permeate the Caribbean religious cosmology. Roman Catholicism, Protestantism, Hinduism, Buddhism, Islam and Pentecostalism abide and dwell in this religious cosmology. In this cosmology, among other features, the world of the spirits intersects and interplays with the historical world.[10]

Moreover, I find myself surprised and excited by the evident and less subtle religious traffic and dynamics between followers of our Caribbean

---

10. I find helpful Andrew Walls' essay "Primal Religious Traditions."

religious cosmology and the recent converted charismatic *evangélicas and evangélicos*. The new generation of charismatic Caribbean *evangélicos and evangélicas* come to our Christian communities with a more permeable *evangélico* worldview and experience—perhaps one important feature of the interplay with the Caribbean religious cosmology. (Interestingly, however, in Latin America and the Caribbean Protestantisms continue to contribute to the diversification of religious experiences in the region, but not necessarily to the interplay among Christian traditions and non-Christian religions.[11]) This permeability allows for new questions as the encounter and interaction between Afro-European Caribbean religions is more open and evident in both the *evangélico* and the *Lukumí* and *Spiritist* communities. Questions are, perhaps, the beginning for new mission studies reflection. Andrew Walls names it well when, discussing the relationship between theology and mission studies, he declares,

> It is the very concept of a fixed universal compendium of theology, a sort of bench manual which covers every situation (referring to Western theological corpus), that mission studies challenges. In mission studies we see theology "en route" and realize its *"occasional"* nature, its character as response to the need to make Christian decisions. The conditions of Africa, for instance, are taking Christian theology into new areas of life, where Western theology has no answers because it has no questions. But Christians (non-Westerners and Westerners) outside Africa will need to make some responses to the questions raised in the African arena. As Christian interaction proceeds with Indian culture—perhaps the most testing environment that the Christian faith has yet encountered—the theological process may reach not only new areas of discourse, but resume some of those which earlier pioneers—Origen, for instance—began to enter.[12]

I have questions. My questions emerge out of many years of interreligious engagement and friendships, but also from discovering that recent Caribbean charismatic *evangélicas and evangélicos* are explicitly giving *testimony* to a different relationship with our Caribbean religious cosmology—the world of living spirits. Implicitly, they are asking different questions and unknowingly challenge an inherited missionary and first-generation Latin

---

11. For an interesting interpretation regarding the role of Protestantism and Pentecostalism with non-Christian religions see Levine, "Future of Christianity."

12. Walls, "Structural Problems," 146.

"WHAT IS JESUS DOING AMONG THE SPIRITS?"

American and Caribbean *tradición evangélica* which dismissed as superstitious or demonic our intrinsic Caribbean religious cosmology.

Questions in the Encounter and Interactions

Raphael's Transfiguration, a mosaic located in St. Peter's Basilica, from the original painting done by Raphael Sanzio, 1483–1521, depicts what many recent charismatic Caribbean *evangélicas and evangélicos* imagine when they read the Transfiguration texts (Matt 17:1–13; Mark 9:2–8; Luke 9:23–36): Jesus relates to Elijah and Moses.[13] Moreover, the readings of these stories catch the attention of both Spiritists and charismatic *evangélicos and evangélicas*. Jesus interacts with spirits, they have a conversation, and God's purpose is revealed. The interpretation of these texts by both Spiritist and *Lukumí* followers and charismatic *evangélicos* generates the following question: How to imagine and construct an *identidad caribeña carismática evangélica* overwhelmed by an active and recognized worldview of spirits who are involved in people's *cotidianidad* or daily life experience?[14]

The world of the spirits is part of the charismatic *evangélico* worldview. Spirits are both good and evil, and their roles are conflicting and ambiguous. For some of the older generation, the good spirits have been "collected" into the Holy Spirit. A distinguished senior pastor from Puerto Rico used to say, "some have many spirits, but remember, our spirit has a first and a last name, the Holy Spirit."[15] It was not clear whether this pastor thought that the other spirits were evil or demonic, but it was clear that a religious and theological distinction was strongly suggested.

More recently, however, good spirits seem to find some space in the charismatic *evangélico* worldview. This space is not created by the ordained leadership of Caribbean Protestant communities, but certainly from the grass-roots *evangélicos and evangélicas* who encounter and interact with good and evil spirits. The good spirits—particularly dead family members and friends—help in decision-making, appear in dreams giving comfort and hope, elicit memories of love and companionship, confirm God's care

---

13. Images of the painting are available on the internet. If the reader conducts an internet search for Raphael's "Transfiguration," multiple sites with the image of the painting are available.

14. *Lo cotidiano* or *cotidianidad* refers to daily life struggles and experiences and the fullness of living: all that is life.

15. These words were spoken by Rev. Domingo Rodriguez, a distinguished Puerto Rican Disciples pastor in a Disciples of Christ pastoral gathering in Bayamón, Puerto Rico, 1985.

in their lives, encourage faithfulness, and give testimony of Jesus' relationship with believers.

Evil spirits, on the other hand, are confrontational and deceiving, they disrupt God's order for the believer. They induce misfortune, illness, and even death. Evil spirits are to be avoided or exorcised. An *evangélico or evangélica* charismatic believer is subject to evil spirits. No one is totally free of their grip.

This kindness of good spirits and threat of evil spirits results in two Christological issues. Confessing the Lordship of Jesus (1) does not clarify the relationship between Jesus and the good spirits and (2) does not assure a total protection against evil spirits. Similar Christological issues are discussed in a seminal essay by Todd Vanden Berg entitled "Culture, Christianity, and Witchcraft in a West African Context," where, based on his anthropological work among Logunda Lutherans in Nigeria, he discovers how the Logunda Lutherans ambiguously understand Jesus' power over witchcraft as a contingent reality based on the faith of the individual Christian. A weak faith renders Jesus powerless to witchcraft power, while a strong faith becomes a force against evil spells.[16] He does challenge African theologians to develop a theology of good and evil that is grounded on the battle between good and evil, rather than a confessional declaration of evil and good based on an orthodox Lutheran theology of the fall and the cross.

Hence, my second question: *What does Jesus do among the spirits?* The traditional confession, still used in altar calls, evangelistic services, conversion experiences, baptisms, and celebrations of the Lord's Supper, "Jesus Christ is my Lord and Savior," does not give us a complete picture of Jesus' role and function in the daily life experience of charismatic *evangélicos and evangélicas*. It seems that the traditional confession serves as an initiation and revolving ritual that strengthens the common idiom of the *evangélico* worldview, while the activity of Jesus among the spirits engenders multiple idiomatic daily life expressions of the Divine which nurture the good and battle the evil: Jesus is our Protector, Jesus is our Healer, Jesus is our Divine Medical Doctor, Jesus is our Deliverer, Jesus is our Counselor, Jesus grounds our lives, Jesus is our Friend.

Our question, *"what does Jesus do among the spirits?"* becomes critical when the typical *evangélico* confession of faith is claimed within one of the Afro-Caribbean religions. In one of my interreligious conversations, a *Lukumí* priest confessed that his *orishas* (spirits) were under the Lordship of Jesus Christ. This is a wonderful confession of faith. However, if *orishas* are the immediate spirit who creates the path of devotees, what does the

---

16. Vanden Berg, "Culture, Christianity."

"WHAT IS JESUS DOING AMONG THE SPIRITS?"

Lordship of Jesus Christ over the *orishas do* (not only mean) to the human-*orishas* relationship? With this confession, it seems that the *tradición carismática evangélica* adds a new agent and sphere of power. The relationship is threefold: Christians, *orishas*, and Jesus Christ. Interestingly, the inclusion of Jesus in the worldview of the spirits also challenges the ritual and symbolic worldview of the Caribbean cosmology, infusing a new interplay and experiences in the Caribbean religions. If this is the case, in the dialogue process Jesus enters the Caribbean religion, but it does not mean that there is a typical *evangélico* conversion. Jesus' participation is the overlapping space between the *tradición evangélica* and this particular *Lukumí* priest and his community.

The confession of my *Lukumí* friend and priest raises a third question: *How do Charismatic Caribbean evangélicos and evangélicas relate to Caribbean religious communities and persons who claim Jesus' presence and work in their lives?* These questions create other critical questions about evangelization and mission: Are those who claim Jesus' presence and work in their lives objects of evangelization and mission? Are they Christians, though the *orishas* or spirits continue to guide their lives? On the other hand, is not the confession, Jesus is the Lord of my *orishas*, a cosmological confession in an integrated cosmology of spirits, the dead and the alive?

These questions show that the *identidad caribeña carismática evangélica* has moved beyond the inherited superstitious and demonic simplistic dismissal of our Caribbean religious cosmology. The movement creates new prayers and religious experiences that consequently raise new questions. These questions and the *participative* agency in the movement generate new theological challenges and opportunities for a grounded-in-life mission practices and theologies. The breakthrough from inherited missiologies includes a discovery of the spirits in Christian Scriptures, a recognition that not all spirits are evil, all spirits need to be discerned, and spirits (and religious traditions) can be in tension, without being exclusive. The possibility of missiological renewal lies in the vitality and synergy found in the discovering of and participation in what Jesus does in the world of the spirits, and what the spirits do in the world of the *tradición evangélica*.

This vitality and synergy also challenges some assumptions in contemporary world Christianity and mission studies. Perhaps another question shows what I consider might be the next missiological challenge in developing contexts: *What does it mean to do contextualization and/or inculturation in a religious context?* Michael Amaladoss, Indian-Hindu Jesuit, suggests that we need to go "beyond contextualization,"[17] as we missiologically

---

17. Amaladoss reference is far from the more well-known metatheology proposed

practice in and reflect on the transfer and traffic of Christian traditions and non-Christian religious traditions in spaces where non-Christian religious traditions instill the cosmology of a people. In our case in point, the transfer and traffic of the *identidad caribeña carismática evangélica* and the Caribbean religious cosmology produce new theological questions such as: *How does the emerging identidad caribeña carismática evangélica reflect the world of the spirits? Where and how will we see the spirits interplay with the historical sources of la fe y tradición evangélica?*[18] Do and will followers of our Caribbean religious cosmology re-discover something new about the gospel of Jesus Christ? If the Caribbean religious cosmology is inherently syncretistic, will our *identidad caribeña carismática evangélica* be syncretistic, more religiously Afro-Amerindian-European than "Christian?"

Conclusions

How do these missiological questions—particular and very contextual missiological questions—contribute to theological formation for Christian ministry in the 21st century? First, theological formation for Christian ministry requires a *participatory* agency in context. The biographical character of participation in mission practices and theological reflection creates a generative theological inquiry. Cross-cultural and inter-religious missiological participation becomes a blood line for the faith of communities.

This *participatory* agency reminds the mission studies scholar that it is critical to study religious traditions as living and organic traditions engaging and interacting with their contexts. Such interactions should include but are not limited to the influence and power of religious worldviews, rituals, and systems of symbols. It should also include the way in which religion shapes and is shaped by daily life struggles and pleasures. It is important to know religious traditions by way of their official literature and theological statements. Yet, the living and organic interplay of religious traditions usually are sources for Christian vitality of religious practices and theological reflection. Regretfully, such vitality can be channeled in different directions ranging from fostering violence to peaceful co-existence. Consequently, from a Christian perspective, our *participatory* agency should encourage and ground religious vitality for the *shalom* of God's creation.

---

by Paul Hiebert in his book *Anthropological Reflections on Missional Issues*.

18. Some of the historical resources of *la fe evangélica* are the Bible, Euro-American and Caribbean hymnody from the 1930s to 1980s, prayer services, evangelistic campaigns, etc. Other less tangible sources are the strongly male-oriented leadership in Christian communities and a sense of progress and individualism due to modernity.

"WHAT IS JESUS DOING AMONG THE SPIRITS?"

Second, the *evangélicos carismáticos caribeños* represent the next generation of charismatic protestants in the Caribbean. I observed above that this next generation has a permeable boundary with the world of the spirits. This is a religious characteristic that is now easily observed, whereas previous generations carried the pressure of an inherited Euro-American missionary theology and an accepted exclusivist claim typical of a minority religious group. Paradoxically, the historical distance from the inherited missionary theologies and exclusivist claim and the growth and new social location of *evangélicos carismáticos caribeños* gives them "permission" to witness or give *testimonio* to a different religious and theological proposition. Generational change can stimulate reformations.

Third, Christological understandings are grounded in the experience of people. Whether our Christological understandings point to syncretistic dynamics, confrontational encounters, or peaceful co-existence, we begin to re-discover Jesus Christ on the terms of *what Jesus Christ does in context* rather than who Jesus Christ is in an assumed universal statement. Moreover, we should remember that such an assumed universal statement or confession was grounded in a particular context.

We assume that texts such as "I am the way and the truth and the life. No one comes to the Father except through me" (John 14:6), "that at the name of Jesus every knee should bow, in heaven and on earth and under the earth" (Phil 2:10), and others have a single interpretation associated with them. The uniqueness of Jesus Christ, as Kwame Bediako and Mercy Amba Oduyoye point out, is not an abstract proposition. For the Jews and Gentiles of the first centuries, the confession "Jesus Christ is Lord" is defiant in the face of the Roman Empire and speaks of new loyalties, loyalties different from those the Empire demanded. To claim that "Jesus Christ is Lord" without context and its socio-religious implications is irrelevant. In fact, the uniqueness of Jesus, as Bediako and Amba Oduyoye discuss, is debated and forged along with other religious and social proposals and alternatives.[19] Hence the uniqueness of Jesus is rooted in history and context—it has living meaning; it demands new loyalties that are not only religious but political and cultural in character. Perhaps this theological argument is best articulated in Matthews' text, "Not everyone who says to me, 'Lord, Lord,' will enter the kingdom of heaven, but only the one who does the will of my Father who is in heaven" (Matt 7:21). Doing the "will of my Father" is coherent with a living faith!

---

19. See Bediako, "How Is Jesus Christ Lord?"; and Oduyoye, "Spirituality of Resistance."

Fourth, practices of ministry, like funerals, counseling in the context of tragedies, and people's relationship with dead family members, can go beyond a traditional therapeutic approach. Perhaps Caribbean Charismatic *evangélicos* and *evangélicas* can provide insights into a theology of the dead that is based on our daily-life experiences and needs and further informs our Eucharistic theology of the saints.

For too long the Reformed tradition has been suspicious about ritual practices and symbols and vague about the world of the spirits and the world of the dead. During my first years of teaching at Columbia I had an excellent student who wrote a thesis on popular religiosity in the sixteenth century and the theological responses of the Reformers. My student was also exploring the possible links between popular religiosity and Reformed Christian ministry and theology in his generation and for his context of ministry. My student raised historical, contextual, and theological questions seeking insight in the living tradition of his dead Reformed ancestors. Yet, both of us experienced suspicion, resistance and indifference in his thesis defense.

These contextual questions push new questions in different contexts of ministry. The theological vitality of one context can potentially generate new theological vitality in another context. The cross-fertilization of missiological perspectives can potentially help us see with new eyes our own context and ask new questions.

Let me conclude with two vignettes—one from my youth as a Presbyterian youth leader in Puerto Rico and another from my teaching context: preparing students for leadership in Christian ministry.

I come from a very ecumenical family. As I indicated above, I was raised a Presbyterian. Yet, I had family members who were Catholics, Methodists, Pentecostals and followers of Caribbean religiosity. Conversations about the world of the spirits and charismatic Christian experiences were common in our dinner meetings and celebrations.

I remember the time when, as a Presbyterian youth leader, our youth experienced a revival. Youth were having charismatic experiences and it was evident that there was an increasing religious fervor in our congregation. With time, the leadership of the church heatedly debated the purposes of these charismatic experiences, concluding that those who wanted to continue fostering them had to leave and go to the Pentecostal churches.

Years after this experience, I read Jonathan Edwards' sermons. I read about the First Great Awakening and the vitality that these religious experiences brought to the United States. I discovered an ancestor, a Reformed ancestor, with whom I could engage in theological conversation. The contextual example of Edwards provides me with *continuity* in my theological inquiry about what Jesus does in the world of the spirits in the Caribbean and Latino/a contexts. Regretfully, I was never taught to interpret Edwards' work in light of my missiological questions. I re-discovered Edwards by way of my own contextual inquiries.

In the seminary where I used to teach, all MDiv students had a mid-course evaluation or assessment. In their second year of study, every student selected two peers, and the administration appointed the adviser and two other faculty members to have an intense conversation about the theological and ministerial development of the student. Students and faculty came together to assess a student's ministerial vocation.

One year I was assigned to an evaluation whose student—a Presbyterian student—was trying to understand some charismatic inclinations he had recently discovered in his internship. The way he articulated his charismatic inclinations and inquiries was by using Harry Potter's language of magic and sorcery. The student claimed that his tradition did not offer any theological language to articulate his charismatic persuasions and inclinations. He was trying to appropriate language from the entertainment world for his recent Christian experiences—he was following a very common Christian method of acquiring theological language. Yet, he was totally ignorant of the fact that the broader Christian tradition—historical figures such as Edwards, Wesley, and Seymour and current ones such as Pentecostals, *evangélicos*, and charismatic Christians—from different historical periods and parts of the world not only have language, but are fully engaged in missiological discourse that considers the encounter and interactions between the world of the spirits and our faith in this dimension of time and space. Perhaps we need to learn that the vitality of the Christian religion is to be found in the wealth of its history and multiple contexts. He certainly discovered that he was not alone in his inclinations and inquiries—both historically, globally, and in his current context—and that grounded theological questions and answers from different Christian communities can contribute to his theological formation and vocation.

I have always been pleasantly surprised by the fact that my Christian faith is eschatological in nature. The Holy Spirit leads us in directions that we rarely expect. I find myself in the same puzzlement that Peter found himself when the Spirit pushed him to go to Cornelius' house and discover that God was at work in that context and in the worldview of those pagans with an inclination for the God of Israel. Yet, I rejoice in knowing that Peter got to Cornelius' house with humility and not with a prepared script. In fact, the curious reader of Acts 10 will notice a peculiar missional practice, rare in our days. Verses 28–29 of Acts 10 reads (NRSV): "and he said to them, 'You yourselves know that it is unlawful for a Jew to associate with or to visit a Gentile; but God has shown me that I should not call anyone profane or unclean. So when I was sent for, I came without objection. *Now may I ask why you sent for me?*" Peter begins his cross-cultural and inter-religious encounter and conversation with a question, an inquiry!

I also begin my missiological inquiry with questions. I want to know "what is Jesus doing among the spirits," so that my answer offers my interlocutors in Caribbean and in Latina/o communities a grounded daily life experience to explore Jesus Christ's work in our living religions and contexts. Perhaps my journey of faith in the Reformed tradition is alive and guiding my passion. Why should I doubt it? I do believe in the never-ending reformation of the Christian community!

Bibliography

Bediako, Kwame. "How Is Jesus Christ Lord?" *Exchange* 25 (1996) 27–42.

Carlos Cardoza-Orlandi, Carlos. *Mission: An Essential Guide.* Nashville: Abingdon, 2002.

———. "Mission at the Borders." In *Teaching Mission in a Global Context,* edited by Patricia Loyde-Siddle and Bonnie Sue Lewis, 25–39. Louisville: Geneva, 2001.

———. "Re-discovering Caribbean Christian Identity: Biography and Missiology at the Shore (Between the Dry Land and the Sea)." *Voices from the Third World: New Challenges to EATWOT Theology* 28 (2004) 114–44.

Fadiman, Anne. *The Spirit Catches You and You Fall Down.* New York: Farrar, Straus & Giroux, 1997.

hooks, bell. *Teaching to Transgress: Education as the Practice of Freedom.* New York: Routledge, 1994.

Levine, Daniel H. "The Future of Christianity in Latin America." Working Paper 340, 2007.

Oduyoye, Mercy Amba. "Spirituality of Resistance and Reconstruction." In *Women Resisting Violence: Spirituality for Life,* edited by Mary John Mananzan, 161–71. Maryknoll, NY: Orbis, 1996.

Phan, Peter. "Doing Theology in World Christianity." *Journal of World Christianity* 1 (2008) 27–41.

Vanden Berg, Todd. "Culture, Christianity, and Witchcraft in a West African Context." In *The Changing Face of Christianity: Africa, the West, and the World,* edited by Lamin Sanneh and Joel A. Carpenter, 45–62. Oxford: Oxford University Press, 2005.

Walls, Andrew. "Primal Religious Traditions in Today's World." In *The Missionary Movement in Christian History: Studies in Transmission of Faith,* 119–39. Maryknoll, NY: Orbis, 1996.

———. "Structural Problems in Mission Studies." *International Bulletin of Mission Research* 15.4 (1991) 146–55.

6

The Holiness of God as Reason for and Promise of a Theological Critique of Religion

Margit Ernst-Habib

A Few Introductory Observations on the "State of Religion"

Hardly a day goes by without reports on how religiously motivated conflicts between members of different religions (or of different branches of the same religion) cause suffering, discrimination, harassment, persecution and even death. All over the world, from Syria to Germany, from the Netherlands to the United States, from France to Nigeria, religious hostilities are rising to new peaks, claiming victims on a daily basis to an almost inconceivable extent.[1] When Christopher Hitchens thus asserts in his bestselling book that "religion kills,"[2] his statement seems to be a rather obvious matter of fact.[3] At the same time, "religion" is one of the principal motivations and forces encouraging people worldwide to resist unjust politics and economics, supporting them in their pursuit of creating a local and global society that is more just and compassionate, and in their manifold efforts for reconciliation, integration and convivence.[4] Looking at the role "religion" plays in the

---

1. According to a new study of The Pew Research Center (the Religion & and Public Life Project), a third of the 198 countries included in that study had high religious hostilities, reaching a six-year peak. The full report may be found under http://www.pewforum.org/files/2014/01/RestrictionsV-full-report.pdf.

2. Hitchens, *God is not Great*.

3. For a more substantiated and balanced discussion of the relation of religion and violence, see Dalferth and Schulz, *Religion und Konflikt*, collecting essays from Christian, Muslim, and Jewish authors; cf. also the theological analysis of Hailer, *Theologische Religionskritik als Gewaltkritik*.

4. On the integrating and conflict resolving power of "religion" see, for example,

life of individual women, children and men all around the globe, this contradictory character of religion in its potential to empower and strengthen on the one hand, and its potential to hurt, oppress, and negate on the other hand is evident—sometimes even in the life of one particular individual. No religion seems to be able to escape this inherent ambiguity.

In Europe's so-called "secularized"[5] countries, for example Germany, we find another significant development concerning the status of religion and its importance for everyday life, which seems to be, at least at first glance, just as contradictory in itself: On the one hand, all established churches, Protestant as well as Roman Catholic,[6] record a drastic decline in membership and a far-reaching loosening of commitment and engagement of remaining church members, who—for a large part—understand themselves as "unchurched" (*kirchenfern*) and no longer as believers in the traditional sense of the word.[7] On the other hand, researchers with a focus on practical theology or the sociology of religion have been claiming for years that not only is "religion" not dead, but that it is actually on the rise, that a vast number of people, inside and outside of the church, understand themselves as "religious," longing for personal spiritual experiences in the broadest sense of the term. Slogans such as "the return of religion" and "megatrend religion" are controversially discussed,[8] and may not provide an adequate description of the religious *status quo* in Germany.[9] Yet they point us towards a fact that should not be overlooked or ignored in order to understand and analyze the role and function of religion in a secularized country like Germany at the beginning of the twenty-first century: Churches, their members and representatives may have become more and more irrelevant in secularized societies, but not so religion in general. It still plays a central role especially in the media, visible in the form of religious

---

Antes et al., *Konflikt – Integration – Religion*. On the concept of "convivence" (found in Latin American Liberation theologies; Spanish: convivencia) in contrast to co-existence, see Sundermeier, *Konvivenz und Differenz*.

5. For a helpful analysis of "secularism," see Pollack, *Säkularisierung*.

6. Which together make up about 95% of all Christians in Germany, and 60% of the population.

7. Cf. Großbölting, *Der verlorene Himmel*.

8. See, for instance, Körtner, *Wiederkehr der Religion?*

9. The most recent research study "Engagement and Indifference" (2014) of the Evangelische Kirche in Deutschland found that 57% of all church members understand themselves to be unchurched and indifferent not only towards the Christian religion, but towards religion and spirituality in general. With Gladkirch and Pickel, *Politischer Atheismus*, 160, we could argue that we cannot speak about a "return of religion" per se, but only of a return of religion to public discussion and attention.

infotainment and a media-hyped, virtualized Christendom,[10] and it is at the same time also ever-present as a perceived threat to society through "other" religions from without and within.[11] Despite all proclaimed indifference, "religion" seems to be at the root of fascination with *and* fear of "the Other" as well as at the root of finding meaningful individual answers to life's fundamental questions.

To sum it up: even in secularized countries, various concepts of and experiences with religion are still vividly present in the midst of society, and the claim that there is "no society without religion"[12] seems to be validated by a simple look around. And it is exactly this central, yet diffuse and ambiguous role religion plays in our daily lives and in the lives of people around the globe that calls for a closer consideration and critique of religion from a theological perspective. It is even more urgent and critical for *Christian* theologies and churches to take the contradictory developments of a perceived "megatrend religion" as well as the growing indifference towards religion into account, not in order to profit from societal developments in terms of increasing membership or adapting to contemporary processes, but in order to look at their inherent presuppositions and implications. What do Christian churches and theologies have to say, on the one hand, about a megatrend religion, that seems to be flourishing and thriving, yet at the same time goes hand in hand with a megatrend "God-forsakenness," (*Gottvergessenheit*)[13] where religion is understood and experienced apart from any notion of a personalized God with whom human beings can live

---

10. Extensive media coverage, for example, of conclave and papal election are routine matters in Germany, and are followed by millions of viewers and readers.

11. This threat is not only perceived to come from the outside, through religiously motivated terrorism, for example, but also from "the others in our midst": When former Federal President Christian Wulff declared in 2010 that "Islam belongs to Germany," he caused a storm of protest from large parts of the population who saw "Christian" culture, heritage, and guiding principles for society endangered by accepting Islam as a part of the religious make up of Germany. See de Nève, *Islamophobie in Deutschland und Europa*, 203–207. As I am writing this, a new right-wing movement in Germany called PEGIDA (Patriotic Europeans Against the Islamization of the Occident), which has organized rallies with tens of thousands people for months, is about to disintegrate due to leadership issues. It has brought the xenophobic and islamophobic attitudes of a considerable part of the German population to the foreground, based on a crude nationalist understanding of "Christian" culture, but also instigated an emphatic and public rejection by large parts of politics, church and public.

12. See, for example, Rendtorff, *Gesellschaft ohne Religion?*; Girard, *Violence and the Sacred*, 221 et passim; both authors argue from a different context, though.

13. Körtner, *Wiederkehr der Religion?*, 31 et passim, uses this expression, in order to indicate that most of the new forms of religiosity are actually contemporary variations of pantheism and monism without a personalized "God." In that sense, human beings have forsaken or forgotten about "God."

in a meaningful relationship? What do Christian churches and theologies have to say, on the other hand, to church members who understand themselves not only as unchurched, but even "indifferent" towards all aspects of "religion"? And how do Christian churches and theologies not only in Germany but worldwide take into account the fact that "religion" is, at the same time, lived and experienced by many people as a nurturing, empowering, liberating, healing dimension of their relationship with God and with others?

With these questions, we have arrived at two central foci this paper will look at: How are "religion" and "God" interrelated? More specific: How does Christian theology from a Reformed perspective understand the relation between who God is and what God does and the human response to this God in the form of religion? How does this theology help to unmask religion, and here first all of *Christian* religion, as nothing more and nothing less than a *human* response, always at risk to invent, proclaim and trust self-made idols and false gods[14] rather than daring to rely on the "Holy Other One"? And finally, how does this theological critique of religion may lead us into a worshipful life, *coram Deo* and *coram mundi*, in which we live all of our life as the *communio sanctorum* in a "holy communion" with God and all of God's creation?

Defining "Religion": More Questions Than Answers . . .

Definitions of religion are indeed legion, and there is no single concept or definition that could claim any degree of universal validity; neither in theology (Christian or other), nor in sociology, philosophy or any other discipline.[15] Religion has been understood and treated rather uncritically for a long time, both, in common usage and in the scholarly world as a general and constant "human feature,"[16] with the result that it seems to belong to the category of what has been called "plastic words":[17] an amorphous stereotype with a quasi-scientific or universal sound, that is used all the time and everywhere, and that seems to be helpful in supporting communication and dialogues of various kinds. As a matter of fact, though, plastic words

---

14. Here, of course, Calvin's warning (*Institutes*, I.11.8) that human nature is a "perpetual factory of idols" comes to mind immediately.

15. For a detailed, critical and very helpful discussion see Feil, *Concept of Religion*.

16. Cf. Masuzawa, *Invention of World Religions*, 1.

17. See Pörksen, *Plastic Words*. Dommel, *Biographien*, 204, even remarks that the term "religion" seems to become more popular in public discourses the less a fixed definition is agreed upon by scholars and laypeople.

are elusive, empty words devoid of concrete and comprehensible meaning, which can be and are indeed customized and molded to fit whatever is needed at a particular moment for a particular group of people, while claiming universal truth, validity and authority for themselves. Recent critical analyses of the term "religion," theological and non-theological, add more facets to this perceived dimension of its elusive and malleable character. Obviously, the scope of this essay does not allow for an extensive and adequate discussion of these analyses; I will list a few of them nevertheless in order to indicate the range of current questions concerning the term religion.

Starting with the most evident observation will demonstrate immediately, how inherently disputable any concept of religion is *per se*. On a global level, we encounter the quite disturbing fact that most languages, cultures and "religions" do not possess a word or concept that could be adequately translated with our word "religion," and thus be used as its pendant. (This is also true, by the way, for the Hebrew Bible which certainly knows about religious phenomena of different kinds, and even of a beginning of what we could call a theological critique of religion, yet does not provide us with even so much as an preliminary attempt at conceptualizing or defining religion.)[18] Deriving either from the Latin term "relegere" (rite, cultic act) or from "religare" (binding back to God), the term religion was used in Western Christianity to describe the "Christian religion"[19] as the true way of worshipping God—at first not in opposition to other religions (which were not in range of view at all until the late Middle Ages), but as distinguished and apart from other expressions of human life such as culture.[20] The plural form, and with it the conceptual understanding of several disparate *religions*, came into usage only after increased contact with Islam through Arabic armed conquest as well as peaceful co-existence in Europe, and secondly, also through the fragmentation of the church in the wake of the Reformation.[21] This euro-centric and "Christian" character of the concept of "religion" became even more evident when colonial powers encountered non-European cultures, categorizing and analyzing them by reference to a concept that was utterly foreign to them; in fact, even inventing

---

18. See Grund et al., *Kultbilder*, 34.

19. See Weinrich, Religion und Religionskritik, 11–24, for a concise and helpful introduction. For a brief, yet informative discussion of "religion" in Luther and Calvin, cf. Plasger, *Ansätze theologischer*.

20. This dialectic of religion and culture is in itself a unique feature of Western thinking, not known to many other contemporary and historical cultures/religion; see, f.e., Dommel, *Biographien*, 204.

21. For an extensive and detailed study of the term "religio" see Ernst Feil's 4 volumes on Religio.

or construing "world religions" according to their own presuppositions.[22] Since all these classifications were neither unbiased nor neutral, but clearly interest driven, they more often than not ended with a hierarchically ordered list of religions, ranging from the so-called primitive natural religions to the sophisticated monotheistic religions, whose climax, of course, was understood to be the Christian religion, the only "true and civilized" one. The disastrous ramifications of these colonial classifications and conceptualizations are still felt today, and are criticized intensely in particular by postcolonial theories and subaltern studies.[23]

In addition, for a long time women in theology and church have been challenging the concept of "religion" for a host of reasons, including its binary Enlightenment perception of private/public, religious/secular, female/male etc., which did not correspond with liberating religious experiences of women, but instead served to suppress and oppress them.[24] It could be even argued, that, especially in the beginning, many forms of feminist theologies developed as a particular form of theological critique of religion (and the concept of "religion" in itself) as an ongoing process of Christian metanoia.[25]

Even more than from the inside of religious institutions or paradigms, religion in Europe was the object of vehement critique from other disciplines (such as philosophy, psychology, sociology) from the eighteenth century on,[26] to which theologians and churches responded for a long time with rather apologetic, even embarrassed attempts at defending religion, or with retreating into the perceived safety of ecclesiastical seclusion. Currently, though, a renewed interest in a *theological* critique of religion and its relevance (and provocations!) for church and society is emerging in Germany; and my essay understands itself as part of this ongoing discourse. What has become central to this discussion, at least from my perspective, is the understanding that any theological critique of religion has to claim and sustain its *theological* perspective—certainly not without assistance from insights of other disciplines, but nevertheless unapologetically understanding itself as a *theo*-logical endeavor. To put it rather simply: even though many,

---

22. Most "Hindus," for example, would not use this term as a self-designation (and may not even know it!), since Hinduism is a European designation for what actually constitutes a cluster of quite different religious traditions in India.

23. See, for example, Jenny Daggers' study *Postcolonial Theology of Religions*.

24. Cf. Serene Jones' description and analysis in *Transnational Feminism*.

25. Cf. my argument in *Stammt Gott vom Manne*.

26. See Michael Weinrich's extensive and detailed study *Religion und Religionskritik*, where he discusses and analyses more than 80 different European (mostly German) theologians, philosophers, sociologists, etc., and their respective critique of religion, ranging from Enlightenment up to present day discussions.

if not most of the popular contemporary expressions of religion (sometimes even within the church) have forgotten about God, a theological critique of religion cannot. Thus an essential first step for theologically *critiquing* religion appears to be an attempt of theologically *defining* religion; and to this task we will now turn.

A Theological Approach to Defining "Religion"

> For it is the God who said,
> "Let light shine out of darkness,"
> who has shone in our hearts
> to give the light of the knowledge of the glory of God
> in the face of Jesus Christ.
> But we have this treasure in clay jars,
> so that it may be made clear
> that this extraordinary power
> belongs to God
> and does not come from us.
> (2 Cor 4:6–7)

What the precedent observations and deliberations aimed to demonstrate is the fact that we cannot treat any concept of "religion" as innocent, scientific, universal, or neutral—religion is quite obviously not a (God-) given human constant, but instead a human construct that as such is prone to all kinds of restrictions, deficiencies and misuses. Before we can develop a critique of religion, then, we will have to deal with the fact that any effort (even if it is theological) to define religion may leave us actually with more questions and problems than with useful and indisputable answers. The following thoughts on defining religion, thus, can and should be understood only as preliminary "approach" (Annäherung) within and for a *Christian* context from a Reformed perspective, with no claim on universal validity.[27]

From this perspective, we would have to claim first that "religion" has to do with human beings and with "God" in a fundamental and essential way, which is, considering the current debate on "religion without God," in fact not as obvious as it may sound. This interrelation between God and

---

27. I am convinced, however, that a stringent, yet humble theological critique of religion might very well turn out be what Weinrich calls "a bridge to a theology of religions" that would not only encourage the desperately needed dialogue of religion, but also serves as the basis of productive, continual self-criticism; see Weinrich, *Theologische Religionskritik*, 33.

THEOLOGICAL CRITIQUE OF RELIGION

human beings could then serve as the basis for a first attempt to describe religion: The *lived faith in God* of actual human beings emerges in religion[28] in a multitude of ways, implicating a particular understanding of who *God* is as well as who *human beings* are. Religion, and this is decisive to keep in mind, is a construct which always relates to at least *three* points of reference: not only God and the individual believer; but God, the individual believer, *and* fellow human beings. In religion, thus, the knowledge of God and of ourselves (Calvin)[29] finds a human, and therefore necessarily finite and fallible expression and actualization: Faith in God is lived out as religion, in words and deeds, in private and public, in spiritual experiences and intellectual endeavors, in structures and encounters, in worship and Christian lives, communally and individually, in liberating and empowering as well as oppressing and destructive ways. This description of the ambiguous character of religion as lived faith provides us with an important distinction we will have to keep in mind as we continue: God, faith, and religion are three separate realities and need to be recognized as such despite their indisputable interrelatedness. Neither is religion to be equated with faith, nor can we claim to "have God" by "having religion" or "having faith." To use the words of Michael Weinrich, the task of theological critique of religion as a function of the church is to draw attention to the fundamental difference of "foundation and form" (Grund und Gestalt):[30] the *foundation* of church, theology and religion lies and remains outside of them in God, the Holy Other One; and thus the *forms* of church, theology and religion are in constant need of critical reevaluation. The Reformed tradition with its particular hermeneutic and inherently *theological* understanding of the *semper reformanda secundum verbum Dei*[31] produced what we could call a "theology of trust and suspicion,"[32] and it might prove to be helpful for our task, too. This theology attempts to counteract the danger of idolatry in all its manifold

28. Ibid., 18.

29. See the opening sentences (I.1.1.) of his Institutes of the Christian Religion on the connectedness of the *cognitio Dei et homine*: "Nearly all the wisdom we possess, that is to say, true and sound wisdom, consists of two parts: the knowledge of God and of ourselves."

30. Weinrich, *Theologische Religionskritik*, 21–23.

31. See Jason Garoncy's article on "Semper Reformanda" in this volume. For a historical discussion of this formula that has actually been coined by Karl Barth in the 1950s, but in fact captures in a remarkable and very influential way analogous assertions of Reformed (and Lutheran!) theologians since the Reformation, cf. Mahlmann, "Ecclesia Semper Reformanda"; and Bush, *Calvin and the Reformanda Sayings*.

32. Green, *Theology, Hermeneutics, and Imagination*, 21, develops the term "theology of suspicion and trust"; I have changed the order to indicate what theologically comes first, as will be developed in the following.

forms by placing all theological constructs *and* religious expressions under continuous scrutiny, while at the same time not only believing God to judge our fallible and sinful human efforts as *unbelief*,[33] but also trusting that this judgment always is already a shadow of God's grace,[34] and includes a divine promise, nevertheless. Trusting faith in God, then, provides the inner motivation for a radical suspicion of all concepts and expressions of religion, and thus for a theological critique of religion; while it relies at the same time on God's grace to not only justify, but also sanctify human responses. The Second Thesis of the *Barmen Theological Declaration* certainly includes "religion," when it confesses that there is no area of our life "in which we would not need justification and sanctification through Jesus Christ"; contrary to popular opinion, no expression or aspect of religion[35] is exempt from this claim. According to Barth, human beings are caught in religion "in a way of acting that cannot be recognized as right and holy, unless it is first and at the same time recognized as *thoroughly wrong and unholy*";[36] with other words: there is nothing holy, that is, nothing that would *not* need justification and sanctification, in or about religion and all of its manifold expressions and aspects *per se,* that is, in and by itself.

Following this line of thought, we would then have to conclude, that religion (from a Christian perspective) is not only a *theological concept*, but, even more specific, a *confessional* concept ("Bekenntnisbegriff"). Apart from our confession to Jesus Christ, "who has been made wisdom and righteousness and sanctification and redemption for us by God" (1 Cor 1:30), and "who is the foundation that has been laid" (1 Cor 3:11), Christian theology cannot even begin to develop a concept or understanding of religion. Not only from a phenomenological perspective, as described above, but even more so from a theological and biblical perspective, we would thus argue with Barth that there is no such thing as *religion per se,* no "consciousness of absolute dependence"[37] (Schleiermacher), not even a "point of contact"[38]

33. See Barth's famous discussion on "Religion as Unbelief," 298–326.
34. Green, *Theology,* 22.
35. And all of its derivatives such as religious experience, spirituality, piety, etc.
36. Barth, *CD* I/2, 299.
37. To use the famous expression of the Reformed theologian Friedrich Schleiermacher; cf. *Christian Faith,* 12: "The common element in howsoever diverse expressions of piety ("Frömmigkeit"), by which these are distinguished from all other feelings, or, in other words, the self-identical essence of piety, is this: the consciousness of being absolutely dependent, or, which is the same thing, of being in relation with God."
38. Emil Brunner, another Reformed theologian, used the term "point of contact" ("Anknüpfungspunkt") in order to describe human nature as being equipped for divine revelation in already having some kind of idea of what revelation is about; Karl Barth responded in 1934 with his famous No!; see Barth and Brunner, *Natural Theology.* For

(Brunner) as a permanent human feature. Human sinfulness has permeated and perverted all aspects and features of human life, *including* religion; and it is only through God's graceful act of justification and sanctification, of God's reconciliation in Christ, that religion *may* become the realm where we reach out and meet God, or rather: where God reaches out and meets us. Accordingly, all theological critique of religion is first and foremost *self*-critique, a continuous process of *metanoia* and new beginnings, with the confession of *our* sin as a crucial part of it.[39] Thus the posture of any theologian critiquing religion is one of repentance and not of arrogance, of praising and trusting God and God's graceful judgment, and not one's own futile efforts of understanding and relating to God; in short, it is a *posture of worship*.[40]

Holiness and the Knowledge of God

With this posture of worship in mind, we now continue our deliberations on the form and content of a theological critique of religion. As we have noted above, Calvin (and with him much of Reformed theology) emphatically underlined the interrelatedness of our knowledge of God and of ourselves, and in our reflections on the character of religion this interrelatedness has already been evident: even though we understand religion to be a *human* response, it cannot be understood without taking into account the subject it is responding to. For this reason, we now turn to consider more closely our "knowledge of God." In doing so, we will focus on what has traditionally been called the *attributes* of God, or, with Wolf Krötke's term, on "God's

---

a brief discussion of this "landmark debate" on natural theology and its continuing importance see, for example, McGrath, *Christian Theology*, 167.

39. Cf. Boulton, *God Against Religion*, 178: "To borrow Luther's term, the genuine Christian cannot avoid the stance of the penitent, for she is 'always a sinner, always a penitent, always righteous.' At every turn, she must confess that, if she is justified, she is simultaneously a thoroughgoing sinner, if her community is a community of saints, it is simultaneously a community of sinners; if her religion is the true religion, it is simultaneously the religion of unbelief, idolatry, and self-righteousness without peer. This emphatically rules out Christian triumphalism, or as Paul puts it, Christian 'boasting.'"

40. Boulton continues, ibid.: "At the same time, however, and just as emphatically, Christian shame and despair are likewise ruled out. For, at every turn, the genuine Christian must constantly confess and rejoice that, if she is a thoroughgoing sinner, she is simultaneously justified by God's grace; if her community is a community of sinners, it is simultaneously a community of saints by God's grace; and if her religion is a religion of unbelief, idolatry, and self-righteousness without peer, it is simultaneously 'reckoned and adopted' by God's grace, that is, reckoned and adopted by God's prodigal love and mercy in Jesus Christ, who enters, adopts, and lifts religion once and for all."

clarities"⁴¹ (*Gottes Klarheiten*), focusing on *one* of them out of a long list of attributes:⁴² God's *holiness*. Given the central role that "holiness" occupies in contemporary discourses on religion, culminating in claims such as "the category of "holiness" or "the holy" lies at the very ground of all genuine religion,"⁴³ our choice may be a rather obvious one. Yet with this choice we are deliberately *not* following the lead of eminent and highly influential theologians such as, for example, Rudolf Otto, who understood human encounters with "the holy" in his phenomenological depiction of the psychology of religion as the fundamental category of all religious experience.⁴⁴ We do not understand holiness primarily as an "experienced phenomenon" which as such could be considered "a very important cognitive 'doorway' to understanding the nature of religion;"⁴⁵ starting point for our considerations is *not* "that which concerns man ultimately"⁴⁶ as Paul Tillich put it in his memorable phrase. Our perspective will also not be determined by religio-sociological perspectives, such as Emile Durkheim's, for example, one of the founding fathers of the sociology of religion, who defined "religion" as "a system of beliefs and practices that binds a community together around those things which it holds *sacred*."⁴⁷

Despite all these exceedingly important and influential conjunctions of religion and "the holy," we will not start by discussing a form of *generic notion* of the holy/holiness;⁴⁸ our focus on holiness, instead, derives from a

---

41. See Krötke, *Gottes Klarheiten*.

42. For a brief discussion of the use of God's attributes in Reformed confessions, cf. Rohls, *Reformed Confessions*, 45–48, on "God's Essence and Properties"; for a discussion of Barth's, Jüngel's and Krötke's use and interpretation, cf. Holmes, *Revisiting the Doctrine*.

43. Opening sentence of Mariña, *Holiness*, 235.

44. Cf. Otto, *Idea of the Holy*. Otto characterized religious experiences with the "Holy" as the "wholly other" as *mysterium tremendum et fascinosum*, trying to establish an universal phenomenological structure in order to systematize and analyze diverse religious manifestations.

45. Tillich, *Systematic Theology*, 215.

46. Ibid., "The holy is the quality of that which concerns man ultimately. Only that which is holy can give man ultimate concern, and that which gives man ultimate concern has the quality of holiness."

47. Nielsen, *Transformations of Society*, my italics.

48. Cf. Webster, *Holiness*, 18, on a theology of holiness as an exercise of holy reason; we could argue analogously for a theological critique of religion. Webster writes: A theology of holiness "can proceed by first of all elaborating a phenomenology of 'the holy,' which will then form the basis of a theological account of God's holiness and its entailments for human sanctification. Or it can proceed directly to the exegetical and dogmatic tasks, bypassing the attempt to root its considerations in a religious phenomenology." With Webster, we would argue for the second option, because within the

quite different perspective and relies on quite different presuppositions, two of which we will briefly introduce here. As we will demonstrate below, this particular choice of a biblical and theological perspective on holiness may not only change our perception of "God's holiness" as such, but also of creaturely holiness, and, as a consequence, also of our understanding of *religion*.

(a) "You shall be holy; for I the LORD your God am holy" (Lev 19:2; cf. 1 Pet 1:15)—this essential biblical claim and assertion opens up our deliberations on the holy, and informs our understanding of holiness, divine and creaturely. As witnessed to in Scripture, the "Holy One of Israel" (Isa 30:12; 45:11) is not to be confused with any generic notion of holiness;[49] the holiness of the *communion sanctorum* is not to be understood apart from God's holiness. As Jason Goroncy rightly notes,[50] divine *and* also creaturely holiness hold a central place in "Holy Scriptures," in the Hebrew Bible as well as in New Testament writings, and therefore call for and demand close attention whenever the knowledge of God becomes the subject of theological reasoning. Holiness, thus, is not an arbitrary starting point for a theological critique of religion, but an indispensable interpretive key. And even though biblical interpretations of holiness[51] may include different and differing, and as such not easy to reconcile notions and convictions of holiness, it seems apparent that the subject of singular and manifold holiness,[52] of the Holy One and the holy many is quite central to both, the Old as well as the New Testament. If one agrees further with Goroncy, who follows the lead of Peter T. Forsyth,[53] that God's and our holiness is "*the* theme in the ministry of Jesus and so of the Scriptures,"[54] and if one understands theology as a contribution to the Christians' task of *hallowing* God's name,[55] than we could,

---

phenomenological approach "the generic notion of 'the holy' has been accorded priority over exegesis, and has in effect swamped the specificity of a Christian understanding of holiness."

49. Cf. Kraus, *Systematische Theologie*, 267: "Der Heilige Israels . . . ist nicht 'das Heilige' Rudolf Ottos und all jener, die das Religiöse im 'Heiligen,' im Numinosen repräsentiert sehen. Die Heiligkeit Gottes ist die Einheit seines Gerichtes mit seiner Gnade. Der kommende Gott ist darin heilig, dass seine Gnade Gericht und sein Gericht Gnade in sich schließt. Gottes Liebe ist heilig. Sie lässt sich nicht annektieren."

50. For a first overview on the centrality of divine and creaturely "holiness" in Scripture cf. Jason Goroncy, *Elusiveness*, and the bibliographical references in his essays.

51. Willis, *Notes on the Holiness*, 85, provides a list of classic Scripture passages "which have informed the history of Reformed interpretation of holiness."

52. Cf. Willis, *Holiness*, 86–90.

53. Forsyth, *Cruciality of the Cross*, 5; I am very much indebted to Jason Goroncy for pointing out Forsyth's relevance to my deliberations on the holiness of God.

54. Goroncy, *Elusiveness*, 204.

55. See John Webster's proposition on understanding the holiness of theology,

and maybe should, conclude that it "stands to reason . . . that Christianity's first concern be 'God's holiness before all else.'"[56] A biblically-oriented theological critique of religion, which is deconstructive as well as constructive in its approach and goal, should thus engage the lens of "holiness" as a way of truly worshipping God and of being ever wary of idolatry.

(b) The main reason for a focus on the holiness of God as an interpretive key, however, is an essentially Christological premise: Christ, the Holy One of God (John 6:69), who has been made our wisdom, is not only the "base of knowledge" (Erkenntnisgrund) for all we can say about God, but also the very place where the Triune God chose to reveal *God's own holiness in human form;*[57] or as Karl Barth writes, "all God's holiness is now *called* and *is* Jesus of Nazareth."[58] The "center of the self-disclosure" of the Holy Other One is thus "Jesus Christ as witnessed to by the power of the Holy Spirit in the scriptures of Old and New Testament."[59] From there, we encounter God's holiness not as a distant, speculative, metaphysical attribute of God, but as God's essential nature in relation to us and all of creation. God's holiness, therefore, is not the *object* of our holy reason, but the *subject* of our holy reasoning, as Goroncy concludes:

> To affirm the Christ-given and -shaped characterization of holiness is to affirm that God's holiness is not the 'object' of our

---

Holiness, 9: "A Christian theology of holiness is an exercise of holy reason; it has its context and content in the revelatory presence of the Holy Trinity which is set forth in Holy Scripture; it is a venture undertaken in prayerful dependence upon the Holy Spirit, it is an exercise in the fellowship of the saints, serving the confession of the holy people of God; it is a work in which holiness is perfected in the fear of God; and its end is the sanctifying of God's holy name." (My italics) Cf. also the Heidelberg Catechism in its prayerful contemplation of the Lord's Prayer's first petition (Q &A 122): "'Hallowed be your name' means: Help us to truly know you, to honor, glorify, and praise you for all your works and for all that shines from them: your almighty power, wisdom, kindness, justice, mercy, and truth. And it means, Help us to direct all our living—what we think, say, and do—so that your name will never be blasphemed because of us but always honored and praised." Cf. also Q & A 190 of the Larger Westminster Catechism.

56. Goroncy, ibid. (again quoting Forsyth). Cf. Willis, *Holiness*, 58: Holiness is "the all-embracing, all-encompassing attribute of God—or, in the language of perfections, the holiness of God is the perfect perfection of all God's perfections"; and Wolf Krötke's understanding of holiness, where he does not list holiness among the four major clarities of God (the clarities of truth, of love, of power and of eternity), but interprets them in the sense of "holy clarities," 116. Cf. Christopher R.J. Holmes' interpretation of Krötke's thesis: "Holiness is so intrinsic to God's identity that the four exemplary clarities are but closer specifications of God's holiness." *Revisiting the Doctrine*, 169.

57. See Goroncy, *Elusiveness*, 199; quoting Forsyth, *Person and Place*, 347.

58. Barth, *CD* II/1, 428.

59. Willis, *Holiness*, 3.

curiosity so much as the 'subject' of our life and being. So to reflect on the self-revelation of holiness is to be ever orientated towards and engaged in holy communion—a willed relationship of the holy with the Holy—a communion which is initiated, established, maintained and perfected by the Holy Trinity and secured forever in Christ's cross. We are saved into holiness—a holiness that is always, for humanity, 'borrowed' holiness, and is sustained by God.[60]

Holiness is who God is and what God does, and creaturely, derived holiness is what the *communion sanctorum*, the sanctified ("made holy") community belonging to the Holy One, lives and grows in. This central biblical understanding of God, translated into our time and context, does not only assist us in efforts for a theological critique of religion, but indeed *commands* it.

God Is Holy Mystery and Wholly Love

Unlike some historical confessional documents of the Reformed tradition, more recent faith documents do not start with a seemingly exhaustive list of God's attributes,[61] describing God's essence and perfections in metaphysical categories. Instead, they insist emphatically on the perennial incompleteness of our knowledge of God—because of *who* God is as the *Holy One*, while at the time respond with awe to this Holy God, who made Godself known to us. One of the most recent confessional documents, the *Song of Faith* of the United Church of Canada from 2006, confesses God's movement towards us and the revelation of God's love as the center of our knowledge of God:

> God is Holy Mystery, beyond complete knowledge, above perfect description. Yet, in love, the one eternal God seeks relationship . . . Grateful for God's loving action, we cannot keep from singing . . . We witness to Holy Mystery that is Wholly Love . . . We find God made known in Jesus of Nazareth, and so we sing of God the Christ, the Holy One embodied . . . Grateful for God's loving action, we cannot keep from singing. Creating and seeking relationship, in awe and trust, we witness to Holy Mystery who is Wholly Love."[62]

---

60. Goroncy, *Elusiveness*, 202.
61. See, for example, chapter 2 of the Westminster Confession.
62. The Song of Faith may be found at http://www.united-church.ca/beliefs/statements/songfaith.

God is Holy Mystery, "beyond the reach of human mind";[63] on our own, we cannot speak about God, and when we try, we ascribe to God human attributes in superlatives, projecting human longing and desires heavenwards. That is, of course, one of the central accusations of a number of critics of religion, beginning with Ludwig Feuerbach, and it has not yet lost its relevance and urgency. Translated into theological terms, it warns all faith, theology, and religion not to succumb to the lures of idolatry—resulting into what we have called before a theology of suspicion. Yet this is only a part of what the *Song of Faith* has to say about God's holiness, and standing alone, it would be not only misleading, but simply wrong from a biblical and theological perspective. The United Church does not confess an unknown and unknowable Holy Mystery, which could be and should be ignored, if we can say nothing about it. Instead, the confession continues by calling our attention not to what *we cannot do* (speak about God), but to what *God has done*: revealing Godself as *Wholly Love* in Jesus Christ. God's Holiness is "that pure love who is God eternally."[64] God seeks and creates relationship, and chooses not to be *totaliter aliter* (wholly Other),[65] but the Holy Other One "who confronts us with purifying love,"[66] creating "a robustly positive—not a cautionary negative relation between the Holy One and the holy many."[67]

---

63. The Confession of 1967 declares: "God's sovereign love is a mystery beyond the reach of human mind. Human thought ascribes to God superlatives of power, wisdom and goodness. But God reveals divine love in Jesus Christ by showing power in the form of a servant, wisdom in the folly of the cross, and goodness in receiving sinful men and women."

64. Willis, *Holiness*, 2: "Holiness is that pure love who is God eternally. This pure love is in every way prior to, is in every way the presupposition of, God's purifying love manifest in creaturely, derivative holiness . . . That pure love is immediate to God eternally and, as purifying love, is mediate temporally, spatially, energetically to constitute creation and redemption."

65. "Der ganz Andere" was a central term in Karl Barth's early theology; see, for example, his famous commentary on *Romans*, 250: "On the brink of human possibility there has . . . appeared a final human capacity—the capacity of knowing to be unknowable and wholly Other; of knowing man to be a creature contrasted with the Creator, and, above all, of offering to the Unknown God gestures of adoration. This possibility of religion sets every other human capacity also under bright and fatal light of impossibility." It would be a gross misunderstanding, though, to reduce Barth's theology to this formula; from an emphasis on the "wholly Other" he moved toward an understanding of the "Humanity of God," and of God's freedom as freedom to and for, and not from human beings; see, in particular, Barth's discussion of this topic in his own theological development in his later essays "Humanity of God" and "Gift of Freedom."

66. Willis, *Holiness*, 36.

67. Ibid., 34.

What we touch upon here is, expressed in classical theological terms, the topic of "immanence" and "transcendence" (among other doctrines); two terms which often create a serious misconception of who God is as the Holy Other One:[68] Transcendence and immanence are often understood as opposing terms denoting first of all a vertical distance, or spatial categories, and God's holiness is more often than not subsumed under God's transcendence. Biblical witness, though, points us to the Holy Other One, who demonstrates an "urgent will to immanence,"[69] who is indeed present in and with creation, yet not bound nor restricted to it, whose immanence is no opposite to divine transcendence, since both refer to the one living Subject. Christian faith, and with it a theological critique of religion, responds in awe to the power of the holy love, which reveals itself, and yet preserves its mystery.[70] "Holiness," thus, points us to a separateness that does not mean remoteness from, but *uniqueness,* a uniqueness that in loves relates to creation. Mayra Rivera, arguing from a postcolonial position, but nevertheless at points surprisingly similar to Willis,[71] calls this uniqueness in relation *relational transcendence;* and even though she never uses the term "holiness" (as far as I can see), what she describes with her term comes very close to what we have said above about the Holy Other One who is Wholly Love. God's creation, and in it the *communion sanctorum,* has been touched and changed by transcendence; "one does not remain unmarked by the costly love of the Holy One."[72]

This robustly positive relation of the Holy One to the holy many, this relational transcendence, has immediate consequences for (1) a theological, confessional understanding of "religion" as well as for (2) a theological, confessional critique of religion, and for (3) our understanding of and encounters with "Others."

(1) With Karl Barth we can maintain that religion as lived faith is indeed "unbelief," a yoke we have to bear,[73] but only in so far as even this unbelief stands under the promise of justification and sanctification by the Holy One. That does in no way equate religion (or spirituality or piety) with the Holy, but it also does not consider them to be irreconcilable opposites; not because of who we are, but, yet again, because of who God is. Religion

---

68. See also for the following, Willis, *Holiness,* 1.
69. Von Rad, *Old Testament Theology,* 279.
70. Cf. Körtner, *Wiederkehr,* 39.
71. Rivera, *Touch of Transcendence.*
72. Willis, *Holiness,* 2.
73. Cf. Barth, *Romans,* 258: "Religion is neither a thing to be enjoyed nor a thing to be celebrated: it must be borne as a yoke that cannot be removed."

as a completely human affair always remains on the "form"-side (*Gestaltseite*), never bridging the gap between form and foundation.[74] In religion, human beings do not embrace or grasp the Holy, but they are embraced and grasped (i.e. made holy)[75] by the Holy One *despite* their religion. Their religion is being judged and negated as unbelief, but this judgment as the judgment of the Holy One is "*Gottes aufrichtendes Urteil*"[76] (the uplifting judgment of God): in Christ, the Holy One embodied, God has not only revealed Godself to all humankind, but has entered and is present in the world of religion, where human beings try to domesticate or take hold of God.

The holy judgment of the Holy One, then, opens up a new future for all humans, since they are no longer bound to sin, and thus not bound to be sinners even and especially in their religion.[77] Thus we also have to maintain with Karl Barth, that the possibility of "true religion" indeed exists, even though we can speak of true religion "only in the sense in which we speak of the justified sinner."[78] No religion is true in itself, it can only *become* true,[79] which is the gracious work of the Holy Spirit[80] in binding us in all aspects and areas of our life to Christ as the Holy One embodied. God's holiness meets us as purifying love, and this holds true for our religion(s), too.[81] In that sense, we would have to state once again, that "religion" from a Christian perspective can only be understood as an inherently *confessional* concept.

(2) A theological critique of religion is, following this line of thought, therefore also to be understood as a confessional endeavor, since it is based upon our confession of the holiness of God and of God's sanctifying grace. By confessing God to be the "Holy Other One," we commit all our religious efforts to God's holy judgment—which is the starting point of all theology in general and theological (self-) critique of religion in particular.

74. See Weinrich, *Theologische Religionskritik*, 21.

75. Willis, *Holiness*, 96, refers to the incarnation as the foundation of human holiness, when he writes: "What makes the humanity holy is the union of the eternal Word with the flesh." In that sense, incarnation as embodiment of the Holy One sanctifies religion, too.

76. See Dahling-Sander and Plasger, *Hören*, 26.

77. See Krötke, *Sin and Nothingness*.

78. Barth, *CD* I/2, 326.

79. Ibid.

80. Cf. ibid., 345: "That there is true religion is an event in the act of the grace of God in Jesus Christ. To be more precise, it is an event in the outpouring of the Holy Spirit."

81. Religion as part of human creatureliness is thus not per se "unholy," but only in its sinful misuse; see Willis, *Holiness*, 48: "'Holiness' is not the opposite of creatureliness but is the right use of creatureliness."

THEOLOGICAL CRITIQUE OF RELIGION

God's holiness calls for and commands a distinct, continual differentiation of foundation and form, not allowing for an equation of our own constructs of God *and* human beings with the Holy One and the holy many. It is wary of all attempts of "*Ent-Heiligung*" (desecration) of God's Holy Name,[82] the worst of which does not come in the guise of atheism or religions, but in the world's (and the church's!) desire and practice to *nostrificate*[83] God:

> This attempt arises when the world . . . believes that he [God] can be very useful and even indispensable to its own goals and aims and aspiration; so that, instead of denying him or coming to terms with him with a bit of religion, it takes the cleverer course of resolutely affirming him, affirming itself in and with him, affirming his deity as its own and its own as his . . . Now it integrates itself with God or God with itself. Now it equates God with itself or itself with God.[84]

Nostrification of God is de-secration, because it replaces God with human-made idols of all possible kinds, dissolving the tension between the Holy Other One and humankind, equating foundation and form, assimilating God's truth to its own. All forms of theological critique of religion, commanded and brought forth by God's holiness, will be especially cautious and attentive towards this fundamental danger and temptation which is not to be avoided by labeling our theology, religion, religiosity, spirituality, piety, but also our culture, politics, economics with the label "Christian." In fact, more often than not, the publicly and ostentatiously used label "Christian" might be a first indication for a need to question and scrutinize the underlying understanding of God. Yet a theological critique of religion that understands itself as a result of the purifying love of the Holy Other One will direct its gaze first of all to its own attempts to nostrificate God and will remain in humble solidarity with all those others, who, just like them, try to domesticate and substitute God with an idol. A theological critique of religion, motivated and stimulating by an encounter with the Holy Other One, will also know of the promise which lies in the openness, incompleteness and fallibility of all forms of religious expressions, in that it expects and seeks "to be touched by that which transcends it and, in the process, transform itself"[85] or, as I would rather put it, be transformed by God's purifying

---

82. See Barth, *Christian Life*, 131.
83. Deriving from the Latin *nostrum facere*, to turn into our own.
84. Ibid.
85. Rivera, *Touch of Transcendence*, 128, with reference to her concept of a "theology of relational transcendence."

love. In short: it will understand itself as "sanctified work"[86] and religion as "sanctified life of faith."

A theological critique of religion that trusts in Christ, the Holy One embodied, the eternal Word made flesh, will also not shy away from the scandal of the cross by ignoring "cruciform knowledge" as "crucial criterion by which doctrine (and religion!) at every point is put to test."[87] Holiness defined and understood apart from the cross of the Risen Christ is an abstract, time- and contextless, unmerciful, unprophetic, unprotesting, distant and neutral holiness of a glorious deity, and not the holiness of the crucified and risen *"Heiland"* (Savior), who came to *"heilen"* (heal), *"heiligen"* (sanctify), and to mend and re-create all that is in *"heil-loser Unordnung"* (hopeless mess) by becoming himself part of this "mess."

A theological critique of religion that relies on the ongoing work of the Spirit in our hearts and minds and all of our life, that relies on the *Holy* Spirit that binds us to Christ,[88] the Holy One embodied, will also take into account the witness of the biblical account—trusting that the Spirit "breathes revelatory power into scripture"[89] while at the same time expecting this Spirit to critically judge us when "we abuse Scripture by interpreting it narrow-mindedly using it as a tool of oppression, exclusion, or hatred."[90] The Bible does not and cannot replace, contain, control or tame the Holy Mystery that is Wholly Love, but witnesses faithfully to God, and a theological critique of religion will hold this understanding of the unique role of Scripture in tension with its limited character as a witness. The promise of a theological critique of religion understood in this way is not primarily the deconstruction and unmasking of all religious idolatries, or the growth of true knowledge about God as a goal in itself, but a *growth in holiness* that is "discovering more and more God's knowledge of us good creatures who are freely forgiven sinners"[91] and being made wholeheartedly willing and ready from now on to live for God, as the first question of the Heidelberg Catechism puts it.

---

86. Cf. Webster, *Holiness*, 17: "in theology the work of human reason is sanctified work."

87. See Willis' discussion on "cruciform knowledge" and "the cross of the Risen Lord," *Holiness*, 9–23, as part of his second chapter "The Holiness of the Cross." Cf. Ibid., 15: "The cross that examines every theological claim is that particular one on which was killed Jesus Christ whom the apostolic community proclaimed to be the same as the risen Lord. It bars cheap grace, and it bars romanticizing suffering."

88. See Calvin, *Institutes* III.1.1.

89. From the already mentioned Song of Faith of the United Church of Canada.

90. Ibid.

91. Willis, *Holiness*, 57.

(3) A theological critique of religion is not a purely academic exercise with relevance to only a few interested scholars, but a fundamental function of the church that understands itself as the *communion sanctorum,* the community elected and made holy for a reason: to witness to the Holy Other One, embodied in Christ, and continually at work in the Holy Spirit, to witness to the Holy Mystery that is Wholly Love, a love that creates, preserves and reaches out to all human beings.[92] A theological critique of religion will examine all expressions of religion in order to determine whether they are, in word and deed, reflections of this utmost *"Menschenfreundlichkeit Gottes"*[93] (God's philanthropy, in the literal sense), or whether they desecrate God's holy name by denying and negating their inherent and indispensable bond of faithfulness to all "others." It is by ignoring and refuting the knowledge of Christ, the Holy One embodied, true God and true human, that human beings assume that they can live with each other just as well as without or even against each other,[94] according to their own preferences and likings. This is no side issue or minor matter for church, theology, and a theological critique of religion, since it is in this "chaotic contradiction [that] the holy name of God is decisively and supremely desecrated in the world."[95] A theological critique of religion will take into account all ambiguity of religion(s) and religious expressions, a few of which we have noted at the beginning of this paper, but not in order to be proved "right" over against others, but in order to honor God's holy name by honoring "each person and all people,"[96] without turning them into objects or, in analogy to our nostrification of God, nostrificating them. Modifying Rivera's modification of Levinas' definition, I would like to propose as a central task of a theological critique of religion

92. And, indeed, all of creation, a perspective which will not be developed further here, but would have to be an essential part of a theological critique of religion.

93. Cf. Zeindler, *Erwählung,* 155.

94. The following thoughts are based on Karl Barth's discussion in *CD IV.4,* 132f. Barth writes: "His [man's] ignorance of God culminates and manifests itself in his ignorance of his fellow man. He regards him as an object to whom he as subject may or may not be in relation according to his own free choice and disposal, whom he may pass by as he does so many other objects, or with whom, if this is out of the question, he may have dealings as it suits himself within the limits of what is possible for him. He does not know him as a fellow subject whom God has set unavoidably beside him, to whom he is unavoidably linked in his relation to God, so that apart from him he cannot himself be a subject, a person."

95. Ibid.; Barth describes this contradiction as follows: "If we wish to know what is the true and final point of the petition 'Hallowed be thy name,' . . . then we had better focus our attention on this one thing, on the evil fact that we humans, whose God in supreme mercy has taken up the cause of each person and all people in Jesus Christ, can be and are both everything and nothing to one another, both fellow men and wolves."

96. Ibid.

to maintain holiness[97] in all forms of relations, with God and with all others, by claiming that *holiness* "designates a reality *irreducibly different* from my own reality, without this difference destroying this reality and without the relation destroying this difference."[98] A theological critique of religion tries to accommodate the tension that all human beings, their religions together with all other aspects of human life, are indeed and will remain irreducibly different from each other *and* from the Holy Other One, and are yet bound together indissolubly by the holy band of God in Christ. With this knowledge, theological critique of religion aspires to assist the holy people of God in living a holy, worshipful life before God and before and for the world God loves so much, while praying: "Hallowed be your name."[99]

---

97. That is, of course, the creaturely and derived holiness of the holy many.

98. Rivera, *Touch of Transcendence*, 82.

99. Cf. Adams, *Exegetical Perspective*, 125: "The first petition is . . . an urgent appeal for God to act. In English it may sound like praise, but it is an imperative. The 'name' is simply a traditional way of speaking of God. May you—your name—be sanctified, that is, vindicated, recognized as holy, and therefore extolled. God is being called upon to reveal God's glory in a world full of ugliness and evil—and to do so soon."

Bibliography

Adams, David R. "Exegetical Perspective on Matthew 6:7–15." In *Feasting on the Gospels: A Feasting on the Word Commentary*, edited by Cynthia A. Jarvis and E. Elizabeth Johnson, 122–27. Louisville: Westminster John Knox, 2013.
Antes, Peter, et al., eds. *Konflikt, Integration, Religion: Religionswissenschaftliche Perspektiven*. Göttingen: V&R Unipress, 2013.
Barth, Karl. *The Christian Life: Church Dogmatics*. Vol. IV, *Four Lecture Fragments*. Translated by Geoffrey W. Bromiley. London: T. & T. Clark, 2004.
———. *Church Dogmatics*. Translated by G. T. Thomson et al. London: T. & T. Clark, 1936–77.
———. *The Epistle to the Romans*. Translated by Edwyn C. Hoskins. Oxford Paperbacks 160. London: Oxford University Press, 1968.
———. "The Gift of Freedom." In *The Humanity of God*, 69–98. Translated by Thomas Wieser. Richmond: John Knox, 1960.
———. "The Humanity of God." In *The Humanity of God*, 37–68. Translated by John Newton Thomas. Richmond: John Knox, 1960.
Boulton, Matthew Myer. *God Against Religion: Rethinking Christian Theology through Worship*. Grand Rapids: Eerdmans, 2008.
Bush, Michael. "Calvin and the Reformanda Sayings." In *Calvinus Sacrarum Literarum Interpres: Papers of the International Congress on Calvin Research*, edited by Herman J. Selderhuis, 286–99. Reformed Historical Theology 5. Göttingen: Vandenhoeck & Ruprecht, 2008.
Calvin, John. *Institutes of the Christian Religion*, edited by John T. McNeill. Translated by Ford Lewis Battles. Philadelphia: Westminster, 1977.
Colpe, Carsten. *Über das Heilige: Versuch, Seiner Verkennung Kritisch Vorzubeugen*. Anton Hein Series 3. Frankfurt: Hain, 1990.
Daggers, Jenny. *Postcolonial Theology of Religions: Particularity and Pluralism in World Christianity*. London: Routledge, 2013.
Dahling-Sander, Christoph, and Georg Plasger. *Hören und Bezeugen: Karl Barths Religionskritik als Hilfestellung im Gespräch mit den Religionen*. Waltrop: Spenner, 1997.
Dalferth, Ingolf U., and Heiko Schulz, eds. *Religion und Konflikt: Grundlagen und Fallanalysen*. Göttingen: Vandenhoeck & Ruprecht, 2011.
De Nevè, Dorothée. "Islamophobie in Deutschland und Europa." In *Religion und Politik im vereinigten Deutschland: Was bleibt von der Rückkehr des Religiösen?*, edited by Gert Pickel and Oliver Hidalgo, 137–64. Wiesbaden: Springer Fachmedien, 2013.
Dommel, Christa. "Biographie als Ort von Religion. Jürgen Lotts Theorie der Erfahrung mit Religion." In *Theo-Web: Zeitschrift für Religionspädagogik* 7 (2008) 202–13.
Ernst-Habib, Margit. "Stammt Gott vom Manne ab? Denkanstöße für eine theologische Religionskritik als Sexismuskritik." In *Theologische Religionskritik: Provokationen für Kirche und Gesellschaft*, edited by Marco Hofheinz et al., 151–78. Forschungen zur reformierten Theologie 1. Neukirchen-Vluyn: Neukirchener Theologie, 2014.
Evangelische Kirche in Deutschland. "Engagement and Indifference." 2014.
Feil, Ernst, ed. *On the Concept of Religion*. Translated by Brian McNeil. Binghamton, NY: Academic Studies in Religion and the Social Order, Global Publications, Binghamton University, 2000.

———. *Religio: Die Geschichte eines neuzeitlichen Grundbegriffes*. Forschungen zur Kirchen- und Dogmengeschichte 36, 70, 79, 91. Göttingen: Vandenhoeck & Ruprecht, 1986–2007.

Forsyth, Peter T. *The Cruciality of the Cross*. 1910. Reprinted, Eugene, OR: Wipf & Stock, 1997.

———. *The Person and Place of Jesus Christ*. The Congregational Union Lecture for 1909. 1909. Reprinted, Eugene, OR: Wipf & Stock, 1996.

Girard, Rene. *Violence and the Sacred*. Translated by Patrick Gregory. 1977. Reprinted, London: Athlone, 2005.

Gladkirch, Anja, and Gert Pickel. "Politischer Atheismus—Der 'neue' Atheismus als politisches Projekt oder Abbild empirischer Realität?" In *Religion und Politik im Vereinigten Deutschland: Was bleibt von der Rückkehr des Religiösen?*, edited by Gert Pickel and Oliver Hidalgo, 137–63. Wiesbaden: Springer Fachmedien, 2013.

Goroncy, Jason. "The Elusiveness, Loss and Cruciality of Recovered Holiness: Some Biblical and Theological Observations." *International Journal of Systematic Theology* 10 (2008) 195–209.

Green, Garrett. *Theology, Hermeneutics, and Imagination: The Crisis of Interpretation at the End of Modernity*. Cambridge: Cambridge University Press, 2000.

Großbölting, Thomas. *Der verlorene Himmel: Glaube in Deutschland seit 1945*. Göttingen: Vandenhoeck & Ruprecht, 2013.

Grund, Alexandra. "Verfehlter Gottesdienst, Andere Götter, Kultbilder: Grundformen der Religionskritik im Alten Testament." In *Theologische Religionskritik: Provokationen für Kirche und Gesellschaft*, edited by Marco Hofheinz et al., 34–64. Forschungen zur Reformierten Theologie 1. Neukirchen-Vluyn: Neukirchener Theologie, 2014.

Hailer, Martin. "Theologische Religionskritik als Gewaltkritik: Ein altes Vorurteil und Bleibendes Problem." In *Theologische Religionskritik: Provokationen für Kirche und Gesellschaft*, edited by Marco Hofheinz et al., 133–50. Forschungen zur Reformierten Theologie 1. Neukirchen-Vluyn: Neukirchener Theologie, 2014.

Hitchens, Christopher. *God Is not Great: How Religion Poisons Everything*. New York: Hachette, 2009.

Holmes, Christopher R. J. *Revisiting the Doctrine of the Divine Attributes: In Dialogue with Karl Barth, Eberhard Jüngel, and Wolf Krötke*. Issues in Systematic Theology 15. New York: Lang, 2007.

Jones, Serene. "Transnational Feminism and the Rhetoric of Religion." In *A Just and True Love: Feminism at the Frontiers of Theological Ethics: Essays in Honor of Margaret A. Farley*, edited by Maura A. Ryan and Brian F. Linnane, 75–108. Notre Dame: University of Notre Dame Press, 2007.

Körtner, Ulrich H. J. *Wiederkehr der Religion? Das Christentum zwischen neuer Spiritualität und Gottvergessenheit*. Gütersloh: Gütersloher Verlagshaus, 2006.

Kraus, Hans-Joachim. *Systematische Theologie im Kontext biblischer Geschichte und Eschatologie*. Neukirchen-Vluyn: Neukirchener, 1983.

Krötke, Wolf. *Gottes Klarheiten: Eine Neuinterpretation der Lehre von Gottes "Eigenschaften."* Tübingen: Mohr Siebeck, 2001.

———. *Sin and Nothingness in the Theology of Karl Barth*. Studies in Reformed Theology and History n.s. 10. Princeton: Princeton Theological Seminary, 2005.

Mahlmann, Theodor. "*Ecclesia semper reformanda*: Eine Historische Aufklärung: Neue Bearbeitung." In *Hermeneutica Sacra: Studien zur Auslegung der Heiligen Schrift im 16. und 17. Jahrhundert*, edited by Torbjörn Johansson et al., 381–442. Historia Hermeneutica, Series Studia 9. New York: de Gruyter, 2010.

Mariña, Jaqueline. "Holiness." In *A Companion to Philosophy of Religion*, edited by Charles Taliaferro, et al., 235–42. 2nd ed. Blackwell Companions to Philosophy 9. Malden, MA: Wiley-Blackwell, 2010.

Masuzawa, Tomoko. *The Invention of World Religions: Or, How European Universalism was Preserved in the Language of Pluralism*. Chicago: University of Chicago Press, 2005.

McGrath, Alister. *Christian Theology: An Introduction*. Hoboken, NJ: Wiley-Blackwell, 2011.

Nielsen, Donald A. "Transformations of Society and the Sacred in Durkheim's Religious Sociology." In *The Blackwell Companion to Sociology of Religion*, edited by Richard K. Fenn, 120–32. Blackwell Companions to Religion 2. Oxford: Blackwell, 2001.

Otto, Rudolf. *The Idea of the Holy*. Translated by J. W. Harvey. New York: Oxford University Press, 1923.

Pew Research Center Religion & and Public Life Project. "Religious Hostilities Reach Six-Year High." http://www.pewforum.org/files/2014/01/RestrictionsV-full-report.pdf.

Plasger, Georg. "Ansätze Theologischer Religionskritik bei den Reformatoren." In *Theologische Religionskritik: Provokationen für Kirche und Gesellschaft*, edited by Marco Hofheinz et al., 65–75. Forschungen zur Reformierten Theologie 1. Neukirchen-Vluyn: Neukirchener Theologie, 2014.

Poerksen, Uwe. *Plastic Words: The Tyranny of a Modular Language*. Translated by Jutta Mason and David Cayley. University Park: Pennsylvania University Press, 2004.

Pollack, Detlef. *Säkularisierung—ein moderner Mythos?* Studien zum religiösen Wandel in Deutschland 1. Tübingen: Mohr Siebeck, 2012.

Presbyterian Church (U.S.A.) "The Confession of 1967." In *Book of Confessions: Part I of the Constitution of the Presbyterian Church (U.S.A.)* 285–97. Louisville: Office of the General Assembly, 2014.

———. "The Westminster Confession of Faith." In *Book of Confessions: Part I of the Constitution of the Presbyterian Church (U.S.A.)* 145–202. Louisville: Office of the General Assembly, 2014.

Rad, Gerhard von. *Old Testament Theology*. Vol. 1, *The Theology of Israel's Historical Traditions*. Translated by D. M. G. Stalker. 1962. Reprinted with a new Foreword by Walter Brueggemann. Old Testament Library. Louisville: Westminster John Knox, 2001.

Rendtorff, Trutz. *Gesellschaft ohne Religion? Theologische Aspekte einer sozialtheoretischen Kontroverse (Luhmann/Habermas)*. Serie Piper 117. Munich: Piper, 1975.

Rivera, Mayra. *The Touch of Transcendence: A Postcolonial Theology of God*. Louisville: Westminster John Knox, 2007.

Rohls, Jan. *Reformed Confessions: Theology from Zurich to Barmen*. Translated by John Hoffmeyer. Columbia Series in Reformed Theology. Louisville: Westminster John Knox, 1998.

Schleiermacher, Friedrich. *The Christian Faith*. H. R. Mackintosh and J. S. Stewart. Edinburgh: T. & T. Clark, 1999.

Sundermeier, Theo. *Konvivenz und Differenz*, edited by Volker Küster. Erlangen: Erlanger Verlag für Mission und Ökumene, 1995.

Tillich, Paul. *Systemtatic Theology*. Vol. 1. Chicago: University of Chicago Press, 1973.

United Church of Canada. "Song of Faith." http://www.united-church.ca/beliefs/statements/songfaith.
Webster, John. *Confessing God: Essays in Christian Dogmatics II*. London: T. & T. Clark, 2005.
———. *Holiness*. London: SCM, 2003.
———. "The Holiness and Love of God." *Scottish Journal of Theology* 57 (2004) 249–68.
Weinrich, Michael. *Die Bescheidene Kompromisslosigkeit der Theologie Karl Barths: Bleibende Impulse zur Erneuerung der Theologie*. Forschungen zur systematischen und ökumenischen Theologie 139. Göttingen: Vandenhoeck & Ruprecht, 2013.
———. *Religion und Religionskritik: Ein Arbeitsbuch*. UTB 3453. Göttingen: Vandenhoeck & Ruprecht, 2012.
———. "Theologische Religionskritik als Brücke zu einer Theologie der Religionen." In *Theologische Religionskritik: Provokationen für Kirche und Gesellschaft*, edited by Marco Hofheinz et al., 16–33. Forschungen zur reformierten Theologie 1. Neukirchen-Vluyn: Neukirchener Theologie, 2014.
Willis, E. David. *Notes on the Holiness of God*. Grand Rapids: Eerdmans, 2002.
Zeindler, Matthias. *Erwählung: Gottes Weg in der Welt*. Zürich: Theologischer Verlag Zürich, 2009.

7

Stepping into the Madness

On Being Skeptical, Doing Justice, and Hoping against Hope[1]

Cynthia L. Rigby

> "The one who expects the possible is great. The one who expects the impossible—the one whose hope takes the form of madness—that one is the greatest of all." —Søren Kierkegaard[2]

Introduction

Skepticism has a bad reputation among people of faith. We see it as blocking the way to our participation in the work of God in the world. We picture skeptics as those who refuse to budge, those who are immobilized by their own disbelief. And so we who identify as Christian believers encourage each other not to be skeptical but to "have faith"—to believe what God has promised will happen. If we have faith that expects what is possible, we can move out into the world and get something done. We can plan our strategies and measure our projects; we can grieve our failures and we can celebrate victories.

The only problem is that what God has promised is *not* possible. Lions lying down with lambs, tears wiped away from every eye, daily bread, forgiveness of sins, deliverance from evil. In order to believe in the possibility

---

1. A version of this essay appeared in the May, 2015 issue of *Studies in Christian Ethics*.
2. Kierkegaard, *Fear and Trembling*, 16.

of these things, it would seem, we would have to diminish them, somewhat. Perhaps we could put well-trained lions across the room from lambs, if the lions were on a leash and well fed beforehand. Or maybe we, in the U.S. context, could swing health care for *a lot more* people than have had it in the past, even if we cannot manage it for *all*. When people of faith believe things can happen that are not impossible, but only highly unlikely, then something is amiss. This is because our confessional claim is not only that God can beat the odds, but that God makes the impossible possible.[3]

I suggest that to bar skepticism from faith in the face of the impossible things God has promised is to impede the work of bringing God's Kin-dom to earth as it is in heaven. This work can be accomplished only by stepping into that which is beyond anything we can ask or imagine. This work is funded not only by all we believe, but also by our leaping into that which we acknowledge is unbelievable. "How can this be?" asks Mary, packing her suitcase to visit Elizabeth with pauses to write poetry about how the poor have been fed, and the rich left empty. "How can a person enter back into his mother's womb?" asks Nicodemus, going on to advocate for Jesus before the Sanhedrin and do his part to make sure Jesus gets a respectable burial. Both of these figures act ethically in the world, taking real risks to participate in God's saving work; both get to the place where they can act by way of a skepticism that allows them to wonder, and then to participate.

Suspecting, then, that skepticism has a significant role to play in creating a space for the work of Christian social ethics, I turn to the major task of this essay: to find a space for skepticism in the context of a Reformed understanding of how we come to know, and participate in, the work of God in the world. I do this, first, by offering a theological argument for how we might do a better job of including and conversing with skeptics in our midst. I then move, briefly, to suggesting we all attend to how skepticism invites us to the wonder that funds perfect participation in the work of God in the world.

Skepticism, the Reformed Tradition, and the Challenge to Re-Think

The Reformed tradition has not typically acknowledged any benefit to skepticism, from the standpoint of faith. While there can be found some appreciation for doubt, as a valid element of faith, and while doubt leans decidedly toward skepticism, there is a sense that skepticism lies too far beyond the boundary of belief to be acceptable. It seems that, if doubt is to

---

3. See, for example, Luke 1:37.

be uncertain about what one believes, skepticism cannot (yet) see its way clear to believe. With this distinction in place, it may be obvious why the Reformed tradition has been more amenable to finding a place for doubt than for skepticism. Our Reformed conviction is that those who confess Jesus as Lord have every reason to trust that they are claimed by God as the elect, regardless of whether they doubt what they believe on any given day.

But what place for skeptics? Is there a place authentically to engage those who visit our churches and cannot see their way clear to say the Creed: that Jesus is *born of the Virgin Mary;* that he will come again in judgment; that the body will be *resurrected?* Is there a place to receive those who do not want to pretend—those who cannot claim these as things they *believe?* Is there a place for acknowledging that much of what Christians confess is, simply, unbelievable? Is there any way in which *not believing* could be seen as a form of faith?

I can almost hear Calvin shouting down from heaven that *no,* "not believing" is not a form of faith. Calvin, after all, went out of his way to argue against the 16th century Roman doctrine of "implicit faith," believing it was not enough for Christians to know they believed "implicitly," by way of the church, if they adhered to the church's teachings.[4] The Roman church had, in the 16th century, wanted to offer what assurance it could to those who were skeptical about their faith. But Calvin, Luther, and the other Reformers wanted Christians to know the joy of *experiencing* faith for themselves. Consider Calvin's "definition" of faith, along these lines: "Faith is the firm and certain knowledge of God's benevolence toward us," he writes, "founded upon the truth of the freely-given promise in Christ, both revealed to our minds and sealed upon our hearts through the Holy Spirit."[5] Certainly, "implicit" knowledge and *not* believing are out of the bounds of what Calvin means by faith.

But what if we were to insert a "yet" between "not" and "believing"? Does Calvin's definition allow that "not yet believing" be a form of faith? And even if it would not explicitly allow for this, is this the direction it is leaning, a direction Reformed theology should be nudged to engage more fully as it moves into the future? Let me explore this possibility, for a moment.

Certainly, to create a space in the life of the confessing community for those who do "not yet believe" would mean entering in fellowship and open dialogue with skeptics who reject what the church confesses. But they would be skeptics of a certain ilk. First of all, they would be skeptics interested in believing, skeptics interested in showing up in church and pondering the

---

4. Calvin, *Institutes,* I.2.2.
5. Calvin, *Institutes,* III.2.7.

truth of members' religious convictions, skeptics who might self-identify as "seekers." They would not be, in other words, the sort of skeptics who have determined that, because it is impossible to believe, it is delusional to do so.[6] They would be skeptics, rather, who are trying to believe what honestly seems impossible to them, and what those who do confess might even admit seems impossible apart from God's intervention. I am suggesting here, in part, that there is a big difference between "not believing" and "not *yet* believing," when it comes to the range of skeptics. It is the difference between walking away from Jesus, with the rich young ruler,[7] and setting up a private meeting with Jesus, alongside Nicodemus, to argue about the logistics of being "born again."[8] It is the difference between self-identifying as an atheist and self-identifying as someone (like Eric Weiner, who will be discussed further, below) who "hopes someday to believe in God."[9]

I think this second category of skeptics should be welcomed into our Reformed communities of faith. I am not expecting they should (yet) be baptized, nor do I expect they would, by and large, want to be. Similarly, I do not think they are interested in becoming church members. (This said, by my observation there are in fact a large number of skeptics who are, already, baptized church members. But they feel in some ways "stuck," I think, because the rules of our ecclesial game have generally precluded them from being honest about their skepticism.)[10] Further, as I will try to show, I believe there are large numbers of those who (in the U.S. context) self-identify as the "religiously unaffiliated" who are skeptics that are seeking. In other words, I believe they fall into the category of skeptics with whom Reformed Christian believers should work to be in better dialogue and closer partnership.

The Reformed tradition prides itself both on being intellectually-minded and on insisting we treat everyone as though they are elect (leaving the matter of their "salvation" to God). When we really are who we pride ourselves as being, I believe we are well-positioned to open our doors and our ears wide to engagement with the "seeking skeptics" that are growing in

---

6. I am thinking, of course, of the growing community of "New Atheists" that follows Richard Dawkins, Daniel Dennett, and the late Christopher Hitchens.

7. Matt 19:16–26.

8. John 3.

9. These, again, are the words of Eric Weiner.

10. In one survey recently done in a large Presbyterian Church, for example, over 40 percent of congregational members indicated they do not believe in the divinity of Jesus Christ, the Virgin Birth, or the resurrection. The point here is that we have by and large precluded honest, mutual conversation with skeptics who are already members of our faith communities.

number, at least in the United States. I will work toward making a persuasive case for broader inclusion in the coming pages, but in order to do so I must first name the resistances that we, with our Reformed sensibilities, will naturally feel to such engagements. These resistances must be taken seriously because they immediately raise the question of what constitutes or distinguishes communities of faith, and whether admitting "skeptics" to these communities violates their identity.

Some Reformed Christians might understandably raise their hackles, for example, in response to the distinction I have made between skeptics who dismiss religious convictions out of hand and skeptics who hope someday to believe. The Reformed might for good reason question whether there is an important distinction to be made between these two categories of skeptics, after all, when it comes to the shape of Christian community. What difference does such a distinction make, it might be asked, when it comes to the *confessional* identity of a faith community? Whether a skeptic is hostile to those who confess or seeking a way "in" to making such confession, their position in relation to the confessional community is the same: they are outsiders to it. As we Reformed Christians point this out, we might reflect on how we do understand that everyone is not equally capable of faith, and that we have, therefore, come to make allowance in our traditions for a certain amount of doubt. The man who tells Jesus he "does believe" Jesus can heal his daughter, and then follows up with, "help me know my unbelief" models what it means to make a confession, but then honestly to doubt one's capacity to follow through on its claim, we might explain.[11] And we might add that we have learned doubt can be an important part of faith, and that we have even pressed Calvin to make more allowance for this.[12] But finally we interpret the unbelief of the father in Mark 9 in relation to a particular confession he has made; a confession he is uncertain about. This kind of uncertainty we can allow, even though we would intercede and hope and pray that certainty might return. But what would we do with a skeptic? How could we help? A skeptic, by contrast to this man, would not be able even to make such a confession. A skeptic would have not yet been able to believe. A skeptic would have rather responded to Jesus, "I don't believe, yet, but I hope to be able to, someday."

---

11. See Mark 9:24.

12. Elsewhere I have criticized Calvin, along these lines, for appealing to God's "secret working" as a way of advising us not to question God. One place that he does this quite starkly is in his commentary on the book of Job. See, for more on this, Rigby, "Providence and Play," 10–18.

Despite periodic attempts on the part of some of our constituencies to revive subscriptionism,[13] Reformed churches have at best resisted forcing everyone to agree wholeheartedly to every doctrinal point, or even to confess to every doctrinal truth we as a community hold dear. But we have, however, expected people to try to say the creed together, as members of the baptized, believing, body of Christ. Must there not be a baseline commitment, after all, to believing the bulk of what the church confesses? Or at very least to confessing even what one doesn't believe, in the hope that one might come to believe it? I have heard more than one Reformed colleague re-tell a story illustrating this approach as offered by Kathleen Norris:

> The student raised his voice: 'How can I with integrity affirm a creed in which I do not believe?' and the priest replied, 'It's not your creed, it's our creed,' meaning the Creed of the entire Christian church. I can picture the theologian shrugging . . . 'Eventually it may come to you,' he told the student, 'For some, it takes longer than for others.'[14]

It seems to me that this story may resonate with the spiritual journeys of some people, but certainly does not resolve the quandary of every skeptic. I am concerned, in fact, that to make such a recommendation to "seeking skeptics" is both to disrespect the shape of their spiritual journeys and to miss out on opportunities for frank conversation and mutual learning. As much as it is important to recognize that the Creed does not belong to any particular member of a church, but to the whole community, it is time for Reformed Christians to acknowledge that there is something less than ideal, something inauthentic, something perhaps even coercive and unjust, about asking a person who does not believe to confess anyway, as a way of coming to belief. The student's question about *integrity*, as it is recounted in this story, is an important one that is laid to the side in the interests of challenging the autonomous character of his question. But, really: isn't there a sense in which saying what you do not believe in the hope that saying it will somehow make it take effect . . . isn't there a sense in which such an enterprise manifests a lack of integrity? Doesn't it risk trading the mystical for the magical in a way that is decidedly *not* Reformed? It is not we who accomplish belief by our own efforts or rituals, according to the Reformed

---

13. Most recently, such an effort is being made by the Evangelical Covenant Order of Presbyterians (ECO), a break-off movement of the Presbyterian Church (U.S.A.) that insists its full-fledged, voting members subscribe to ten "essential tenets" (including that marriage be only between a man and a woman). See http://eco-pres.org/static/media/uploads/resources/Essential%20Tenets/eco-essential-tenets-confessions.pdf.

14. From Norris' *Amazing Grace*, as quoted in Kuiken, "Living Edge of Faith," 111–130, 125.

view. Christians are free to act in ways consistent with who they already are as disciples of Christ, not bound to act in certain ways in order to conjure preferred Christian identities.

The "religiously unaffiliated" (commonly identified as the "Nones,"[15] these days, in U.S. culture), certainly eschew any suggestion that they "fake it 'til you make it," when it comes to their spirituality. They care a great deal about integrity and authenticity, and have no patience at all with what they perceive to be hypocrisy. The idea that one would confess things one doesn't believe in the hope that one might be "lured into" believing them not only does not hold weight. Such a strategy argues, for them, against being religious. Frankly, I can see their point.

A "None" from whom I have learned a great deal, along these lines, is Eric Weiner. In his book, *Man Seeks God*,[16] Weiner recounts how he has spent a block of time "trying on" each of several religions, and what his experience of each was like. In December of 2011, in an op-ed piece for the *New York Times*, he says very directly that "he has a dog in this hunt" for meaning. "I hope someday to believe in God," he explains, insisting that "Nones" should not be perceived as atheists.[17] In an interview on PBS, Weiner explains that he came to respect the religious communities in which he took part; that he "was surprised" by the fact that members of religious communities were not as "narrow minded" as he had thought, but were instead "filled with intellectual curiosity" and "a deep doubt that nurtures their faith." But when asked by the interviewer why he couldn't quite "take the leap" and join any of these communities; when asked "What is holding you back?" Weiner replies, "I'd say it is my skepticism." Weiner goes on to explain that the difficulty, as he understands it, is that faith requires him to "be devoid of all skepticism," but that this would entail him laying to the side something he feels gives him protection. Skepticism, he argues, keeps him from being "lured into something dangerous."[18]

It is an interesting point Weiner makes, that skepticism helps keep us on our guard against that which is dangerous. Certainly, to the degree to which skepticism provokes us to pause and to consider whether or not claims about what constitutes the good are of God, it would be welcomed in a Reformed theological framework. The question, then, is why is there pressure to lay skepticism to the side if one is to be a person of faith? A

---

15. These are those who do not identify with any particular religious tradition, but also who do not identify as "atheists." They may include the so-called "spiritual but not religious," though this language is becoming dated.

16. Weiner, *Man Seeks God*.

17. Weiner, "Americans Undecided."

18. "In *Man Seeks God*, Author Eric Weiner Hunts for Divine," at video.pbs.org.

"None"-turned-Christian—believer named Christian Wiman has made it a project of his to argue otherwise. A poet who was brought back to Christian faith by way of falling in love with his wife, being diagnosed with a terminal illness, and entering into relationship with a thoughtful pastor with whom he has been able to engage in consistent and open dialogue, Wiman takes speaking engagements around the country where he tells his story while standing firm in his skepticism, despite sincere attempts by his interlocutors to undue it. "But . . . have you discovered a progressing state?" one questioner asked Wiman, in the context of a congregational Q and A session. "Do you mean have I found a resting state? A place of equanimity?" Wiman responded. "No. It seems to be my fate to experience God as anxiety. My whole life is wrestling with it."[19] Silence. What can possibly be done with such a statement, in the context of a faith community?

In his memoir, *My Bright Abyss*, Wiman develops this point at length. What is striking about his narrative is how tenaciously he seeks, even when he cannot believe. His search itself, it seems to me, is a kind of belief—a kind of belief that, one suspects, would not run nearly as deep were it void of skepticism. At one point Wiman writes,

> I have tried to learn the language of Christianity but often feel that I have made no progress at all . . . I understand that my understanding must be forged and re-formed within the life of God, and dogma is a means of making this happen: the ropes, clips, and toe spikes whereby one descends into the abyss. But I am also a poet, and I feel the falseness—or no, not even that, a certain inaccuracy and slippage, as if the equipment were worn and inadequate—at every step. And that's in the best moments. In the worst, I'm simply wandering through a discount shopping mall of myth, trying to convince myself there's something worth buying.[20]

In this we see the fatigue of an endlessly-seeking seeker, the frustration of a skeptic who wants to know that he knows, but who has learned to value the search itself, and the ways that have been given (e.g., theological language; doctrines) to enter that search.

Where I see skepticism, in addition to doubt, is in Wiman's reference to "myth." This reference goes beyond reflecting that it is difficult to hold onto what one believes. It raises the question of whether what one believes is true, or whether it is false and misleading. It leans toward the concern raised

---

19. Interview found at http://www.christchurchcville.org/events/an-evening-with-christian-wiman/.
20. Wiman, *My Bright Abyss*, 115.

by Wiener in his PBS interview: that laying aside skepticism for the sake of belief puts us in real "danger." The danger is that we might indeed enter into the realm of delusion, even as Dawkins, et. al. have been warning us. And of course those who nonetheless make confessional claims despite this danger, including Wiman, would say the even greater danger is that we will protect ourselves so well by means of skepticism that we will miss out on experiencing the presence of God, even in the abyss. As faulty as confessional claims might be, they indeed serve as the "ropes, clips and toe spikes" by which we make our way *to* meaning.

But there is a third danger I am becoming aware of, and this is the one I am suggesting we need take into account, as we move into the future. It is the danger inherent not to letting go of skepticism, nor to clinging fast to it, but of not allowing it to have any place in faith. Wiman, in my view, is stepping fearlessly into his own fear, into his own anxiety, into his own disbelief, as an exercise of faith. But we hardly know what to do with this. Like the man who tried to push him into claiming some form of "equanimity," we want a mature faith (at least) to have overcome skepticism. Again: doubt has a place, but disbelief? Disbelief is something that seems to us to fund fear, when what we want (with Calvin) is some modicum of confidence.

In her essay "Fear in the Reformed Tradition," Lyn Japinga notes that the Reformed tradition has a reputation for being fear-full. We are known for the fear that drove the Salem witch trials, founded in questioning who was truly "in," and who was threatening, the community of faith. We are known for the over-read and quoted "Sinners in the Hands of the Angry God," warning that we cannot know for sure whether *we* are "in" or "out," when it comes to the Kingdom of God. Given these stereotypes and historical realities, Japinga notes, "It is ironic that the Reformed tradition is theoretically deeply confident about God and salvation."[21] I wonder: Could it be that what the Reformed tradition fears most is being straightforward about our skepticism? Are we on some level worried that honesty such as Wiman's might lead us to be labeled "witches," of one sort or another? Are we afraid we might *be* "witches," if we are, in fact, skeptical? Do we fear that we might be doing an injustice to God claiming us *unconditionally* by naming out loud our fear that what we claim to believe is untrue?

I realize that at this point I have "gone to meddling," as they say in the southern United States. I am not thinking only, any longer, of making a place for *those who are skeptics* in our ecclesial communities. I am pressing also on the matter of *acknowledging and including our own skepticism* in our faith practices.

---

21. Japinga, "Fear in the Reformed Tradition."

With these matters in mind, and hoping I have made some case both for what skepticism is and why we should give it renewed consideration, I turn to what resources I believe we have, in the Reformed tradition, for making a place for it.

Making Space for Skepticism in the Reformed Tradition

The Divine Sovereignty & Philosophical Skepticism

If there is any conviction that most characterizes Reformed theology, it is that God is sovereign. God is the ruler over all; the Almighty Father who is the Governor of the universe. God is infinite; we are finite. But the Reformed tradition does not leave the relationship of God to creation at that. On the contrary, it insists that the God who is transcendent to the world is also near to us; that the God who is beyond our comprehension "accommodates" Godself to us. As Calvin famously puts it, "God . . . lisps to us," as a nurse talks baby-talk to the child in her charge.[22]

Central to Calvin's beautiful articulation of the divine accommodation is the idea that God remains incomprehensible, even as God is truly known to us on the basis of God's self-revelation. Calvin invokes this incomprehensibility frequently, both in order to honor the infinite character of God and also to celebrate God's graciousness. It is only when we remember God is utterly unknowable to us that we can revel in the fact that God is known. For God, in revealing Godself to us, has accomplished what is impossible: We know the unknowable God who knows us. In relation to this, it makes sense that Calvin would define faith as "firm and certain knowledge of God's benevolence to us, founded upon the truth of the freely-given promise in Christ, both revealed to our minds and sealed upon our hearts through the Holy Spirit." God accommodates us through the work of the Son by way of the Spirit so that we might have "firm and certain" knowledge.

Where all this gets tricky, for Calvin, is when our certainty wavers due to life circumstances that do not seem to reflect God's benevolence. In such cases, Calvin makes an interesting recommendation. He advises us not to question God, and certainly not to disbelieve, but rather to put our trust in God's "inscrutable will," trusting in God's "hidden plan."[23] What it comes down to is: we understand what we have been given to understand, and we have to trust God to handle what we don't understand, since we (as finite

---

22. Calvin, *Institutes* I.13.1.
23. Ibid.

creatures) do not understand everything. Skepticism is avoided by appeal to the "secret workings of God."

I must boldly say, in relation to this, that this marks a problem in Reformed theology (particularly in Calvin's thinking) that we should correct, as we head into the future. The claim that God is sovereign and that God's ways are never fully known to us need not leave us with no faithful option but blindly to trust. On the contrary, the Reformed insistence that God is sovereign creates a space for our doubts to be named and for our skepticism to be placed out in the open. We don't see where you are in this, God. We don't believe you are there. We demand you make things right.[24] We think you have forsaken us.[25]

Interestingly, the Reformed emphasis on the sovereignty of God maps fairly well over a concept called "philosophical skepticism." If skepticism is disbelieving that something exists or is true, philosophical skepticism is the idea that what exists or is true is not knowable, anyway. When Reformed theologians say the sovereign God is "inscrutable in God's ways," they are saying, similarly, that God and God's ways cannot be known. The divine accommodation, again, does not make God more knowable, but *adds to* God's unknowability the fact that God is known through God's acts. God is truly known, Reformed theology teaches, in the person of Jesus Christ. But God remains at the same time unknowable, and (as Barth teaches) is incomprehensible even in that which we know. The way I think about this is by imagining myself looking over the side of the manger in Bethlehem, and marveling that the baby lying there is the one "without whom anything that was made was made." The baby Jesus is, in Calvin's terminology, God's "accommodation" to us. But seeing God manifest in Jesus makes me wonder, all the more, at God's incomprehensibility. "How can it be?" it leads me to ask.

In relation to this, it seems to me, skepticism is useful for honoring the mystery of God and our own relationship to it. It authorizes us to say, even in the face of what *is* known, "I don't believe it." Now: expressing disbelief while looking over the side of the manger may be one thing (especially when it is coupled with Christmas joy, etc.), and saying it while looking at a hard-to-believe line of the Apostles' Creed may be another. Either way, though, when one a person ponders a confessional claim like "I believe . . . in the resurrection of the body" and says—with genuine skepticism—"I don't believe it!," she opens herself to experiencing the wonder of coming to know something that truly is impossible. Skepticism ensures that we don't

---

24. See Psalm 44.
25. See Psalm 22.

have to suspend rationality or "limit reason to make room for faith," as Kant advised. This is a good thing for social ethics, since if shutting down our reasoning processes were required, there would be no possibility we could function as actual subjects or agents in relation to what God is doing in the world.

In short, the fact that God is sovereign creates space for us to be skeptical without compromise to faith. Our skepticism ensures we are brought back to wonder at who God is and what God has done. It also ensures that we are distinct subjects who may join *with* Christ in the ministry of reconciliation. We are not absorbed by the one in whom we abide. Like Mary and Nicodemus, we act in relationship to him.

The Extra Calvinisticum & Openness to Other Divine Accommodations

Related to the idea that the sovereign God is unknown even when known is the idea that God is not exhausted even in God's self-revelation in Jesus Christ. According to Calvin, for whom this idea is named, the divine logos remains ubiquitous even while it is incarnate. While Jesus Christ truly reveals who God is, then, there is always "more to" God's living Word than what we see in him. This idea can be remembered as a guard against the idolatry of certainty that takes the form of making faith claims that assume exhaustive knowledge. Again, there is more room for skeptical "play" when what is known is not all it is possible to know. To be skeptical in the face of what is not (yet) known is potentially to be driven to explore beyond claims of certainty that can stymie spiritual and ethical pursuits rather than urging them on.

Election & Fearlessness

Reformed theology's trademark doctrine is probably the doctrine of election. Many of us agree that it could use some refurbishing, as we head into the future. If Japinga is right that the Reformed tradition has a reputation for promoting fear, election is the doctrine that precipitates the knocking together of knees and the quickening of the pulse.

Many are surprised to learn that the doctrine of election is meant not to evoke fear, but to instill confidence. From a pastoral care perspective, the doctrine of election reassures us that "nothing can separate us from the love of God." Neither death nor life; neither doubt, nor skepticism. The claim we make that we are elect; the belief we have that any particular person we talk to may be elect (and just not know it—yet) should inspire us to cast off fear in favor of interesting and honest theological conversation.

Because God is sovereign, because God is up to more than even what we know, because nothing can separate us from the love of this One who has claimed us: because of these things, we are free to engage, listen, speak, question, explore, testify, work, risk, and create. There is no need to prove we are "in" by pious actions or statements; there is no need to judge whether others are "in" or not. There, the only "true religion" is one that is practiced sincerely before God, even if it includes honest skepticism.

Skepticism and Wonder

> *I made "Star Wars" to try to awaken a certain kind of spirituality in young people—more a belief in God than a belief in any particular religious system. I wanted to make [Star Wars] so that young people would begin to ask questions about the mystery. Not having enough interest in the mysteries of life to ask the question, 'Is there a God or is there not a God?'—that is for me the worst thing that can happen.*[26] – GEORGE LUCAS

I remember reading Lucas' words, said in the context of an interview with Bill Moyers, and being quite surprised. This is because he said them in the guise of a person filling in a gap. From Lucas' point of view, young people were not asking questions about mystery. The problem, according to Lucas, was not that they were skeptical. It was that they were apathetic.

When we disallow skepticism in our churches, I wonder if we are promoting apathy. Building on the prior section, my suggestion is that if we reconstrue the divine sovereignty and its related doctrines in ways that invite doubt, questioning, and even skepticism, we may well nourish people in their spiritual journeys. It may be that creating a space for skepticism might even be opening an opportunity to stand in wonder in the face of impossible things that we can help make actual.

Calvin calls us to "wonder" almost every time we witness something that is seemingly impossible. In his commentary on Psalm 145 he even recommends "pursuing" God in relation to the incomprehensible gifts of the natural world, believing it will "stir us deeply" and cause us to stand "in wonderment."[27]

Calvin seems to associate contemplation with a form of disbelief. Granted, it is a disbelief that immediately submits to what God has in mind,

---

26. Lucas, quoted in "Conversation," 92. My emphasis.
27. Calvin, *Commentary on Ps 145*.

such as the kind Mary has when she moves immediately from saying "How can this be?" to "Let it be unto me as you have said." Still, it seems that in the moment of the disbelief there is incredulity, even skepticism. Writes Calvin, in relation to the Abraham who has just been shown stars, and promised descendants:[28]

> Like the Virgin Mary, when she inquired of the angel how his message would come to pass, and other similar instances in Scripture, Abraham asked how this could happen, but it was the question of a person struck with wonderment.

And Calvin moves from here to suggesting we, like Mary and Abraham, are called to participate in wonder:

> When, therefore, a message is brought to the saints concerning the works of God, the greatness of which exceeds their contemplation, they break out into expressions of wonder, but from wonder they soon pass on to contemplation of the power of God.[29]

Again, my suggestion here is that there is a place, in the mechanics of "wonder," for a kind of disbelief that refuses to be resolved, that continues to ask questions, and that endures even as that which is impossible becomes actual.

Conclusion

I have set out, in this essay, to make a case for how the Reformed tradition might be more open to skeptical "Nones" as we head into the future. I have also tried to show how our tradition might better welcome into worship, study, and conversation the skepticism of its confessional members, thereby allowing them to feel "at home," in church, for who they are. And I am further suggesting that creating spaces for skepticism will benefit both the Reformed community of faith and the world in which it lives. This is because *not* jumping too quickly to belief, in the face of the impossible things God has promised, leaves us open to wonder at the possibility that the impossible will be made possible. To *not* believe—in the face of God's absence—creates a context in which God can be called to account, or met somewhere in the absence, in Sheol, in the abyss, in the injustices of the world.

---

28. See Gen 15.

29. Calvin, *Commentary on Gen 17*, as quoted by David Steinmetz, *Calvin in Context*, 71.

If not believing is ruled out of bounds, the danger is we will miss the ways in which God enters even into it. To be skeptical that God will keep God's promises in relation to the kidnapping of schoolgirls in Nigeria; the beheading of journalists, taxi cab drivers, and aid workers in Syria; the killing of unarmed civilians in Ferguson and Staten Island; the Ebola epidemic in Africa is to honestly name the fact that healing seems impossible. We can give up altogether, we can invoke God's "secret will," or we can do what Jesus taught us to do: stomp our feet and demand of God, hope against hope, "Thy Kingdom Come!" Praying this, we wonder at the magnitude of God's promise as it meets the magnitude of the pain of the world. And we recommit to the work of doing justice, again. We jump into the mad, doubtful, impatient hope that, somehow—even though we don't really expect it—that which is impossible will be made, by God, possible. And we find ourselves praying, again: "Thy will be done."

But we do not stop even there. Because we know what God's reign looks like and we want it to be established. Because God's will is not inscrutable, just impossible to fathom. In wonder that we do have something to say about how things should look differently, then, we stomp our feet again, first demanding daily bread, and then forgiveness of sins, and finally deliverance from evil. *This* is what the Kin-dom looks like! we insist, claiming the impossible promises of God. And then, still skeptical, we begin gathering ingredients to make the bread.

Bibliography

Calvin, John. *Institutes of the Christian Religion*, edited by John T. McNeill. Nashville: Westminster, 1960.

ECO: A Covenant Order of Evangelical Presbyterians. "Essential Tenets and Confessional Standards." http://eco-pres.org/static/media/uploads/resources/Essential%20Tenets/eco-essential-tenets-confessions.pdf/.

Japinga, Lyn. "Fear in the Reformed Tradition." In *Feminist and Womanist Essays in Reformed Dogmatics*, edited by Amy Plantinga Pauw and Serene Jones, 1–18. Louisville: Westminster John Knox, 2006.

Kierkegaard, Søren. *Fear and Trembling*. Translated by Howard Hong and Edna Hong. Princeton: Princeton University Press, 1983.

Kuiken, Rebecca. "The Living Edge of Faith: Doubt and Skepticism in the Formation of Pastor-Theologians." In *The Power to Comprehend with All the Saints: The Formation and Practice of a Pastor-Theologian*, edited by Wallace Alston and Cynthia Jarvis, 111–30. Grand Rapids: Eerdmans, 2009.

Lucas, George. "A Conversation between Bill Moyers and George Lucas on the True Theology of *Star Wars*." *Time*, April 26, 1999.

Norris, Kathleen. *Amazing Grace*. New York: Riverhead, 1999.

Rigby, Cynthia L. "Providence and Play." *Insights* 126 (2011) 10–18.

———. "Stepping Into the Madness: On Being Skeptical, Doing Justice, and Hoping Against Hope." *Studies in Christian Ethics: Critical Directions and Developments in Reformed Theological Ethics* 28 (2015) 175–86.

Steinmetz, David. *Calvin in Context*. Oxford: Oxford University Press, 2010.

Weiner, Eric. "Americans Undecided About God." *New York Times*. December 10, 2011.

———. *Man Seeks God: My Flirtations with the Divine*. New York: Twelve, 2011.

———. "In *Man Seeks God*, Author Eric Weiner Hunts for Divine." http://video.pbs.org.

Wiman, Christian. "Christ Church Artist Series with Christian Wiman." http://www.christchurchcville.org/events/an-evening-with-christian-wiman/.

———. *My Bright Abyss: Meditations of a Modern Believer*. New York: Farrar, Straus & Giroux, 2013.

PART 3

Reformed Theology and Doctrine

8

Spirit, Vulnerability and Beauty
A Pneumatological Exploration

Deborah van den Bosch

Introduction

PEOPLE OFTEN UNDERSTAND VULNERABILITY as being synonymous with weakness and frailty. The common understanding of vulnerability is that it is a state one does not want to be in, because it implies lack of control, power, vitality and independency. It is not surprising that this negative understanding of vulnerability has led to different strategies of invulnerability. Insurance policies, the building of dykes, having airbags in the car, vitamin pills—these are just a few illustrations of how people try to safeguard themselves against their own vulnerability.[1]

However, there is a growing body of theological voices that aims at resisting the negative interpretation of vulnerability. These voices introduce an approach to vulnerability that is *beyond* deficiency and lack of power. According to these voices, vulnerability is so much more than we tend to think. The myth of invulnerability and the illusion of control are being denounced, while new understandings of vulnerability are being explored.

Various disciplines of theology reveal an exciting turn towards the notion of vulnerability. Within the HIV/AIDS discourse, for example, theological methodologies have been developed in order to give voice to marginalized and infected people.[2] The field of disability studies emphasizes

---

1. Culp, *Vulnerability and Glory*, 88.

2. See West and Zengele-Nzimande, "Medicine of God's Word"; West, "Reading the Bible"; and West, "Reading Job". See also Dube, "Theological Challenges"; Dube,

the idea that it is objectionable to disqualify physical and mental disability. On the contrary, vulnerability is an essential aspect of theological reflection on the *imago Dei*.[3] And within body theologies discourse, we encounter a high appreciation of the vulnerable body that, contrary to the myth of invulnerability, is seen as the very source of God-talk.[4] And there are other fields of theology that reveal how the notion of vulnerability can spur a particular hermeneutical development; see for example various contributions on empire,[5] on interreligious dialogue,[6] on practical theology,[7] on ecclesiology.[8] One might say that the different hermeneutical understanding of vulnerability has not fully surfaced yet, but it is already obvious that it implies a meaningful development for Reformed theologies in a world that normalizes the denial of vulnerability. The various theological voices make us aware that the common definition of vulnerability is the product of the illusion of control, and that a reinterpretation of vulnerability opens fruitful avenues for understanding human life in relation to God.

In his contribution to *Towards the Future of Reformed Theology*, William Placher[9] refers to the theme of vulnerability as an important topic in Reformed theologies. He contends that the relevance of the theme of vulnerability is closely related to the biblical witness to God of the Bible. When Christian theologians reflect on vulnerability, they are "only reclaiming their own birthright, for it is just such a God that we encounter in the Bible."[10]

Like Placher, a number of other Reformed theologians have developed inspiring proposals regarding the understanding of the vulnerability of human life in relation to the biblical God. The constructive theological contributions offer an important kind of hermeneutics of vulnerability. These novel insights carry great weight for Reformed theology because they disclose blind spots in our God-talk and in our ecclesial practices. The value

---

"Grant me Justice"; and the important contributions of the Circle of Concerned African Women Theologians.

3. See Eiesland, *Disabled God*; Reinders, *Future of the Disabled*; Berinyuu, "Healing and Disability"; Yong, *Theology and Down Syndrome*; Reynolds, *Vulnerable Communion*.

4. See Nelson, *Body Theology*; Isherwood and Stuart, *Introducing Body Theology*; van Niekerk, *Towards a Theology*.

5. See Rieger, *God and the Excluded*; Rieger, *Christ and Empire*; and Snyman, *Empire*.

6. See Yong, *Hospitality and the Other*; and Moyaert, *On Vulnerability*.

7. See Meylahn, *Folly of Vulnerability*.

8. See Koopman, *Vulnerable Church*.

9. Placher, "Vulnerability of God," 192–205. See also Placher, *Narratives*.

10. Placher, "Vulnerability of God," 194.

of reconstructing vulnerability is that vulnerability can be recognized as an existential quality in relation with God.

In this article I first turn to some inspiring constructive theological accounts of vulnerability. I will provide a brief overview of the work of William Placher, David Jensen, Thomas Reynolds, and Kristine Culp.[11]

The brief overview of constructive theologies presents us with an interesting perspective on vulnerability: it is complex and ambiguous. This new perspective transcends the idea of vulnerability as an undesirable condition of creation. The theological accounts of Placher, Jensen, Reynolds and Culp link the concept of vulnerability to the relational life of the triune God, the vulnerable life of Christ who was crucified and resurrected, human being as carrier of the *imago Dei*, human life *coram Deo*. It turns out that vulnerability is a complex and multilayered concept within Reformed theology.

The brief overview also reveals the absence of pneumatological interpretations of vulnerability. We do find Trinitarian relational perspectives on vulnerability. But where would an exploration of human vulnerability from a pneumatological point of view lead us? I am not proposing to move away from what already has been said about vulnerability from a Christological and Trinitarian perspective, but to offer additional interpretations of vulnerability.

The second part of my contribution will focus on the Holy Spirit in relation to human vulnerability. Starting with a biblical understanding of the vulnerable Spirit, it will transpire that vulnerability can be understood as the realm of the Creator Spirit. The insight that vulnerability and the Holy Spirit are inextricably linked invites questions regarding the meaning of vulnerability being the realm of the Spirit. What kind of theological proposal emerges from the connection between Spirit and vulnerability? Is it possible to construct a new perspective on vulnerability when vulnerability and the agency of the Holy Spirit are joined together?

My hypothesis is that the agency of the Holy Spirit leads to a extended hermeneutics of vulnerability. The link between Spirit and vulnerability bestows a particular quality to human vulnerability, because the person of the Holy Spirit is fully involved in the vulnerability of creation. This particular quality turns vulnerability into a non-passive, dynamic condition of life, because when vulnerability is understood as the realm of the Spirit, then being vulnerable means being involved in the beautification of life. Being vulnerable thus implies a resistance against the myth of control. It also entails a spirited attitude towards life.

---

11. Placher, *Narratives*; Jensen, *Graced Vulnerability*; Reynolds, *Vulnerable Communion*; and Culp, *Vulnerability and Glory*.

This pneumatological exploration is just an exploration, a search for constructive thoughts about the notion of vulnerability in relation to the work of the Holy Spirit. Since the Holy Spirit in Reformed theology is closely related to creation but not (yet) to vulnerable life, it makes sense to concentrate on the agency of the Spirit. My contribution is motivated by the significance of the theme for Reformed theologies in a world in which vulnerability is usually denounced, despite the fact that vulnerability is a given in human existence. The aim is to present existing constructive proposals of vulnerability in Reformed theology, and to consider the agency of the Holy Spirit with regard to vulnerability.

Reformed Voices on Vulnerability

Some Reformed theologians have offered an incentive to theological reflection on vulnerability. Bonhoeffer,[12] Barth, and Moltmann drew attention to the notion of vulnerability by referring to God's strange power as a kind of weakness revealing His love for mankind. They wrote from their own particular experience about a God who suffers with creation because of his love. Liberation theologians presented their own perspective on God's preference for the weak and the vulnerable. And this movement raised theological awareness of notions of weakness, suffering and vulnerability. A novel perspective in God-talk was introduced: God became associated with vulnerability rather than with power and omnipotence.

This association has existential consequences for human life. What does it mean to witness to a vulnerable God who loves vulnerable people? William Placher, David Jensen, Thomas Reynolds and Kristine Culp developed their views on this question. Below I will offer a brief overview of their invigorating, constructive contributions to vulnerability theologies. I do not attempt to give a complete presentation of the various constructive proposals; the main focus will be on how each approach interprets vulnerability, and how this interpretation is accounted for. This overview provides the constructive background for a pneumatological exploration of vulnerability.

William C. Placher

In his book *Narratives of a Vulnerable God: Christ, Theology and Scripture*, Placher seeks to recover particular interpretations of God by looking at the

---

12. "Christ helps us not by virtue of his omnipotence, but by virtue of his weakness and suffering . . . Only the suffering God can help." Bonhoeffer, *Letters and Papers*, 360.

biblical narratives, especially the gospel stories about Jesus. Placher wants to move away from a generic understanding of God as an all-powerful God who is in charge of everything, because the Scriptures tell a different story of this God. In the biblical narratives God reveals himself as a God who is willing to be vulnerable to pain in the freedom of love. Vulnerability, Placher says, is a perfection of loving freedom.[13] It is the willingness to risk pain and suffering. And this loving freedom, this divine willingness to take the risk that his love remains unanswered, presents us with a paradigm for our own life and love: "The kinds of risk that the security of knowing God's love permits, are not just a kind of bonus but part of what it means to be fully human, just as the capacity for vulnerable love without limit is part of what it means to be God."[14]

Placher develops his ideas about the vulnerable God by paying attention to the notion of eternity. The biblical stories witness to a loving God who is faithful even when He takes the risk of being hurt and rejected. God's faithfulness seems to be at odds with vulnerability, because God's faithfulness may refer to a God who is unchanging and immutable. But Placher's interpretation of time is such that he defines eternity as "a 'time' neither of invulnerable changelessness nor of shifting and unreliable relations but the 'time' where fully vulnerable love can be trustworthy."[15] Speaking of an eternal God implies speaking of God in trinitarian terms, because God's love is about God's being: God is a community of equals united in mutual love,[16] and this perichoretic love is a love that dares to risk being vulnerable. After all, the biblical stories tell about Jesus Christ, the vulnerable God who can most be with us in our sufferings.

In the final part of his book Placher explores what it means for Christian communities to worship the triune, vulnerable God. He translates the meaning of divine vulnerability into various practices for believers: being the church of a vulnerable God means that believers open themselves to outsiders and strangers of the world on the basis of biblical stories about the crucified Christ. By holding on to the narratives and the sacraments, Christians make known the vulnerable God. Focusing on the biblical vulnerability narratives also has implications for the roles that believers assume in academic settings and in the wider social contexts where they work and

---

13. Placher, *Narratives*, 19.
14. Ibid., 20.
15. Ibid., 45.
16. Ibid., 73.

live: Christians have to become outsiders themselves[17] and move beyond their comfort zone to be made whole by the vulnerable God.

David H. Jensen

In his book *Graced Vulnerability: A Theology of Childhood*, Jensen develops a theological perspective on childhood. He convincingly shows that such a theology of childhood includes practices of vulnerability. Jensen starts with uncovering a blind spot of Christian theology: while the birth of the divine child is granted a central place in Christian faith, theological attention to children is more or less absent. Jensen's advocacy theology draws attention to the vulnerable, broken, and downtrodden in this world,[18] and aims at representing the children neglected by theology.

Jensen starts off with the biblical covenantal perspective and with Jesus' attitude towards children, and he claims that children are included in the covenant. This means that we should be paying special attention to the meaning of vulnerability in light of the relationship with the covenantal God. With Jensen, the theological meaning of vulnerability is anchored in the *imago Dei*. The raison d'être of every person is warranted on the basis of the belief that every human being is uniquely created in the image of God. But the *imago Dei* should not be interpreted as a common denominator of human characteristics (like rationality, power of dominion, morality, capacity for love, possession of an eternal soul), because the image of God is not 'a mold that shapes human life in uniformity.'[19] On the basis of the biblical text in Gen 1:27, Jensen points out that there is *difference* in the image of God: 'male and female he created them.' When one chooses to understand difference as the core idea of the *imago Dei*, one sees that difference implies openness to others and thus to vulnerability. Jensen contends that openness and vulnerability are incorporated in the image of God: "The God of the Bible is not a monad enclosed upon itself, but a God who becomes vulnerable in relation to others, who calls us to live in vulnerability with others."[20] So, God is the source of differences, and thus of openness and vulnerability. At distinctive moments in history, this God of difference and openness reveals himself as a God with a preference for vulnerability. The covenantal relationship with Israel, the divine revelation in vulnerable flesh, Jesus' acknowledgment of vulnerable and marginalized people, the strange

---

17. Ibid., 178.
18. Jensen, *Graced Vulnerability*, xiv.
19. Ibid., 14.
20. Ibid,. 15.

vulnerability of the cross and of the resurrection, the communal life of the triune God—in multiple ways the biblical God reveals a God who opens himself to others, thus a God who is inclined to vulnerability.

After having constructed a theological meaning of vulnerability (relationships, differences and openness), Jensen points out that childhood is one very essential dimension of the vulnerable, related existence into which human beings are called. His theological perspective on childhood has particular implications for believers witnessing to a vulnerable God. Whoever seeks shelter in the covenant with God will come to understand baptism as a communal expression of vulnerability and resistance to violence against children. Peacemaking and nonviolence ought to be typical traits of the baptismal practice of vulnerability. A church community could be a sanctuary for children as well, for it is God's space for physical safety and a harbor for emotional and spiritual growth.[21] And prayer is a crucial locus of ecclesial practices of vulnerability, since prayer is a relational act that makes us open and vulnerable to God and to the world. Jensen's vulnerability ecclesiology approaches children as full members of the covenant community, and places them in the presence of the vulnerable God who prefers differences and openness.

Thomas E. Reynolds

In his book *Vulnerable Communion: A Theology of Disability and Hospitality*, Reynolds offers a theological account of disability. His aim is to reach novel understandings of disability in order to develop counter practices that reveal abundant hospitality. Reynolds' personal experiences with raising and loving a son with disabilities form a delicate part of this exploration.

Reynolds' careful rethinking of human disability starts with critiquing the ruling 'cult of normalcy'. This cult of normalcy refers to the social processes and relationships people enter when they seek a place of welcome and acknowledgment. Human beings are involved in social contexts, such as school, sports, employment, family, friendship, and these social contexts cultivate their own performance expectations and criteria of value measurement. This means that ideas about what is normal are made desirable, and that they are enforced in public venues as the standard.[22] Reynolds emphasizes that there is a standardizing power underneath a society's conventions and the norms that remain unquestioned. This standardizing power carries

---

21. Ibid., 113.
22. Reynolds, *Vulnerable Communion*, 60.

the tyranny of normalcy, and assigns aberrancy to what is perceived as different, disable, abnormal, the other.

Reynolds suggests a counter-discourse by painting the contours of an anthropology that is based upon the understanding that human beings are relational beings. Human beings are incomplete, vulnerable, and they need others to become complete. In being relational by definition, human beings are vulnerable. We are open to and in need of relationships and community. Human vulnerability is thus a testimony to the fact that our nature involves receiving our existence from each other.[23] The aim of centralizing vulnerability and disability is neither to valorize vulnerability nor to trivialize it as an instructive tool for those who perceive themselves as healthy, but to reach the understanding that each person is vulnerable and open to being wounded. Privileging disability, Reynolds says, calls us to responsibility as agents capable of loving and welcoming others on the basis of our human vulnerability.

Vulnerability, thus, must be protected against the tyranny of normalcy, and must be interpreted as an acknowledgment of weakness and limitation that is made concrete in relations of mutual openness and dependence. This perspective draws Reynolds into a religious space of orientation. This is where his theological account begins. Reynolds forges a path into a theology of disability by understanding life as a gift. This is how the sense of God arises in human life: God is the creator of life, and 'to exist is good, a grace received.'[24] Recognizing one another's vulnerability and value is embracing this gift of life. Creation opens up to God, and senses an extraordinary possibility in vulnerable ordinariness. God's relationship with creation reveals God's own vulnerability: "As God becomes relationally open to God's gift of creation and lovingly embraces creatures as distinct and valuable beings, God shows vulnerability."[25] In other words, vulnerability and disability are part of the world God loves. Particularly in the light of creation theology, Reynolds warns that one should be mindful not to view vulnerability and disability as tragedy, because that is the song of the cult of normalcy, which might even be called "sinful."[26] He therefore proposes to reconsider the *imago Dei* as *imitatio Dei*, for God is a vulnerable, creative, relational and available God.[27] Created in God's image, human beings are gifted with the capacity to respect, be faithful to, and show compassion to others.

23. Ibid., 106.
24. Ibid., 139.
25. Ibid., 165.
26. Ibid., 169.
27. Ibid., 179.

Jesus Christ is the icon of a vulnerable God.[28] In being crucified and in being resurrected, Jesus overturns the established powers and principalities, and He reveals the transformative power of love by redeeming us from our fear-based anxiety of the abnormal, the vulnerable and the disabled. This is what Reynolds calls "reversing disability's disability." In Christ, human beings are brought into relational wholeness with one another.

Reynolds started his constructive theology of disability and hospitality because he experienced painful rejection of his son with disabilities within the church community. His aim was to rethink human community into communities of abundant hospitality, and along this line he closes his book: 'the nature of this creative-redemptive love fosters a recognition and acceptance of human vulnerability and disability as bearing the image of God. And it does so in a gesture of trusting welcome. The moral thrust of Christian community has its origin here.'[29]

Kristine A. Culp

In her book *Vulnerability and Glory: A Theological Account*, Culp presents the contours of the meaning of human vulnerability before God. She starts off with Paul's reference to human life as earthen vessels that contain a glorious divine treasure: the human being is vulnerable, but capable of bearing glory. With Augustine, Luther and Calvin, Culp explores the relation between human fallibility and divine power, between corruption and transformation. She taps into a variety of sources of her theological account of vulnerability, and she contends that vulnerability is much more than a reference to deficiency or lack of strength. Culp makes a surprising move by untangling vulnerability from the idiom of risk assessment and devastation. Culp does not deny the daily reality of this world, nor does she downplay suffering or ignore evil. She just refuses to offer a simple understanding of vulnerability and rejects the general contemporary interpretation of vulnerability as a condition to be overcome. Vulnerability is not just something that refers to damage and threats. Rather, it is an ambivalent and multilayered concept that embraces both devastation and glory.

Culp's theological account of vulnerability is actually an account of life before God. Human life is a gift of the living God. This gift turns human life into life that is not only susceptible to harm, but also to bearing glory. This is what vulnerability means: that human life by definition embraces both ill and good, both rejection and welcome. In other words, being alive implies

28. Ibid., 197.
29. Ibid., 211.

that one is susceptible to being "changed in ways that may be destructive or transformative."³⁰

In the second and the third part of *Vulnerability and Glory*, Culp addresses the theological and practical implications of vulnerable humans and creatures *coram Deo*. She engages two Protestant marks of the church to elaborate on the meaning of being vulnerable, of being involved in transformation towards the glory of God, which means that one opens oneself to participating life with and for other in the sight of God. These Protestant marks are the call to resist idolatry and inhumanity, and the journey of delight and gratitude. Culp indicates that "in a world marked by suffering and in which creatures are vulnerable to devastation and transformation, such testimony and resistance and such delight and gratitude may provide a baseline for living with others before God."³¹

Evaluation

How is vulnerability defined in the contributions by Placher, Jensen, Reynolds and Culp? This brief evaluation will show that vulnerability is a complex and multifaceted concept.

Placher defines vulnerability as the willingness to *risk* pain on the basis of love. He positions vulnerability within a Trinitarian framework: it is divine perichoretic love that is the source of vulnerability, and Jesus Christ reveals how the biblical God chooses to become vulnerable out of love. Placher's important contribution to the theme of vulnerability is the focus on the biblical narratives of vulnerability. These narratives reveal that vulnerability is the crux in the relationship between God and humankind.

Unlike Placher, Jensen does not explicitly define vulnerability. In Jensen's approach, vulnerability is the opposite of violence and oppression. It receives a meaningful interpretation when it is linked to differences and to openness towards one another in order to celebrate differences. Being vulnerable implies openness and tolerance. Like Placher, Jensen understands vulnerability as related to the trinity: the communal life of the triune God means that God's being is open and vulnerable. God's vulnerability is found in the brokenness of Jesus Christ, and in the story of God's covenant with his people. Jensen then shifts his focus from the divine image of vulnerability to vulnerability in society and church, and he shows how God's vulnerability changes our understanding of children (and other vulnerable groups) in ways never seen before in church history.

---

30. Culp, *Vulnerability and Glory*, 95.
31. Ibid., 130.

Reynolds does not interpret vulnerability within a Trinitarian frame, as Placher and Jensen do. Instead, Reynolds develops his ideas about vulnerability from a sociological perspective: vulnerability is part of disability discourse and of the abject cult of normalcy. From the reflection on and the experience with disability, Reynolds moves to a theology of disability that hinges on the idea that disability is not something less than normal. In theological terms, Reynolds approach to vulnerability is quite plain. He defines vulnerability within the frame of creation theology: God creates difference, and God's self is vulnerable in his relationship with creation. In this light, the cult of normalcy can be called sinful, and the redemption of Christ implies the turning over of the tyrannical cult of normalcy. Human being, created in the image of God, is called to imitate God (*imago Dei* as *imitatio Dei*) by resisting the cult of normalcy and by releasing transformative power into creation. For the Christian community this transformative power means welcoming every person (in particular those who are abandoned by the cult of normalcy). Vulnerability and disability, then, are notions interconnected with Christ-like hospitality in church and society.

Culp defines vulnerability as complex and ambivalent. She leaves traditional ideas about vulnerability as synonymous with damage and with being wounded behind by creating space for a concept of vulnerability as a *dynamic* condition of human life. By definition life is vulnerable, meaning that a person is susceptible to devastation, suffering and grief; but a person is also susceptible to growth, change and meaning. Being vulnerable is being open to wounds and to healing. In addition to the ambivalence of vulnerability, Culp emphasizes that vulnerability is a condition *coram Deo*. Before the face of God there is room for damage and for transformation; God's presence embraces the dynamics of human life. In theological terms, Culp's approach to vulnerability focuses mainly on the glory of God. Vulnerability is related to daily life in practices such as resistance to idolatry and inhumanity, and the expression of gratitude and joy for the good things in life. Culp's theological move is that vulnerability is closely related to the glory of God, and that it is a dynamic testimony of faith.

In summary it can be said that the concept of vulnerability emerges in different ways in the various constructive proposals. Vulnerability is associated with the vulnerability in God's self (triune community, inner-trinitarian relationships, inner-divine openness). God's own vulnerability is also revealed in the cross of Christ, the icon of the vulnerable God. And God's vulnerability is not separated from the vulnerability of creation. Notions such as *imago Dei*, *imitatio Dei* and *coram Deo* reinforce the relation between divine and human vulnerability. The vulnerability of creation in light of divine vulnerability is further translated in vulnerability as feature of community life and ecclesial practices. Vulnerability is about an ambivalent way of life: it is devastation as well as transformation that can be practiced through sanctification, hospitality, resistance to degradation of life, and thankfulness. All these different aspects of vulnerability reveal that vulnerability is *a multi-layered, complex, ambiguous concept.*

It is remarkable, however, that in the wide range of colors of vulnerability, the work of the Holy Spirit is not painted in bright colors. What can be said about the Holy Spirit in relation to the theme of vulnerability? Will a pneumatological interpretation of vulnerability bring about further thoughts about human vulnerability? The next part of this contribution is an exploration of the relationship between the Holy Spirit and vulnerability.

Spirit and Vulnerability

In the following part I will consider the relationship between the Holy Spirit and creation. I will argue that this relationship includes vulnerability, because God's Spirit becomes vulnerable by being involved in creation. The relationship between Spirit and creation is such that vulnerability may be viewed as the realm of the Holy Spirit. Since Jürgen Moltmann is the only Reformed theologian who has addressed the issue of Spirit/creation/vulnerability specifically (in his *Spirit of Life*), I will briefly describe his ideas here as well.

The Vulnerable Spirit

The Spirit of God is often associated with creation. The Bible opens with the Spirit hovering over the water. The Bible continues with the creation narrative of the Spirit as the life-giving breath of God, and later draws attention to the Spirit as the groaning companion of creation. These biblical perspectives encourage the idea that the Spirit of God specifically embarks on those matters that tie human beings to their created existence.

The Spirit of God is also associated with the vulnerability of creation in such a way that the Spirit's own sensibility and vulnerability surfaces. Biblical texts such as 1 Thess 5:19 ("do not put out the Spirit's fire") and Eph 4:30 ("do not grieve the Holy Spirit of God, with whom you were sealed for the day of redemption") show that the Holy Spirit is not an unaffected and invulnerable power that blows wherever the Spirit pleases. In fact, the Spirit of God can even be tested and insulted (Acts 5:9, Heb 10:29). In other words, the Holy Spirit is committed to creation in a personal way. Or, in the words of Eugene Rogers Jr., "the Spirit is a Person with an affinity for material things. The Spirit characteristically befriends the body."[32]

The vulnerability of God's Spirit transpires in what the Spirit *does*. It is reflected in the agency of the Spirit: the Spirit suffers with the suffering, is grieved and quenched, and rejoices when creation rejoices.[33] As Rom 8:22–26 shows, the vulnerability of the Spirit has to do with the Spirit's preference for creation. By indwelling in creation, the Spirit bonds with creation, and fully identifies with the vulnerable condition of creation in the sense that the Spirit groans with us and helps us in our weakness.[34] The Spirit seeks to befriend and to look after God's good creation in such a way that the Spirit self, working on the inside of creation, becomes vulnerable.

Vulnerability as the Realm of the Spirit

In a fascinating article on the hidden works of the Spirit in the cosmos, John Polkinghorne[35] elaborates on how God is at work within the contingent processes in the world. Polkinghorne's proposal is to be considered in light of the dialogue between faith and science. He addresses the idea that God, creator of this world, is involved in the world in such a way that God is not only present in the disrupting, interventionist moments of life, but in the continuous unfolding of history as well. Here Polkinghorne follows the ideas of John V. Taylor[36] who contends that, if there is a creator God at all, He is present in the whole process of life and not only in the gaps of divine intervention. In connection to Taylor's rejection of the interventionist idea of a God who enters when human knowledge fails, Polkinghorne twists the concept of the "God of the gaps" by suggesting that these gaps should be considered as rather benevolent, because they match very well with the intrinsic features of this world. Polkinghorne proposes to understand the gaps of contingency as gaps that belong to the reality of creation. And these contingent spaces of life form the hiding place of God's Spirit. The "Spirit of gaps" is present, hidden and veiled, right there in the historically unfolding fruitfulness and in the change and decay that are inescapable features of this world.[37] These gaps are the loci of pneumatological involvement with the travail of creation. The gaps of contingency have nothing to do with

32. Rogers, *After the Spirit*, 60.
33. Moltmann, *Spirit of Life*, 51.
34. Polkinghorne, "Hidden Spirit," 181.
35. Ibid., 179.
36. Taylor, *Go-Between God*, 28.
37. Polkinghorne, "Hidden Spirit," 181.

interrupting power exercises of the Spirit, but they constitute the realm where the Spirit works on the inside of creation, keeping the fruitfulness and contingency, the order and the disorder of human life closely together. In other words, in the gaps of our contingent, creaturely life the Spirit is at work, dissolving our self-constructed ideas of infinity and restoring our longing for fullness.

The contingency of creation is where the Spirit resides—in those places and moments where human beings have to deal with unforeseen events and uncertainties. The realm of the Holy Spirit may thus be seen as the sphere of open spaces where human vulnerability becomes most palpable. In a sense the presence of the Holy Spirit holds creation's goodness and vulnerability together. Under the reign of the Spirit we come to see that God's creation is simultaneously vulnerable and existentially good (cf. Reitsma).[38] The agency of the Holy Spirit firmly unites quality and vulnerability, flourishing and suffering, in such a way that these two conditions cannot be separated from one another. In other words, through the work of the Spirit every living being is invited to accept the experience of vulnerability and finality of life. And denial of vulnerability may be interpreted as denial of the Spirit's creation, because creaturely life is supposed to be vulnerable, finite, and restricted.[39] It is precisely *in* the finality, contingency and vulnerability that the quality of life emerges.

Jürgen Moltmann on Spirit and Vulnerability

The Reformed theologian Jürgen Moltmann is widely characterized as one of the most productive and creative contemporary theologians. His theology has guided many people to new ways of thinking. In this section, I will focus on just a small part of Moltmann's pneumatology, which permeates his overall theology, and which is also specifically addressed in *God in Creation* and *The Spirit of Life*. The intention here is to explore specifically Moltmann's perspective on the Spirit and vulnerability, since he is one of the very few theologians who address the theme of vulnerability (and disability) in relation to the work of the Holy Spirit.

---

38. Reitsma, *Geest en schepping*, 165.

39. Restrictedness should be understood as bound to the *quantity* of life, not as a reduction in *quality* of life. Any form of life that is called by the Creator Spirit, is final. Embodied life is restricted life by necessity, since life owes its value to its restrictedness. If there were no boundaries to human life, life would lose its value and its quality.

Moltmann's theology of the Holy Spirit reveals a clear emphasis on the quality of creation. The purpose of creation, according to Moltmann,[40] is becoming God's home, where God's indwelling involves all of creation, not only human life. The homecoming in creation is the work of the Spirit. According to Moltmann, the Spirit dwells in creation (in its totality as well as in individual living beings) with the power of life. The understanding of the cosmic breadth of the Spirit is closely linked with the idea that creation is destined to become God's dwelling place. The eschatological condition of creation is the hope that inspires the current condition of creation: in the cross of Christ, the Spirit is committed to the historical condition of this world, where the Spirit displays the power of life that points toward the restoration and the affirmation of creaturely existence.

The future of creation requires an attitude of affirmation and sanctification of life. Moltmann's emphasis on the reverence of the life of all living creatures is about the retrieval of the holiness of life by respecting it, particularly life that is perceived as weak and insignificant. It is also about accepting the boundaries of life, rejection of violence pertaining to life, and the quest for harmony and balance. Reverence for life hinges on the themes of creation and re-creation: any form of life is holy because it is created by God and is desired by God for his coming inhabitation.[41]

The Spirit of life is the love between the Father and the Son in the cross event.[42] This divine love assumes and embraces all life, and that applies also to forms of life that we usually exclude on the basis of weakness and disability. Moltmann emphasizes that the charismatic and healing powers of life also apply to inflicted life: "we have to recognize that *every handicap is an endowment too*. The strength of Christ is also powerful in the disablement."[43] The Spirit of life, who is the Spirit of Christ, bequeaths every form of life with gifts that ought to be lived out in the service of the kingdom. This is what Moltmann labels "the calling" of every living being: "when a person is called, whatever he is and brings with him becomes a charisma through his calling, since it is accepted by the Spirit and put at

---

40. Moltmann, *God in Creation*, 64; *Spirit of Life*, 31–38.

41. Moltmann, *Spirit of Life*, 178.

42. In Moltmann's theology, the cross event is fully Trinitarian. The Son's utter isolation and the Father's mourning are embraced and translated by the Spirit into a history of surrender and love. The Holy Spirit is present in the cross, thus identifying with the suffering of the Son, even though the suffering of the Spirit is not the same as the Son's suffering. In the cross event, the Spirit becomes the love between the Father and the Son. This love generates life and brings life closer to its purpose.

43. Moltmann, *Spirit of Life*, 193; italics original.

the service of the kingdom of God."[44] Those who are physically or mentally impaired, ill, infected, or subordinated, are also called to the service of God's kingdom. Moreover, in the pains and disabilities they suffer, they reveal the suffering power of the God who relates himself to the weak with his own broken and humiliated body.

Moltmann also addresses the vulnerable human body when he says that the Spirit is "a living energy that interpenetrates the bodies of men and women and drives out the germs of death."[45] The relation between the Holy Spirit and human body is expressed in the transfiguration of the body in this life. With the transfiguration of the body he means the change and the transit invoked by the Spirit of Christ, who is the Spirit of the resurrection of the dead. The Spirit embraces embodied life with the love of God, and places life in a new perspective. The Holy Spirit regenerates human life, gives new opportunities to mortal bodies, and invites man to look forward. The direction is the future, and the process toward vitality is rooted in God's eternal love that transfigures the body. In his Gifford lectures Moltmann explains that vitality and vulnerability are about one's attitude that reveals one's humanity.[46] It is the power of the soul to deal with the difficulties and afflictions in life; it is the strength to live, to suffer, and even to die. Therefore, vitality (or "true health" as Moltmann also calls it) is attainable for anybody, regardless of age, presence of disease or other kinds of disabilities, because it is grounded in the affirmation of life, in the will to live in the light of hope.

All in all, Moltmann's pneumatology offers a fresh perspective on the relationship between creation and vulnerability. Moltmann constructs a strong link between the work of the Holy Spirit and the condition of creation by showing that the vulnerability of the triune God and the vulnerability of creation are joined in the love who is the Holy Spirit. The vulnerability of creation is assumed by the loving God. Moltmann attributes a notion of responsibility to vulnerability when he refers to vulnerable life as life that is called to renewal by the Holy Spirit. The call of vulnerable life includes the disabled and the outcast of society. They, too, receive the call and the responsibility in life that is endowed and renewed by the Holy Spirit. It is not very clear how the calling and its practices materialize in light of the coming kingdom. Moltmann mentions the transformation of the vulnerable body by the work of the Holy Spirit, but he does not substantiate how this transformation takes shape in the process of the Spirit drawing creation closer to God's kingdom.

44. Ibid., 182.
45. Ibid., 190.
46. Moltmann, *God in Creation*.

Spirit, Vulnerability, and Beauty

Crucial to Moltmann's understanding of Spirit and vulnerable creation is the close arrangement of quality and vulnerability by the work of the Holy Spirit. I will follow this path, considering what this pairing of quality and vulnerability means for human life.

Vulnerability Dialectics

On the basis of constructive approaches to vulnerability, and considering Moltmann's pneumatological understanding of vulnerability, one could say that the Spirit of God introduces vulnerability as a *qualification* of the relation between a loving God and his creation. Vulnerability not only means that creaturely life is receptive to damage and disappointment. It also means that one can find particular quality in the experience of vulnerability. Vulnerability *is* the capability to be kept safe and whole, to be healed and lifted. This vulnerability, which becomes most tangible in the sensitive human body, turns out to be a quality under the reign of the Holy Spirit.

The pairing of vulnerability and quality is framed by the idea that vulnerability is the realm of the Spirit. Where the Spirit is at work, vulnerability means susceptibility to love and mercy. That is because the Holy Spirit puts human life in touch with cross and resurrection of Christ. Creation needs the Spirit to see the depth of the cross, and to be introduced to the impaired, crucified Christ who demonstrates a new understanding of vulnerability. The wounds of Christ's body undermine our illusion of auto-salvation and they deconstruct our cult of normalcy. Seeing the depth of the cross, thanks to the Spirit, means responding to the scandal of vulnerability. It involves nailing one's ideas about vitality to the cross, surrendering one's strategies of power, and betraying one's own understanding of what is normal. The Spirit of the incarnated God creates a relationship between the cruciform death of Christ and the cruciform experiences of human life, for the sake of gracing our vulnerable life and maintaining the quality of creation. Through the cross of Christ, the Holy Spirit reveals the truth about God's love for creation and about its God-given quality. Moltmann convincingly explains that the story of the suffering of the Son is the story of the suffering of God's Spirit as well.[47] However, "the Spirit does not suffer in the same way, for he is Jesus' strength in suffering, and is even the 'indestructible life' in whose power Jesus can give himself vicariously 'for many.'"

---

47. Moltmann, *Spirit of Life*, 64.

The Spirit aims to transform vulnerable *afflicted* life into vulnerable *restored* life. It does not mean that the Spirit turns affliction and evil into something smooth and positive. The Spirit does not 'fix' life by re-establishing the former condition of life, just as the Spirit did not reverse or negate the wounds and scars of Jesus' body after the cross. Instead, the vulnerable and broken body of Christ is included in his resurrection. The glorified body is a site of deep wounds, because this is how God reveals himself: He is the Lord of life who endows vulnerable life with resurrection quality, with an inclination towards glory, love and reverence. Resurrection of vulnerable life does not imply the move from vulnerability to invulnerability but the transformation from damaged vulnerability into restored vulnerability through God's love and grace. Human life will always remain vulnerable. But by being in the realm of the Spirit, vulnerability draws us into an intensity of life that makes us search for earnest ways of being who we are.

When the Spirit nudges us into accepting our vulnerability as part of life that belongs to a vulnerable God, the Spirit retrieves the quality of life that is bestowed upon creation. But it is not a plain, effortless quality. It involves a *vulnerability dialectics* of cross and resurrection, of being wounded and being raised, of affliction and restoration. This dialectics, which means that one cannot speak of vulnerability without using both words, emphasizes the complexity of vulnerability. It is not only about the attitude of openness or the effort of being in relationship at the risk of being hurt. It is also about claiming the wounds of fear, rejection and failure that are part of us, perhaps just as Jesus claimed his wounds when He revealed himself to his disciple Thomas. Nancy Eiesland says that the resurrected Christ with his impaired hands and feet transforms the taboos surrounding vulnerability and disability of the body, and links them closely to new abilities.[48] Daniel Louw even states that in the disfigurement of the resurrected Christ a new theological model of wholeness and a metaphor for life within disfigurement can be discerned.[49] The new hermeneutics of vulnerable life is thus a discontinuous continuity, because vulnerable life is now considered as life that belongs to God who has bound death, and at the same time has bound life by death.

Vulnerability as Beauty

The vulnerability dialectics of surrendering and claiming describes human life in the presence of the Spirit. Patrick Sherry relates the presence of the

---

48. Eiesland, *Disabled God*, 101.
49. Louw, *Cura Vitae*, 100.

Spirit to the notion of *beauty*, because 'beauty' will help us to understand how God reaches out to his creation through the Holy Spirit.[50]

Beauty may refer to notions such as excellence, glory, symmetry, proportion, harmony, consent, union, love and holiness.[51] This perspective has been developed by Jonathan Edwards, who viewed the triune God as a society of love and beauty. Creation, all beauty in creation, may be perceived as the overflow of inner-trinitarian beauty that is communicated by the Holy Spirit. The Holy Spirit is God's infinite beauty, "and this is God's infinite consent to being in general"[52] so that the very structure of being can also be understood as beauty. This idea of divine beauty as the archetype of earthly beauty can also be found in the writings of the Cappadocians, Augustine, Karl Barth and Hans Urs von Balthasar.

Von Balthasar developed the idea that the Christian understanding of beauty hinges on the *ugliness* of the cross: the ugliness of the cross is the utter denial of God's glory and the destruction of God-given life.[53] Yet this revolting cross event discloses God's love for creation, and it reveals His beauty and inclination to perfection of life. Viladesau says that "Christ—precisely on the cross—is the supreme revelation of God's being, God's form, glory, and beauty."[54]

The Holy Spirit, who is the beauty of God and who is present with Christ in the ugliness of the cross, produces a *redefinition* of beauty. In the realm of the Spirit beauty no longer means absence of ugliness. The Holy Spirit did not obscure or deny the wounds of Christ's body, but instead taught him to claim his wounds and brokenness. God's Spirit, as divine infinite beauty, thus assumes ugliness in such a way that glory and delight prevail. Rather than rejecting everything that does not exemplify God's beauty, the Holy Spirit chooses to redefine God's beauty itself. Instead of understanding damage and ugliness as conditions that do not correspond with beauty, beauty itself is transformed and opened up so that the Holy Spirit still can communicate God's life in creation. God's life of beauty and glory now engages the opposite, the presence of suffering, the complex condition of vulnerability. In other words, under the reign of the Holy Spirit, who beautifies all things, we may learn to live with a *converted* sense of beauty.

This converted sense of beauty brings forth the understanding that the Holy Spirit beautifies our vulnerability by assuming both our being

50. Sherry, *Beauty of God*, 12.
51. Venter, *Trinity and Beauty*, 187.
52. Edwards, "The Mind," Entry 45.
53. Von Balthasar, *Glory of the Lord*, 124.
54. Viladesau, "*Theosis* and Beauty," 186.

wounded and our being raised. Just as the Holy Spirit was present in the disfiguration *and* in the transfiguration (beautification) of Christ's body, so the Spirit repetitiously is present with each form of vulnerable life. In the realm of the Holy Spirit, life turns out to be a discontinuous continuity: our vulnerable life is drawn in the beauty of God's life through the ugliness of the cross.

Our vulnerable life thus becomes beautiful life when we embrace our existential condition in the sense that we *consent to being vulnerable.* This consent to being vulnerable does not imply that we acceptingly endure our vulnerable and finite condition as if that is the only way to approach vulnerability. Vulnerability is a discontinuous continuity with the promise of beauty. Vulnerable life becomes beautiful life when we move with the Spirit and learn to see that human life is *meant to be* vulnerable and limited. Because *in* the vulnerability and finiteness lies the quality of life through which God is glorified. In other words, if life would be invulnerable and boundless, then life would lose its meaning and quality. It would be life outside the realm of the Spirit, the creating life-giving breath of God.

The redefinition of vulnerability by the work of the Holy Spirit is thus an invitation to human beings to own their vulnerability, to consent to being susceptible to wounds as well to wholeness. The embrace of vulnerability means involvement in the Spirit's mission of beautifying creation, because accepting vulnerability is an act of beautifying life—my own life and the life of others.

The pneumatological perspective on vulnerability as redefined beauty, as beauty that is touched by ugliness, emphasizes that vulnerability is a multi-layered concept that carries notions of openness, hospitality, reverence for life, resistance of the cult of normalcy, of joy and gratitude. Yet in relation to the work of the Holy Spirit, vulnerability also includes a sense of danger—not in the "traditional" sense that vulnerability means the danger of being wounded, for that is a definition of the cult of normalcy. But way beyond that traditional definition the Spirit teaches us that vulnerability means the danger of losing oneself, of being drawn out of one's own comfort zone in order to comfort others in the name of the Father, the Son and the Holy Spirit. It is the gracious work of the Spirit, who challenges the idea that our human life should be defined by strength or influence, or be shielded from risk and frailty. When feeling weak and wounded, we simply want our strength to be restored. But the Spirit wants our identity to be restored. The Holy Spirit teaches us a dangerous thing: our true identity does not depend on human capacities, but on God's grace and beauty.

Conclusions

The growing body of theological voices, aiming at resisting the commonly defined, negative interpretation of vulnerability, necessitates the exploration of new understandings of human vulnerability. Four particular voices of Reformed theologians (Placher, Jensen, Reynolds, Culp) have been discussed here. Dismissing the understanding of vulnerability as an undesirable condition of life, these voices claim that vulnerable life is always *complex, ambiguous and multilayered*, since it is life that is influenced by God's own intricate vulnerability. These constructive proposals show that it is an illusion to refer to vulnerability as a simple and straightforward condition of life, whether aspired or not.

Despite the emergent contributions to the discourse of vulnerability, there is still need for *pneumatological explorations of vulnerability* in order to broaden vulnerability hermeneutics. Jürgen Moltmann is one of the very few theologians who explicitly address the theme of vulnerability in relation to the work of the Holy Spirit.

Moltmann's close arrangement of the notion of quality (of creational life) and vulnerability through the work of the Spirit allows for additional constructive ideas: (1) vulnerability may be seen as the *realm of the Spirit*, (2) vulnerability as a quality under the reign of the Spirit involves a *vulnerability dialectics* of cross and resurrection, of affliction and restoration, (3) the Spirit, who is the beauty of God and who is present with Christ in the ugliness of the cross, produces a *redefinition of beauty*. Through the work of the Spirit vulnerable life becomes beautiful life (in its converted sense) when we move with the Spirit and consent to being vulnerable. Embracing vulnerability is thus an act of beautifying life.

Bibliography

Balthasar, Hans Urs von. *The Glory of the Lord: A Theological Aesthetics*. Vol. 1, *Seeing the Form*. Translated by Erasmo Leiva-Merikakis. Edited by Joseph Fessio and John Riches.. San Fransisco: Ignatius, 1982.

Berinyuu, Abraham A. "Healing and Disability." *International Journal of Practical Theology* 8 (2004) 202–11.

Bonhoeffer, Dietrich. *Letters and Papers from Prison*. Translated by Reginald H. Fuller et al. New York: MacMillan, 1972.

Culp, Kristine A. *Vulnerability and Glory: A Theological Account*. Louisville: Westminster John Knox, 2010.

Dube, Musa W. "Grant Me Justice: Towards Gender-Sensitive Multi-Sectoral HIV/AIDS Readings of the Bible." In *Grant Me Justice! HIV/AIDS & Gender Readings of the Bible*, edited by Musa W. Dube and Musimbi Kanyoro, 3–24. Pietermaritzburg: Clusters, 2004.

———. "Theological Challenges: Proclaiming the Fullness of Life in the HIV/AIDS & Global Economic Era." *International Review of Mission* 91 (2002) 535–50.

Edwards, Jonathan. "The Mind." *The Works of Jonathan Edwards, with a Memoir by Sereno E. Dwight*, edited by Edward Hickman. Edinburgh: Banner of Truth Trust, 1979.

Eiesland, Nancy L. *The Disabled God: Toward a Liberatory Theology of Disability*. Nashville: Abingdon, 1994.

Isherwood, Lisa, and Elizabeth Stuart. *Introducing Body Theology*. Introductions in Feminist Theology 2. Sheffield: Sheffield Academic, 1998.

Jensen, David H. *Graced Vulnerability: A Theology of Childhood*. Cleveland: Pilgrim, 2005.

Louw, Daniel J. *Cura Vitae: Illness and the Healing of Life: A Guide for Caregivers*. Wellington: Lux Verbi, 2008.

Koopman, Nico. "Vulnerable Church in a Vulnerable World? Towards an Ecclesiology of Vulnerability." *Journal of Reformed Theology* 2 (2008) 240–54.

Meylahn, Johann-Albrecht. "The Folly of Vulnerability Beyond Epistemic Injustice and the Power of Knowledge: A Vulnerable Praxis of Thinking (Practical Theological Ethos) in Global Conversation." *HTS Theological Studies* 68 (2012). http://dx.doi.org/10.4102/hts.v68i2.1304.

Moltmann, Jürgen. *God in Creation: A New Theology of Creation and the Spirit of God*. Gifford Lectures, 1984–1985. London: SCM, 1985.

———. *The Spirit of Life: A Universal Affirmation*. Translated by Margaret Kohl. Minneapolis: Fortress, 1991.

Moyaert, Marianne. "On Vulnerability: Probing the Ethical Dimensions of Comparative Theology." *Religions* 3 (2012) 1144–61. www.mdpi.com/2077-1444/3/4/1144/pdf.

Nelson, James B. *Body Theology*. Louisville: Westminster John Knox, 1992.

Placher, William C. *Narratives of a Vulnerable God: Christ, Theology, and Scripture*. Louisville: Westminster John Knox, 1994.

———. "The Vulnerability of God." In *Toward the Future of Reformed Theology: Tasks, Topics, Traditions*, edited by David Willis-Watkins et al., 192–205. Grand Rapids: Eerdmans, 1999.

Polkinghorne, John C. 2006. 'The Hidden Spirit and the Cosmos." In *The Work of the Spirit: Pneumatology and Pentecostalism*, edited by Michael Welker, 169–82. Grand Rapids: Eerdmans.

Reinders, Hans S. *The Future of the Disabled in Liberal Society: An Ethical Analysis*. Notre Dame: University of Notre Dame Press, 2000.

Reitsma, B. J. G. *Geest en Schlepping: Een Bijbels-Theologische Bijdrage aan de Systematische Doordenking van de Verhouding van de Geest van God en de Geschapen Werkelijkheid*. Zoetermeer: Uitgeverij Boekencentrum, 1997.

Reynolds, Thomas E. *Vulnerable Communion: A Theology of Disability and Hospitality*. Grand Rapids: Brazos, 2008.

Rieger, Joerg. *God and the Excluded: Visions and Blind Spots in Contemporary Theology*. Minneapolis: Fortress, 2001.

———. *Christ and Empire: From Paul to Postcolonial Times*. Minneapolis: Fortress, 2007.

Rogers Eugene F., Jr. *After the Spirit: A Constructive Pneumatology from Resources outside the Modern West*. Grand Rapids: Eerdmans, 2005.

Sherry, Patrick. "The Beauty of God the Holy Spirit." *Theology Today* 64 (2007) 5–13.

Snyman, Gerrie. "Empire and a Hermeneutics of Vulnerability." *Studia Historiae Ecclesiasticae* 37 (2011) 1–20.

Taylor, John V. *The Go-Between God*. London: SCM, 1972.

Van Niekerk, Pieter I. "Towards a Theology of the Body: A Spirituality of Imperfection." *NGTT* 53 (2012) 369–75. ngtt.journals.ac.za/pub/article/viewFile/275/386.

Venter, Rian. "Trinity and Beauty: The Theological Contribution of Jonathan Edwards." *NGTT* 51 (2010) 185–92.

Viladesau, Richard. "*Theosis* and Beauty." *Theology Today* 65 (2008) 180–90.

West, Gerald O. "Reading the Bible in the Light of HIV/AIDS in South Africa." *Ecumenical Review* 55 (2003) 335–44.

———. "Reading Job 'Positively' in the Context of HIV/AIDS in South Africa." *Concilium* 4 (2004) 112–24.

West, Gerald O., and Bongi Zengele-Nzimande. "The Medicine of God's Word: What People Living with HIV and AIDS Want (and Get) from the Bible." *Journal of Theology for Southern Africa* 125 (2006) 51–63.

Yong, Amos. *Hospitality and the Other: Pentecost, Christian Practices, and the Neighbor*. Faith Meets Faith. Maryknoll, NY: Orbis, 2008.

———. *Theology and Down Syndrome: Reimagining Disability in Late Modernity*. Waco: Baylor University Press, 2007.

9

Integrating Different Values
Beyond Literal vs. Oral, Word vs. Image in the Reformed Spirit

MEEHYUN CHUNG

Introduction

THROUGHOUT HISTORY, A HIERARCHICAL dualism has manifested itself as a dichotomy between literality and orality or narrativity, which reflects the dichotomy between word and image, maleness and femaleness, and reason and emotion to a certain degree. The Reformed Tradition, too, has underscored the written word of God and weakened the oral image, creating an imbalance between literality and orality and word and image, among other dualities. In order to find and integrate different values, this essay initially explores the idea of Barth's threefold meaning of the Word of God. Secondly, it deals with the issue of Jesus's hermeneutics regarding John 7. This essay then explains this dichotomy using examples of Korean culture and customs. The aim is to overcome the one-sided hierarchical domination and rediscover the other side of value dialectically; both values should be integrated to understand the Word of God.

The Threefold Meaning of the Word of God

Karl Barth defines his theme about the word of God as a touchstone to volume one of his *Church Dogmatics*.[1] Proclamation of the word of God

---

1. Barth, *Doctrine of the Word*, 117.

makes the Church fulfill its duty as the Church. The message of God can be delivered to us as the proclaimed, written and revealed word of God. The revealed word of God is recognized through proclamation, which is based on the Bible. Hence, in order to understand the proclaimed word of God, we need to know the written word of God. The proclaimed word makes God's word God's word. The proclaimed word is consigned as the basis of proclamation in the church. The word of God is the object of the proclamation. However, it is different from any other objects because it is not merely given, but promised for the proclamation. The word of God itself is the touchstone of this event. This is a miracle event in which human words are transformed into the word of God. The proclamation itself as such is not the Word of God. However, the word of God is the proclaimed word. The words of a human being remain as the words of a human being. God's word through proclamation is already the spoken word. If the proclamation implies a succession of apostolic witness, it could be the true spoken word of God.

This apostolic word encountered by human beings is canon. Canon is the written word. As written text, canon has the highest value. Oral tradition remains dependent within the church tradition; it even implies its own meaning. "Whatever such spiritual-oral tradition there may be in the Church, obviously it cannot possess the character of an authority irremovably confronting the Church, because it lacks the written form. In the unwritten tradition the Church is not addressed, but is engaged in a dialogue with herself."[2] The spiritual-oral tradition has its own value. However, it is not comparable to the written form. "Self-defense against possible violence to the text must be left here as everywhere to the text itself, which in practice has so far always succeeded, as a merely spiritual-oral tradition simply cannot, in asserting its own life against encroachments by individuals or whole areas and schools in the Church, and in victoriously achieving it in ever fresh applications, and so in creating recognition of itself as the norm."[3]

All real prophetic and apostolic succession can be understood as an event which refers to the event of Jesus through expectation and memory. "In this event the Bible is the Word of God, i.e., in this word the human word of prophets and apostles represents the Word of God Himself."[4] To confess that the Bible is God's word does not signify human beings as capturing the Bible, but the Bible capturing human beings. "This very fact of the language of God Himself becoming an event in the human word of the Bible

---

2. Ibid., 117–18.
3. Ibid., 119.
4. Ibid., 122–23.

is, however, God's business and not ours."⁵ Thus, the Bible is God's word, not the words of human beings.⁶

Nevertheless, the Bible is not as such the revealed word of God. It becomes the concrete means through which the church remembers the events of Jesus. Through this recollection of grace "the Bible speaks to us of the promise, that prophets and apostles tell us what they have to say to us, that their word is imposed upon us, and that the Church from time to time becomes what she is because she is faced with the Bible, is God's decision and not ours—that is grace and not our work."⁷

The word of God is encountered by humans in three forms: The Word of God is firstly the Word, secondly God's Act, and thirdly God's Mystery. Proclamation refers to the word, the written text refers to the act and the word of revelation refers to mysterion.⁸ The Word of God means "God speaks."⁹ The unity of the threefold form and the threefold form in unity are *analogia entis* to the trinity of God.¹⁰ In order to recognize the word of God both literally and orally, words and images are combined and different values are integrated.

First, it means that this word occurs as an event of incarnation. However, this word of God occurs as a spiritual event. Secondly, it has character of personification. Personification does not refer to something out of literality. The word of God is the act of God. This mysterion of God's word is related to the secularity of this world, as it should be spoken to the world. It is related to the revealed and unrevealed word. The word of God remains in spirituality. Human beings cannot understand the word of God. This is a precondition to accept the Word of God as the Word of God. Barth expressed the knowability of the Word of God, which could be founded in God's Word itself. With the concept of *analogia fidei*, Barth explained the relationship between God's revelation as the language of God and the knowability of human beings as acts of believing. A human being has not taken faith unto himself and herself. A human being has not personally created his faith himself or herself; the Word of God has created it. A human being has not reached faith; rather faith has reached a human being through the Word. Faith has been gifted to human beings by the Word.¹¹ My

5. Ibid., 123.
6. Ibid.
7. Ibid.
8. Cf. Ibid., 141–212.
9. Ibid., 150.
10. To speak with Bruce McCormack it is a "*unity*-in-differentiation." McCormack, "Being of Scripture," 59.
11. Cf. Barth, *Doctrine of the Word*, 280.

argument here is that Barth's threefold Word of God—incarnate, written, spoken—overcomes the possible destructive dichotomy between the literal and the spoken, including words and images, by grounding both of them in the Word Incarnate, namely, Jesus Christ, or God as a human being. Word in each case still requires the Spirit to complement the Word and give it life.

Given this background, it is important to examine the possibility of rediscovering disregarded value in the reformed tradition in order to understand the Word of God in our contemporary context. The development of Christianity, based on Hebraism, is very much affected by alphabets, literacy, written cultures and therefore hearing.[12] The 16th Century Reformation with its hostility toward images and statues is difficult to deny.[13] The reformers wanted to hear God's word without any distraction by seeing.[14] Reformers in the 16th century had not encouraged visual images and depictions to understand God's word and to use in the church. However, visual depictions were important to individual pious practice and could serve didactic purpose in commemorating events of Jesus's life. The Reformation further accentuated providence as the arena of our interaction with God, which includes the whole self and engages the whole of creation. If images encourage one to contemplate the word of God and to become awake with sensual awareness, images should not be disregarded in a Reformed church, as iconophobia in the Reformed tradition is in our context no longer appropriate.

Law of Moses and Hermeneutics of Jesus: John 7:53—8:11

The Teaching of Jesus consists of not only hearing but also of seeing images and understanding parables. Therefore, it is closer to the right brain than

---

12. Patriarchal religion which is based on the text disregards other religions which are based on oral tradition and flexibility.

13. Questions about images after reformation require differentiated observations. It is not easy to say that the written word replaced the image. Cf. Jürgenson, "Arts and Lutheran Church Decoration," 356.

14. Conflict against pictures during the Reformation was not only related to the prohibition of images according to the Ten Commandments, internalized piety, an opponent of reformation, but also involved a fight against rich people on behalf of the poor. The crucial point was the distribution of wealth. To summarize, it was not merely theological thought but also social reform to support a reduction of poverty and a redistribution of material goods. According to Luther and Erasmus, images and pictures could be used in the church for educational purposes. Zwingli did not agree with this intention, but he was not completely against the use of pictures. For Zwingli, images and pictures could make faith more vivid and were therefore not completely forbidden. It depends on how these materials were used and for which purposes. Cf. Christ-von Wedel, "Bilderverbot und Bibelillustrationen," 315–16.

the left. Jesus's events were based on words. We cannot deal with the Word without particular words, but the words by themselves have to be gathered into a focused meaning, hence the Word. The person of Jesus Christ is the one who focuses the words of the Old Testament and the New Testament. Spirit is still essential to make both the Word and words come alive to us. It later became literate language.

The passage of John 7:53—8:11 brings out the conflict of Jesus with the scribes and Pharisees.[15] The Scribes and Pharisees were committed to the law as it was written. In contrast, Jesus functioned to a certain extent as a lawbreaker;[16] not only in his redefinitions of religious matters, but also in regard to the jurisdiction of the Roman Empire. In the community where John's gospel erupted, there must have been heated debate between Pharisaic scholars and the followers of Jesus. The Pharisaic scholars emphasized written regulations and the traditional authorities of office. The followers of Jesus, however, were drawn to the charismatic authority rooted in the powers of direct speech.[17] As shown in John 8:7, Jesus brought to bear his word, coupled with grace and truth (John 1:17), to openly oppose written scripture and the thick-headedness of the scribes. His word, actively taking the side of the most vulnerable, proved superior to their commentary.

The text does not show whether Jesus ever wrote down his thoughts. The text does indicate that through his actions Jesus sets aside the limitations of scripture. He demonstrates the superiority of the spoken word of love to the power of written legislation. Through speech he fulfills the true spirit of the law. We can say that it was the Word Incarnate that was the subject of the action.[18]

In the story in John, a woman is accused of being an adulteress, although her partner in the act is not mentioned. Compare this to Lev 20:10, where both the adulterer and the adulterous are mentioned, but in John's story there is not a single word about the male; only the adulteress is mentioned. Nor is the woman given a chance to recount what happened or to share her side of the story. As is usual in the Bible, the woman is either

---

15. I appreciate this insight of Merwyn Johnson. This expression should be understood relatively, as it is not easy to generalize certain tendencies. The Pharisees and Scribes in the New Testament also belong to the orality side of Scripture, while the Sadducees regarded the Law only as Scripture (Pentateuch). The former wanted the Law to be supplemented by the oral tradition as represented by the prophets. Furthermore, all the rules and regulations practiced by the Pharisees/Scribes vis-à-vis Jesus are in the category of orality. They were not written down.

16. Cf. Chung, "Das Geschrei vom Stummen hören," 151–72.

17. Schnelle, *Einführung*, 511–15.

18. Cf. Kim, "Adultery or Hybridity?" 122.

victimized, objectified, or both. "The power to speak is directly related to the power to act; so far this is commonplace. The linguistic powerlessness of some categories of subjects is congruent to their physical objectification."[19]

It is thus that in patriarchal societies, the sacrifice and innocence of the women is soon forgotten, while the lost honor of the men remains important.[20] In the story of adultery as John tells it, Jesus uses the power of direct speech to clarify the true nature of law, how it is meant to support and guide life among us all, and not to become an instrument of death and oppression. Indeed, Jesus showed the power of the spoken word. Jesus reinterprets this law toward life and breaks custom in order to transform culture. Jesus does not set himself over against the law as a description of God's righteous presence or the covenant in God's name. Jesus affirms the Law in order to save life. Indeed Jesus came to fulfill it, not set it aside (Matt 5, 17). To the extent that the law *describes* God's presence and activity with us, the law points to God and our place in God's covenant. However, written law is not merely work per se. Like the Reformed Tradition—explicitly Calvin's third use of the law and Barth's command of God—it should be used as guidance for life and ethical practices.[21]

The Split between the Literal and the Oral in Religion and Culture in Korea[22]

This section considers the ideological dichotomy with regard to cultural and religious aspects in Korea. The rise in literacy promoted the rapid

---

19. Bal, *Death and Dissymmetry*, 243.

20. These attitudes, prejudices and social perceptions were obstacles to the public discussion and understanding of critical historical events. The voices of the comfort women were silenced for a long time and were only heard in 1992 through the efforts of a dedicated women's group. Since then, every Wednesday, there have been peaceful weekly demonstrations in front of the Japanese Embassy on this issue. It is through such perseverance and commitment that difficult information has entered the public sphere, leading in 2014 to recognition of the problem by a US Senator in the American Senate. Cf. https://www.womenandwar.net/contents/home/home.nx

21. I appreciate Merwyn Johnson for the improvement of expression regarding law and orality. The third use of the law delineates who God is, where God is, and what God is doing. That is far more that "a guide to Christian life." The law only becomes problematic when it takes on a life of its own, i.e., when it becomes a means or instrument of revelation/salvation/wisdom that does not depend upon God. What Jesus does is replace it with himself (God with us) and so redirect our attention to the lawgiver whenever we contemplate the Law. The law *after Christ* still retains a remarkable role for us in the Reformed tradition, but no longer as a demand-requirement.

22. Cf. Chung, "Das Geschrei vom Stummen hören," 155–61.

enlargement of Western culture's left hemisphere, wealth and knowledge, the power of the authoritarian church, as well as hunter-killer values.[23] The male-oriented ethos and logic of left-brain values was emphasized strongly, while the right-brain values of love, kindness, equality, respect for nature, nurturing, protecting the weak and compassion for others were reduced.[24]

The point in this section is to illustrate certain religious and cultural dichotomies in Korea. To define and to generalize the difference between femininity and masculinity is not easy. Even to describe their characteristics carries certain limitations and dangers of prejudice. In spite of these boundaries, we can note certain specific characteristics, as follows: The oral or spoken word is generally related more to femininity, while masculinity is related more to the literal or written word. The elites possess power to control with these written texts. While the oral is related to flexibility, the literal is related to rigidity. Even when literacy contributed to a democracy of knowledge, the literal remains as the power of dominance against culture, economy, and not least of all, religion.[25] The power of writing is simultaneously related to political, cultural, and economic power in general. The gap between literacy and orality remains in certain degrees, as always. It is as if the male body functions as a symbolic support of literacy, while the female body symbolizes the carriers of the oral. This gender-related order describes the two cultural forms of the literal and the oral.

The dichotomy and confrontation between male- and female-oriented languages and their cultures can be illuminated in the Korean context.

1. First example: Shamanism and Confucianism

"Ownership" of literacy and the associated scientific authority are connected. The cultural shift from spoken to the written word pushed women increasingly to the periphery, while men took over the power of writing as well as the creation of the definitions of the norms of society, culture and religion.[26] Shamanism is an ancient religion that has deeply affected Korean culture and religiosity. Confucianism prevailed for more than 500 years as a political philosophy and ideology in Korea after its canonization in Chinese

23. Leonard Shlain describes the essential expression of the left brain as masculine energy which is connected to written culture. According to him, every society that has acquired alphabetic literacy became violently self-destructive a short time afterward. Cf. Shlain, *Alphabet versus the Goddess*, 377.

24. Ibid., 322.

25. Cf. von Braun, "Gender, Geschlecht und Geschichte," 10–51.

26. More about Confucianism and shamanism in Korea, cf. Chung, *Reis und Wasser*. Buddhism also plays a strong role in Korean culture. To delve into this and/or a comparison with Buddhism exceeds the range of this article. It could be a subject for further research.

antiquity. Both religions have an impact on Korean language, culture, tradition and society.

More than shamanism, Confucianism is characterized as related to literacy.[27] It belongs to strict forms of religion and philosophy.[28] Despite the existence of traditional writing systems, shamanism is usually preserved by oral tradition and is designed to be flexible over time. The problem of gender stereotypes in patriarchal societies is more evident in Confucianism than in shamanism.

"While the details of the Confucian ancestral worship are defined in ritual books, in shamanism, there are many religious activities of women without legislation. It is rather an oral improvisational performance."[29] These two written and oral traditions actually are also associated with masculinity and femininity by the power of men through Confucianism and women in their long journey through history with shamanism. A sexually embossed difference is also evident in the participation characteristics in ceremonies and their contents: In Confucianism women may only prepare the ritual food, while they themselves are excluded from the ritual. In contrast, the women in shamanism are active both as shamans as well as participants in the ritual."[30] This reflects a significant formal difference between the dialogue-designed rituals between shamans and lay participants in shamanism, and the more monologue-designed rituals in Confucianism,

---

27. There is some commonality between Confucianism and shamanism, as both of them are cosmic religions. Conversion from these cosmic religions to a metacosmic religion is easier than it is the other way around. cf. Pieris, *Feuer und Wasser*, 17. Regarding Confucian ancestor worship and shamanism. cf. Nam-Beck, *Protestantismus und Ahnenverehrung*, 23–34, 199.

28. There are three social duties in the Confucian-oriented social order: loyalty, children's filial duty, and rites through ancestor worship and respect in front of other people. Like other practical duties of society, it is important to have inter- and intra-human relationships. Five classical books and four classical books of great teachers were canonized as norms. Ironically, the standard of Confucius, "Lunyu" (論語), was not written by him but was collected through his disciples.

29. Deuchler, "Konfuzianismus und Schamanismus," 89–105.

30. In contrast to institutional religions, including Christianity, for women practicing shamanism, it is easier to become a priest. Nevertheless, the role of the shaman could and should be critically evaluated in Korea. Physically, it is noted that females were the majority leading shamanistic rituals. However, the content of the shamanistic ritual was not helpful for women's liberation.

Though it is not proper simply to offer a critique from a feminist viewpoint, there are certain aspects of shamanism that supported the maintaining of the Korean patriarchal system and fixed the female domain within this structure. For instance, the preference for sons and fertility as the women's role are major issues of shamanistic rituals. This helps to adjust to the dominant culture and structure rather than leading to a transformation of society.

read in certain specified forms and following the processes of traditional written rules. The strict preserved order of Confucianism does not allow for flexibility, while shamanism includes more spiritual freedom of reflection.

2. Second example: Chinese Writing and Korean language

Chinese characters are a logographic script that implies certain icons and images. In that sense Chinese characters are rather right-brain oriented because it is related to specific graphemes. Compared to Korean writing, however, Chinese writing as written character was recognized more as a left-brain function. Despite centuries of the dominance of Chinese culture in Korea, people (*Minjung,* ordinary people) could use their language and develop their own culture, even if it was always despised and oppressed.[31] While the higher layer in society was familiar with Chinese characters, the social underclass and women of all classes as well were more connected to their own language: This language with the Korean alphabet *Han-gul* is *"Eun-Mun"* (言文), literally.[32] This alphabet was translated into "oral writing," and created by King Sejong (1397–1450) against the following background: "With Chinese writing we cannot express our thoughts. The uneducated multitudes therefore have no way to express what they want to say. Regretting this, I have had an alphabet of 28 letters created that is easy to learn and use."[33]

The founder of the Korean liberation theology, *Minjung* theologian Byungmu Ahn,[34] emphasizes the importance of the written Korean language, but also underlines its subordinated position in Korean society: "*Eun-Mun* is created in contrast to the use of Chinese characters as an alphabet. This has made it possible for the *Minjung* to lay down experiences and words from real life in writing. But the gentry despised the alphabet and only used Chinese writing. *Han-gul* or *Eun-Mun* was called the Korean

---

31. Cf. Ahn, *Draußen vor dem Tor*, 10.

32. Korean "oral traditions" and the Korean alphabet, which is written but counted as "oral" are two different things. Korean culture embraces oral tradition in terms of songs, stories, myths, and so forth. With the Korean alphabet it is written the way it sounds, i.e., phonetically. Moreover the language has become an "oral" language in comparison with Chinese, which is a written language.

33. Ibid., 87.

34. Within Minjung theology, there are differences between written theology and theological-oriented movements. Thus, the literality of Minjung theology does not always have the same meaning. The text according to the meanings and norms has a performative effect. Theology is written generally by males, while movements and diaconal works are produced by females. About the Minjung diaconal work and movement, see http://www.kordiakonia.or.kr/ (09 April 2012).

alphabet and described as the writing of the *Minjung*. So it was pressed from the outset with the stamp of contempt."[35]

The two writing styles also helped to establish social structures with a few exceptions of women from the higher social class. Women of the higher social classes and men and women from the low social class belonged to the class of *Eun-Mun*, while men from the higher social class belonged to the *Han-Mun* class (using Chinese characters).[36] In the traditional social *Minjung* movement, this "oral writing" is used considerably because it is possible through it to express informally, quickly and unobtrusively the voice from below. In contrast to scholars who dominated the Chinese script and conformed to Chinese culture, the Minjung layer has therefore retained more of its own Korean cultural identity.[37]

Byungmu Ahn emphasizes the importance of "oral writing" for the Church's life and draws a parallel with the language of Jesus:

> Real language can arise therefore only when you design life accordingly. If the Church really wants to make the language of *Minjung* its own, there is no other way for her than to live with the *Minjung*, their experiences, to share their suffering, in short, to identify with the *Minjung*. Without a common experience there can never be a common language . . . We need to return to the language of Jesus. His language, especially the parables, is typical language of *Minjung*. The language of Jesus was just the oral writing, which allowed direct access to the common people. It was living-related, concrete and meaningful. Jesus's language was word for word of the *Minjung*, *Eun-Mun* language. Children, women, the elderly, the illiterate, all marginalized people could also be included as those who could understand it. The more immediate the language is associated with life, the more original.[38]

Byungmu Ahn emphasizes the life-related characteristics of the language of Jesus as it is directly reflected in the Minjung language. "If one is connected to the real life, the form of expression remains simple . . . Looking at the

---

35. Ahn, *Draußen vor dem Tor*, 87.

36. The missionaries in nineteenth-century in Korea noticed this gap of society in terms of language. They were focused on Korean oral writing in order to reach a majority of people. Since women were excluded from the educational system at that taught Chinese writing, women were forced just to use oral tradition. After the Korean translated Bible is introduced and distributed to women, it contributed to their capability for reading the Korean alphabet.

37. Cf. ibid., 88–89.

38. Ibid.

language of Minjung in this context, it is a language which is closely related to real life. The oral narrative is therefore actually referring to Minjung in this regard."[39] Jesus also is actively involved in the everyday discourses of law and justice in a manner which substantiates the restoration of the justice of God as a present and formative perspective. Jesus's Word speaks to people's hearts, not only to their brains.

Conclusion

The rise of alphabetic literacy and the written word brought about a suppression of females and the oral tradition in many different ways. In many places of our contemporary world, the situation has changed. Along with recovering oral language, the value of images has increased as well. Therefore, in the twenty-first century, the importance of images, logos, icons, and storytelling is rising. Re-exploring of the value of narrativity does not merely imply a focus on orality. It means finding a method of integration and reciprocity between various values.[40]

Everyone needs a different approach to understand God's Word. Diverse methods and media can be used to support this understanding, according to the age, sex, culture and physical condition. The Word of God contains substantially the three forms of proclamation, written text and revelation, implying dialectical dynamics between the literal and oral and the word and image. The Reformation was not a once-for-all event. To be a Reformed church means to continue to reform, i.e., with non-stop reformation. The message of a reformed church was delivered by preaching, not by images. Image could not replace the Word of God per se. However, images could be used to help understand God's word and to keep faith more alive, without falling to idolatry or personal cultism. Therefore, to understand the incarnated Word of God, it is important to reevaluate the value of seeing as well, as even the Reformation was a non-visual event which created a word-based form of religion.

This essay revisits the lost value of the Reformed tradition because the strength of the Reformation is in its sharing of information and decentralizing Christianity. The translatability of the Christian canon makes Christianity possible as a mainline religion. The translatability also helps

---

39. Ibid., 85–86.

40. The recognition of other values is still important. Narrative implies story-telling, images, bodily sensuality, body language, and visual materials could be used as a medium of wisdom and biblical message.

with the decentralization and polycentrism of Christianity.[41] The Reformed spirit recognizes locality, not just center-oriented ideas. It does not intend to generalize or unify everything monotonously. Therefore, the low values of orality and narrativity should be reinvestigated and strengthened. A process of conceptualizing for a metaphysical dimension is necessary. However, this does not imply narrativity over conceptuality, but narrativity with conceptuality in order to recognize the different values of both processes.

To be reformed means to keep examining this critical reflection of whether the proclamation of the church is suitable to the Word of God. The Bible has authority because it is the Word of God. Even the Word of God has special authority as written word; it should be proclaimed, interpreted and integrated as revealed and spoken language with the help of the Holy Spirit.

It cannot be generalized that the literal cuts off imagination (the ability to draw images), while the oral is never wooden. There are positives and negatives to be drawn for both the oral (spoken) and the literal (written). The literal, including words, and the oral, including images, could be complementary at their best. As Paul distinguishes between the letter that—by itself—kills and the Spirit, which gives life—but not by itself (2 Cor 3:5), the Reformed tradition could deal with this issue in terms of the Word and Spirit constantly interacting with each other—never one without the other. "The Word of God becomes knowable by making itself knowable . . . The possibility of knowing the Word of God is God's miracle on and in us, just as much as are the Word itself and the utterance of it."[42] In the light of the Word of God, the split between literality and orality is unnecessary.

I have imagined a dialogue between literality and orality in the Reformed tradition for mutual correction and growth. Presbyterian doctrine, including catechisms, is often employed as a synonym for literality in Korea while Pentecostalism is regarded as orality. Orality, however, is not merely a monopoly of the Pentecostal Church. It is also related to the Reformed tradition in origin, if it is defined as the proclamation and interpretation of the Word of God. A renewed focus on positive values and common ground could provide impetus toward mutual improvement and development in reciprocity.

---

41. Cf, Sanneh, *Translating the Message*.
42 Barth, *Doctrine of the Word*, 282.

Bibliography

Ahn, Byung-Mu. *Draußen vor dem Tor: Kirche und Minjung in Korea: Theologische Beiträge und Reflexionen.* Edited by Winfried Glüer. Theologie der Ökumene 20. Göttingen: Vandenhoeck & Ruprecht, 1986.

Bal, Mieke. *Death and Dissymmetry: The Politics of Coherence in the Book of Judges.* Chicago Studies in the History of Judaism. Chicago: University of Chicago Press, 1988.

Barth, Karl. *The Doctrine of the Word of God.* Translated by G. T. Thomson. Edinburgh: T. & T. Clark, 1969.

Braun, Christina von. "Gender, Geschlecht und Geschichte." In *Genderstudien: Eine Einführung,* edited by Christina von Braun and Inge Stephan, 10–51. Stuttgart: Metzler, 2000.

Christ-von Wedel, Christine. "Bilderverbot und Bibelillustrationen im reformierten Zürich." *The Myth of the Reformation,* edited by Peter Opitz, 315–16. Refo500 Academic Studies 9. Göttingen: Vandenhoeck & Ruprecht, 2013.

Chung, Meehyun. "Das Geschrei vom Stummen hören: Macht der Schrift und Sprachmächtigkeit." *Journal of the European Society of Women in Theological Research* (2012) 151–72.

———. *Reis und Wasser: Eine feministische Theologie in Korea.* Theologie/Religionswissenschaft 12. Berlin: Frank & Timme, 2012.

Deuchler, Martina. "Konfuzianismus und Schamanismus: Männerreligion und Frauenreligion in Korea." In *Homo Religiosus,* edited by Hans-Jürg Braun and Karl H. Henking, 89–105. Ethnologische Schriften Zürich 9. Zürich: CVB Buch+Druck, 1990.

"Dignity and Justice to the Victims of Military Sexual Slavery by Japan!" https://www.womenandwar.net/contents/home/home.nx.

Jürgenson, Martin Wangsgaard. "The Arts and Lutheran Church Decoration." *The Myth of the Reformation,* edited by Peter Opitz, 356–80. Refo500 Academic Studies 9. Göttingen: Vandenhoeck Ruprecht, 2013.

Kim, Jean K. "Adultery or Hybridity?" In *John and Post-colonialism: Travel, Space and Power,* edited by Musa W. Dube, et al., 111–28. Bible and Postcolonialism 7. London: Sheffield Academic, 2002.

McCormack, Bruce. "The Being of Scripture is in Becoming." In *Evangelicals & Scripture: Tradition, Authority and Hermeneutics,* edited by Vincent Bacote, et al., 59. Downers Grove, IL: InterVarsity, 2004.

Nam-Beck, Lee. *Protestantismus und Ahnenverehrung in Korea: Entwurf einer Theologie der Erinnerung.* Ecumenical Studies 12. Münster: Lit, 2001.

Pieris, Aloysius. *Feuer und Wasser: Frau, Gesellschaft, Spiritualität in Buddhismus und Christentum.* Theologie der Dritten Welt 19. Basel: Herder, 1994.

Sanneh, Lamin. *Translating the Message: The Missionary Impact on Culture.* American Society of Missiology Series 13. Maryknoll, NY: Orbis, 1989.

Schnelle, Udo. *Einleitung in das Neue Testament.* 6th ed. Uni-Taschenbücher 1830. Göttingen: Vandenhoeck & Ruprecht, 2007.

Shlain, Leonard. *The Alphabet versus the Goddess: The Conflict between Word and Image.* New York: Penguin, 1998.

10

Jeffrey Stout, Original Sin, and Christian Faith

William Greenway

"Above all . . . the idea of original sin is blight on the human spirit." —Jeffrey Stout[1]

"'That is my place in the sun.' That is how the usurpation of the whole world began." —Pascal[2]

Despite valiant efforts to the contrary, the "more militant atheist" in Sabina Lovibond cannot help but suggest that, "Christian belief *per se* is symptomatic of a 'rationality deficit.'"[3] This worry results in wary affirmation of Jeffrey Stout's *Democracy and Tradition* (2004), for Stout, an atheist, refuses to declare theism irrational. Stout is sympathetic with Lovibund. In his very first book, Stout recalls, he too argued at length that, "social and intellectual developments since Hume's day have brought it about that no one in the modern period is rationally entitled to hold religious beliefs."[4] However, Stout continues firmly, since then "much has changed in the philosophy of religion," and he has now "come to think that I can no longer responsibly impugn the rationality of modern theists en masse."[5]

---

1. Stout, *Democracy and Tradition*, 20.
2. Pascal, *Pensees*, 112, as cited in Levinas, *Otherwise Than Being*, vii.
3. Lovibond, "Religion and Modernity," 627–30.
4. Stout, "Comments on Six Responses," 713.
5. Ibid.

Accordingly, in *Democracy and Tradition* Stout refuses, "to rule out a class of claims simply because they refer to something *beyond* or *above* the ontological framework assumed in the natural sciences."[6] This refusal lies at the heart of what Stout sincerely intends to be a generous engagement with Christianity. Stout's open spirit of engagement is critical to his defense of secular democracy, for his project is politically viable only to the degree he convinces Christians they can embrace secular democracy without facing prejudice and without abandoning their beliefs at the gate to the public square. Stout's generous spirit of engagement led Stanley Hauerwas to declare *Democracy and Tradition* "a gift to . . . to all Christians" because "Jeff Stout thinks theology matters."[7]

Stout's generous spirit, however, is severely compromised by metaphysical convictions he continues to share with Lovibond (and a powerful segment of intellectual elites). For Stout's reflections are decisively conditioned by an inherently atheistic metaphysical naturalism (henceforth designated "physicalism"). As a direct result, Christians across the theological spectrum have shied from Stout.[8] Even Hauerwas, in his promotional blurb on *Democracy's* back cover, continues to contrast "advocates of democracy" with "those who hold substantive Christian convictions." Stout's affirmation of people, faith, and churches in his more recent, *Blessed Are the Organized*—"if one subtracted churches from . . . organizing networks, then grassroots democracy in the United States would come to very little"—while appreciative, remains equally equivocal.[9]

I argue that Stout's physicalism prevents him from discerning a vital axiological challenge that sets the context within which Christianity's significance is manifest. Stout's moral spirit is redolent of Jesus and the prophets, but Stout's physicalism renders him *incapable* of thinking theology really matters (other than in a *de facto* political sense). On Stout's account, Christian faith may not be demonstrably irrational, but Christianity has no valid, non-instrumental significance. I argue that the moral spirit Stout shares with Jesus and the prophets should lead him to not merely withholding of judgment, but to affirmation of the reality and character of a spiritual reality that is congruent with a realist Christian affirmation that God is love.

---

6. Stout, *Democracy and Tradition*, 256.

7. Hauerwas, *Performing the Faith*, 217.

8. Gaston, "Augustine or Emerson?" 25. See the similar conclusions of Meilander, "Talking Democracy," 27; Lovin, "Christian and Citizen," 34; and Long, "Jeffrey Stout," 172.

9. Stout, *Blessed Are the Organized*, 4–5.

Affirmation: Stout's Promising Political Proposal

Jeffrey Stout is concerned about the future of secular democracies. Though not himself a person of faith, Stout frankly acknowledges that modern political theory and non-religious cultural elites have demanded believers leave religious reasons behind if they want to enter public debate. He realizes this is a condition faithful Christians (or faithful Hindus, Muslims, Jews, and so forth) cannot accept—indeed, this condition makes democracy and people of faith implacable antagonists. Given the number and influence of Christians (especially in the United States), Stout sees this as a serious problem for secular democracies.

Fortunately, Stout argues in *Democracy*, the source of the problem is a relatively recent "secularist" account of the secular. Stout reminds us that modern secular democracies had their origins in societies that were overwhelmingly Christian. Historically, Stout points out, the secular is the product not of rejection or marginalization of theism, but of diversity *among* theists. Secular democracy resulted from attempts in early-modern Europe to minimize sectarian violence by tailoring "institutions and vocabularies to accommodate diverse reasonable perspectives on theology and the good."[10] "Secular," Stout suggests, should be understood accordingly. "Secular" should mean not a-religious but multi-religious. It should mean only, "that participants in a given discursive practice are not in a position to take for granted that their interlocutors are making the same religious assumptions they are."[11]

In addition to this historical argument, Stout articulates an internal theological/idealist reason for the faithful of any one tradition to affirm a wider pluralism: epistemological humility. Stout argues for a recovery of classic Christian understanding of Understanding that transcends (finite, Fallen) understanding. The Cartesian pretension to Knowledge led to an idolatrous equation of truth and Truth. Forgetting that the equation truth/Truth is itself Cartesian, many mistakenly conclude that the demolition of Descartes' pretension entails the demolition of the idea of Truth. But it entails only the demolition of the idolatrous equation. With the fall of Cartesian epistemology, Stout realizes, realist Truth and Christian Truth endure as reasonable but super-human possibilities, and all human truth claims are accordingly humbled.

Along these lines, Stout makes clear he means to recommend a pragmatic epistemology that can be affirmed by atheist and Christian, by

---

10. Stout, *Democracy and Tradition*, 127.
11. Ibid., 97.

nominalist, naturalist, idealist, moral and theological realist alike. He explicitly affirms the reasonableness of belief in Truth in moral realist/idealist terms. With regard to moral truth, Stout affirms for believers God's own moral understanding as Truth, and for classically realist philosophers an "imaginative projection," the exhaustive and completely coherent "*Concise Encyclopedia of Moral Truth*."[12]

The idealist/religious idea of absolute Truth, Stout points out, precisely because it is always beyond the grasp of finite beings, plays a cautionary role, keeping us humble and relatively open-minded by preventing us from ever identifying our finite understanding with ultimate Understanding.[13] Notably, this means that *even if Christianity is true, Christians do not gain any specific epistemic privilege when adjudicating ethical quandaries*. To the contrary, belief in God's perfect Understanding entails relative humility regarding one's own understanding.

For parallel reasons regarding human finitude, the *Concise Encyclopedia* should humble all idealist philosophical claims to Truth. In short, both the theist and the philosopher may believe that their understandings imperfectly but faithfully approach God's understanding or Ultimate Truth, and they may indeed be correct, but neither has a position of epistemic privilege over the naturalistic nominalist, for given our finite (plus, for traditional Christians, Fallen) understanding, neither has the ability to appropriate either the *Encyclopedia* or God's understanding in order to establish or justify their positions. Any attempt to do so Stout rightly rejects as "metaphysics in the pejorative sense."

For Stout, then, epistemological humility entails ontological openness and both philosophical idealism and theological realism entail epistemological humility. Stout does not believe that there are eternal truths in the realist/idealist Augustinian or Platonic sense. Humbled epistemologically, however, Stout explicitly rejects the idea that those who do believe in Platonic Truth or God are necessarily less than rational. He also asserts explicitly that pragmatism, "understood strictly as a critique of metaphysics in the pejorative sense," does not quarrel, "with the God of Amos and Dorothy Day, or even with the God of Barthian theology, but with the God of Descartes, and with the God of analytic metaphysics.[14]

Stout's public square subsists not by virtue of theoretical appeal to objective Reason or any single metaphysic, and not by excluding the moral wisdom of religious traditions, but by virtue of practices pivoting about

---

12. Ibid., 245.
13. Ibid., 243.
14. Ibid., 268.

epistemic humility and the desire to cultivate virtues and institutions that maximize possibilities for a peaceable coexistence wherein all flourish. His public square is neither naked nor uniform, but full of folks dressed in various metaphysical garb whose epistemic humility and virtuousness gives each reason, on internal grounds, to participate in and mutually sustain a democratic public sphere which blends sufficient consensus (think of the "overlapping consensus" of Rawls' *Political Liberalism*) with significant ethical, metaphysical, and religious pluralism.[15]

Stout's political proposal is promising. The success of his proposal, however, turns upon the ability of atheists like himself truly to understand and respect the significance of Christianity. Stout's physicalism precludes that possibility. I will argue that it is reasonable for anyone with Stout's moral passion to leave physicalism behind.

Stout, Original Sin, and the Significance of Christian Faith

Stout's Physicalist Blinders

Despite sincere intentions to the contrary, Stout remains firmly in the grip of the metaphysical naturalism (i.e., physicalism) that quietly anchors Western intellectual elites' disdain for faith in God. Nancy Frankenberry, a professor of religion at Dartmouth, illustrates the contemptuous attitude physicalism authorizes towards believers even among scholars of religion:

> To many investigators, the phenomenon of religion resembles a petri dish brimming with exotic specimens and puzzling data. Viewed under the microscope, it teems with strange cultures. Even to a trained eye, the study of religion—its structure, persistence, and meaning—poses acute interpretative challenges . . . *Radical Interpretation in Religion* consists of original chapters by ten prominent authors in these fields who propose a variety of new ways of interpreting believers . . . they stand in a critical tradition that explains religion in entirely naturalist [i.e., physicalist] terms, rather than on supernatural or faith-based premises.[16]

Frankenberry's portrayal of herself in the role of a natural scientist is not innocent. It surreptitiously asserts that there are no truths beyond the physicalist parameters of modern science. By contrast, Stout's

---

15. See Rawls, *Political Liberalism*.
16. Frankenberry, "Preface," xiii–xiv.

epistemological humility and claimed openness to truths "*beyond* or *above* the ontological framework assumed in the natural sciences" stands in sharp relief.

Then again, Stout, a contributor to Frankenberry's volume, may find her words not untrue but unhelpful. In his contribution, Stout interprets religion within the wholly physicalist framework of Robert Brandom's *Making It Explicit*.[17] Brandom's physicalist horizon precludes ontological truths beyond the metaphysical arc of modern science. It leaves no conceptual space for any religious "more." In Brandom the idea is not even refuted. The requisite ontological space is thought not to exist, so no question of any "more" can even arise. Stout calls Brandom "ideal" for interpreting religion because he affirms no ontological truths beyond modern scientific ontological parameters. So it is little surprise that, despite his claimed ontological openness, Stout's "public philosophy" in *Democracy* and in *Blessed* remains within the bounds of physicalism.

Consider, for instance, Stout's imposition of physicalist boundaries when he argues for "a *social* theory of moral objectivity."[18] Stout dismisses the classically realist / idealist question with a rhetorical wave of the hand: "But what about the question of whether the individuals really have the right we have attributed to them? This question gets us on the wrong track if we take it as an invitation to do an inventory of everything there *really* is."[19] "For practical purposes," Stout says, we can replace this question by asking more concrete questions. For instance:

> 'Do we (really) have sufficiently good reason, all things considered, to attribute the right not to be smashed on the head with a sledge-hammer?' This question is analogous to the question, 'Do we have sufficiently good reason to remain committed to the rule against tackling from behind in soccer?' Both of these questions have the merit of directing our attention explicitly to reasons, to rational considerations that would count for or against the rule being discussed. The answers to both of these questions happen to be clear, for we have every reason to remain committed to our conception of these particular properties.[20]

There is no essential difference with controversial cases, where, similarly, "what we are actually faced with is a conflict or balance of rational

---

17. Brandom, *Making It Explicit*.
18. Stout, *Democracy and Tradition*, 275.
19. Ibid., 275.
20. Ibid., 275.

considerations, not an absence of such considerations."[21] In every case, it is such "rational considerations" which form the basis for debate.

It is critical to affirm that, insofar as rejection of metaphysics in the pejorative sense is concerned, there is no problem with Stout's argument. Theists, idealists, and moral realists enjoy no epistemological edge when it comes to adjudicating ethical quandary cases. Problems arise, however, when Stout conflates the epistemological and the metaphysical by leveling norms in ethics with ideals in (American) soccer.

Stout says the only critical distinctions he sees between ethical norms and the ideals of soccer are that "ethical norms are much more important in most contexts, and much harder to assess critically, than the properties and ideals of soccer are."[22] That claim depends upon a metaphysical, not an epistemological, premise. Classic moral realists, for instance, would be aghast at a failure to draw a *metaphysical* distinction between prohibitions against murder and tackling from behind in soccer. They would also be baffled at Stout's blanket contention that ethical norms are "harder to assess critically" than the ideals of soccer—does Stout really think this vis-à-vis killing for profit, torture for personal pleasure, pedophilia, rape, genocide, and a multitude of other horrors?

"Why," the classic realist asks, "is murder more important?" Because, the realist answers, "murder is a violation of what is Good; a tackling from behind in soccer violates *only* a social construction" (murder is *also* a social construction, but for moral realists it is not *only* a social construction). "An innocent person should not be smashed with a sledge-hammer" is not a "right" we "attribute" but a moral truth by which any sane person is seized (here we work with a defining trait for sanity). The question here is not about epistemological certainty in the unattainable Cartesian sense, not about adjudication of quandary cases, and not about the admitted strength and essential role of socio-cultural formation.

The question is whether or not the fullness and depth of our moral convictions are adequately and most reasonably expressed when we equate their ontological status to that of the rules of soccer. Why, for instance, does Stout feel the need to use language of "moral *objectivity*" (emphasis mine) in relation to socially contingent standards, language that sounds bizarre if applied analogously to the rules of soccer (i.e., who would claim that the rules of soccer are objective in such a strong sense?). Why, with regard to some moral offenses, does Stout feel the need to speak of the "horrendous," of "evils," of our "deepest concerns and passions," violation of the "sacred,"

---

21. Ibid., 276.
22. Ibid., 275.

and "reverence"? Why does Stout *not* think he is discerning some ontological reality?[23]

Absent some strong reason to affirm the contrary, it is wholly reasonable to conclude that ethical convictions by which we are seized and over which we have no real doubt are *misrepresented* and *weakened* insofar as they are understood to be epiphenomenal, wholly contingent, socio-cultural products. We are speaking here not of quandary cases, where ethical judgments are by definition unclear and contestable. We are speaking of ethical convictions over which there is no real debate. We are speaking of the evil of the torture of children, of pedophilia, rape, genocide, sex trafficking, on the one hand (the list of horrors is long and painful), and we are speaking, on the other hand, of the good of aiding those who are wounded, visiting those unjustly imprisoned, defending and/or meeting the needs of those who are hungry, naked, exploited, and so on. And with reference to such evil and good it is wholly reasonable to affirm moral realism, for it is wholly reasonable to conclude that, as Charles Taylor says, our "deepest moral instincts, our ineradicable sense that human life is to be respected" is "our mode of access to the world in which ontological claims are discernible and can be rationally argued about and sifted."[24]

We will always face ethical quandaries in our complicated world. But that ineradicable epistemological challenge does not entail rejection of a realist moral ontology, most especially with regard to that host of ethical ideals over which we have no real doubt and over which there is historically deep and wide cross-cultural consensus. The question is, why, given the clear depth and certitude of Stout's central moral convictions, and given that he says it is not unreasonable to affirm truths beyond the ontological boundaries of modern science, why does Stout not make the next, wholly reasonable step and affirm that moral convictions over which we have no real doubt provide access to "the world in which ontological claims are discernible" (Taylor)?

My hunch, again, is that Stout is in the grip of a powerful ideology prominent among modern Western cultural elites, namely physicalism (or, "naturalism"). But why does Stout remain committed to physicalism? If I am correct, the real answer to that question *must remain hidden in order to remain effective*, because the real answer is that physicalism *allows people to shield themselves from moral condemnation by dismissing moral realism*. Accordingly, Stout subverts the question of moral realism by arguing that the realist distinction is empty and by claiming to avoid metaphysics altogether.

---

23. Stout, *Blessed are the Organized*, 211–12.
24. Taylor, *Sources of the Self*, 8.

In fact, however, Stout works within the metaphysical parameters of physicalism. Stout is not deliberately deceptive. He is in the grip of an ideology that is especially powerful among modern Western cultural elites, an ideology that is both unwarranted and that subverts (Stout's own) concerns over social justice. Stout is sincere when he explicitly portrays his pragmatism as metaphysically innocent. He is sincere when he subtly and unwittingly elides the metaphysical question and identifies metaphysics with theology:

> Pragmatism comes into conflict with theology in ethical theory mainly at those points where someone asserts that the truth-claiming function of ethics depends, for its *objectivity*, on positing a transcendent and perfect being. Metaphysics asserts the need and then posits the divine explainer to satisfy it. Pragmatism questions the need and then doubts the coherence of the explanation.[25]

On the basis of this illicit identification of theology and metaphysics, Stout advertises "ethics without metaphysics."[26] But what he actually delivers is ethics within the boundaries of a physicalist metaphysic.

In the above quote, moreover, Stout misrepresents the "need" of classic Christian theology, which does not posit the divine in order to secure the objectivity of its ethical truth claims. Certainly, some Christians construe God as a posit necessary for human certainty (e.g., those duped into attempting to meet Cartesian criteria for rationality). But this betrays mainstream Christian theology, for which God is neither an explanation nor a needed posit. Theological talk of the God who is righteous, just, gracious, steadfast, love, and so forth, is how theists name and unfold experiences of moral reality, evil, good, horror, joy, reverence, love, forgiveness, and grace with a complexity and sophistication that far surpasses Stout. By reducing "God," Cartesian-style, to a "divine explainer" or "human justifier" (the conclusion, posit, or lynchpin of some human system or logical contention), Stout caricatures Christian faith, making it easy to group and dispatch Christianity's metaphysical claims as a species of "metaphysics in the pejorative sense."

Once metaphysics in the pejorative sense is dispatched, Stout simply cannot see anything significant at stake in theistic faith. Stout's respect for Christians feels genuine. In accord with his physicalism, however, he cannot but render realist Truth- or God-talk essentially decorative. Thus, in reference to the *Concise Encyclopedia* Stout stresses without qualification that

---

25. Stout, *Democracy and Tradition*, 268.

26. "Ethics Without Metaphysics" is the title of Chapter 11 of *Democracy and Tradition*.

there is "no harm in granting that there is a set of truths like this, provided that we rigorously avoid treating it as something we could conceivably know and apply."[27]

Stout applies the same rationale to God. Christianity's "controversial" and "questionable" ontological claims are allowable because they are harmless additions to important ethical affirmations.[28] They are harmless because belief either in God's Truth or the *Concise Encyclopedia* has been accepted only to the degree that even believers "rigorously avoid treating it as something [they] could conceivably know and apply."[29] On Stout's account, God has no more significance or power than an imaginative projection, which is why an imaginative projection can do equally well for atheists what God does for Christians. Aside from concern over "metaphysics in the pejorative sense," Stout treats God as a difference who makes no difference. Faith in God amounts to flowery embellishment of ethical convictions that can stand as solidly on their own.

Stout's naturalistic bracketing of God's significance is patent when he consistently casts the stakes of the metaphysical question in exclusively epistemological terms. "My complaint about realism," he says, "is that I do not see any explanatory value in the notion of correspondence that realists lay over it."[30] Once pejorative metaphysics is neutralized, Stout simply cannot discern anything in the demise of moral realism that constitutes an appropriate "focal point for large-scale cultural angst."[31] For Stout, realism amounts to nothing more than an empty distinction, as if the moral realist is simply insisting, "murder is not just really wrong, it is Really Wrong." Even when Stout makes passing reference to human despair, his epistemological focus upon pejorative metaphysics stunts his moral and spiritual reflection:

> Especially for those on the verge of despair, it might well be a saving comfort to believe that our highest ideals are instantiated in an actual being—not only a perfect paradigm of goodness but a power capable of seeing to it that everything will eventually turn out well. I do not gainsay people of good will and common decency who accept faith in such a God. Who am I to judge them? Yet I do question the wisdom of treating the objectivity

---

27. Ibid., 240.
28. Ibid., 259–60.
29. Ibid., 240.
30. Ibid., 249.
31. Ibid., 252.

of ethics as if it depended, in effect, upon a faith shared by only some of the people.[32]

Here, Stout both caricatures Christian hope and misses the significance of his own words. The caricature of Christian hope may be understandable, for even many pastors turn Christianity into a crude, self-centered game whose *raison d'etre* is life after death in heaven (and, even worse, material success in the here and now). Such caricature in a scholarly study purportedly committed to serious consideration of theology, however, is not innocent. Indeed, as will become clear, Stout's seemingly sympathetic move here is part and parcel of an unwitting but significant misunderstanding of faith.

Stout is right to focus upon despair. But he is wrong to think the Christian response to despair depends upon affirmation of a "power capable of seeing to it that everything will eventually turn out well." Given the character of life, it would be mean-spirited not at least to hope in such a power. But even if there is some sort of literal heaven, it is not clear how that addresses the religious/moral issue of despair. The abuser giving his wife expensive presents tomorrow does not undo the violation of yesterday—and in the only life we know it is always "yesterday."

Stout should be afflicted by the same aching despair. The critical question is not about faith being essential for affirmation of ethical objectivity. This misunderstands the genesis and meaningfulness of faith. Stout is right to forbid Christians metaphysics in the pejorative sense, faith in God yields no epistemological advantage. But Stout's paradigmatically modern fixation upon epistemology and God as an Archimedean point or as the means to a literal heaven forecloses upon the possibility that he might recognize the devastating challenge that the pervasive suffering and injustice suffusing reality poses to our ability to affirm existence and ourselves. That is, Stout masks the existential challenge posed by evil. As a result, a critical dimension of the origins and meaningfulness of faith is elided. Stout is the victim of an unconscious protective strategy, a powerful, unconscious, modern Western ideology that elides the existential challenge and encourages people to shield themselves from moral censure by dismissing moral realism.

The Moral/Religious Significance of Evil: The Challenge of Affirmation

Stout's too easy reference to those "on the verge of despair" should provoke a more searching interrogation of the precise character of religious and/or

---

32. Ibid., 268.

moral despair. What sort of person, perceiving the overwhelming suffering and injustice permeating reality, would not taste bitterness, would not despair? Who, aware that their own existence is inextricably tied up with all who exist, aware that their being has been purchased at a price which includes all the suffering suffusing reality, would not confess bitterly that, as Pascal put it, "the I (*mon*) is hateful"?[33] Who would not resonate with the apparent ethical sensitivity of Dostoevsky's Ivan Karamazov, who needs not multitudes, but for the tears of one child would give back his ticket to this world?[34]

As Emmanuel Levinas put it, "One comes not into the world but into question."[35] *Ab initio*, one finds oneself *already* complicit in all the evils of the world. This, continues Levinas, is a "guiltless responsibility, whereby I am none the less open to an accusation of which no alibi, spatial or temporal, could clear me."[36] The question, then, is, "the question of my right to be which is already my responsibility for the death of the Other, interrupting the carefree spontaneity of my naïve perseverance."[37] For Levinas, consciousness of this question, ethical consciousness, marks the truly human:

> The human is the return to the interiority of non-intentional consciousness, to *mauvaise conscience*, to its capacity to fear injustice more than death, to prefer to suffer than to commit injustice, and to prefer that which justifies being over that which assures it.[38]

The properly self-regarding "why me?" remains, but as a species of a prior and overwhelming, "why evil?" Levinas' philosophical genre can cloak the enveloping angst of the question. One does not grasp this question. It is not out there, a puzzle. One is seized, shaken. The issue is not accepting death but accepting life. Not "ask not for whom the bell tolls" but, "*I* hurt them, *I* torture them, *I* kill them." Indictment of existence and of our own selves screams out from and at us, a desperate, pained cry in an enveloping abyss. *Why, God damn it all, why? How now joy, affirmation, yes?* Not amorality or moral relativism but supremely convicted moral sensitivity to all the suffering and injustice that immediately delivers damnation. That is the

---

33. Pascal, *Pensees* as cited in Levinas, "Ethics as First Philosophy," 82.
34. See *The Brothers Karamazov*, close of Book V, Section 4, "Rebellion."
35. Levinas, "Ethics," 81.
36. Ibid., 83.
37. Ibid., 86.
38. Ibid., 85.

abyss. That is where every human qua fully awakened moral being, beyond any possible protestation of personal innocence, lives.

Charles Taylor acutely depicts this existential plight as a "dilemma of mutilation": we either acknowledge our deepest moral intuitions and, given our complicity in this damnable cosmos, instantly damn ourselves, or we manage *yes* by denying our deepest moral intuitions, and so mutilate ourselves spiritually.[39] Is there any escape? As Levinas warns, all-embracing physicalism appears to offer one avenue of escape, for the challenge itself turns upon a "responsibility for my neighbour, for the other man, for the stranger or sojourner, to which nothing in the rigorously ontological order binds me—nothing in the order of the thing, of the something, of number or causality."[40] As Taylor knows, Nietzsche, grandson and son of Lutheran pastors, possessed of the moral conviction of Ivan, knew the question, knew the abyss, and thought it would be negated if the challenge could be elided. Nietzsche had no illusions about the ontological order of modern science, the ontological order of the thing:

> the acting man is caught in his illusion of volition . . . his assumption that free will exists, is also part of the calculable mechanism . . . Man's complete lack of responsibility, for his behavior and for his nature, is the bitterest drop which the man of knowledge must swallow.[41]

But Nietzsche, having discounted the possibility of divine grace, saw in this bitter pill our only hope for salvation. For in the "ontological . . . order of the thing" the moral accusation that accompanies life in this vale of tears is elided. Nietzsche urged us to swallow the pill, to affirm the ontological order of the thing, to elide the human qua moral being, to effect the self-overcoming which empowers a post-moral *yes* to "becoming who you are" and to all that is.

At the turn of the twenty-first century, neo-Nietzschean Bernard Williams also confessed the truth entailed by modern scientific reasoning to be "bitter." It obliterates, he says, an ideal presented in "most moving" fashion by Kant: "the ideal that human existence can be ultimately just," for the truth (of physicalism) reveals there is no hope of "a voluntariness that will . . . cut through determination, and allocate blame and responsibility on the

---

39. Taylor, *Sources of the Self*, 518–21.
40. Levinas, "Ethics," 84 (emphasis mine).
41. Nietzsche, *Human All Too Human*, 74.

ultimately fair basis of the agent's own contribution."⁴² The truth, modern knowledge has discovered, is that morality in this sense is illusory.

Williams realizes the illusion is built into socially sustained frameworks of meaning. Individuals (e.g., Nietzsche) cannot singly escape. But from a physicalist perspective, frameworks, wholly socio-cultural products, are plastic. Over time, perhaps, the frameworks can be shifted. Accordingly, in his final work, *Truth and Truthfulness*, Williams embraces hope in a post-moral future in which salvation from the dilemma of mutilation, now dimly glimpsed, might be realized. Williams was unsure if society could ever transparently be aware of such bitter truth, but he hopes we can avoid ongoing mystification. Williams closes *Truth* urging us develop the institutions and vocabularies necessary to effect the needed transvaluation of the foundations of our values (unlike Nietzsche, Williams prizes liberal democratic values) so that some future people might be enabled to live contentedly without belief in voluntariness and in accord with a post-moral ethic—as Williams says, might be enabled "to see the [physicalist] truth and not be broken by it."⁴³

Since the vital challenge of affirmation of the world and our own selves is moral, it is illusory on Williams' account. Nonetheless, insofar as even for Williams the challenge currently does in fact arise as certainly as do equally mistaken beliefs about free will and morality, it is significant that Williams' summary of Kant subtly elides the challenge of affirmation in the face of Taylor's dilemma of mutilation. Williams' framing makes it seem as if Kant's ideal of just existence is devastated by loss of free will and moral responsibility in and of themselves. This elides moral realism and, here again, protects modern thinkers from the challenge of affirmation, which is axiological (i.e., he perpetuates physicalist ideology). It also profoundly misrepresents Kant.

First, free will and morality immediately deliver not fairness and justice, but the challenge of affirmation from within the abyss. Second, Kant realized this, which is why he postulated God, afterlife, and ultimate realization of perfect justice with precisely the same conviction with which he postulated free will. Of course, insofar as Williams successfully encourages readers to elide the challenge, he cultivates advance toward the post-moral society of which he and Nietzsche can—confined yet within inescapably moral frameworks of meaning and, if we are right, striving, *per impossible*, to deny the essential, moral dimension of reality—can only dream.

In stark contrast to Williams and Nietzsche, in the face of the dilemma Taylor gestures towards, "a hope that I see implicit in Judaeo-Christian

---

42. Kant, *Ethics and the Limits*, 195.
43. Williams, *Truth and Truthfulness*, 268–69.

theism . . . and in its central promise of a divine affirmation of the human, more total than humans can ever attain unaided."[44] Taylor does not develop this gesture, but correlations are easily sketched. In classic Christian theology, "God" names a finite but opening extant experience of "yes," the experience of being seized by a surpassing grace even as one lives in the abyss. The abyss is named "Fallenness." Our complicity *ab initio* is one aspect of "original sin." Far from being threatened by Ivan's indictment, classic Christianity (if not modern theodicy) accentuates and embraces it, plumbing our cosmic embeddedness even more fully. Ivan's stance presumes the paradigmatically modern and deluded assertion of a primordial personal innocence (e.g., implicit in Descartes' *cogito* and Locke's *tabula rosa*). Pascal's "the 'I' is hateful," also critical for Levinas, plumbs the depths of our cosmic embeddedness more acutely because it rightly acknowledges that the self, wholly the child of this Fallen world, first becomes conscious of itself already complicit and full of selfish, destructive desires.

Christianity (along with all theistic faiths) joins Levinas and Taylor in affirming our most profound ethical and spiritual intuitions as intimations of the Real (i.e., *not* plastic, *not* to be elided), rejects the belief that modern scientific metaphysics is exhaustive, and embraces the transcending, extant reality of a "yes" that seizes us within the abyss and frees us to live and work in assurance of the lived experience of divine grace.

For Christianity, unflinching confession of complicity and depravity only extends the reach and profundity of the enduring divine "yes," for the dynamic existential experience of the two moments of the experience of oneself as simultaneously justified and sinful (*simul iustus et peccator*) is directly proportional. Lighten one's hatred of the "I" apart from God, and one compromises the joyful release of 'yes' and affirmation of "I" in God. For classic Christianity, the mortal mistake is, *per impossible*, denial of complicity, proclamation of innocence, any attempt at an autonomous "yes."

From a Christian perspective, then, Stout's pivotal mistake is signaled by his lack of despair. Stout is rightly offended when realists contest his ethical sensitivity. For Stout, like Ivan, Levinas, and Taylor, fully affirms the classic, essentially Jewish, Christian and Platonic ethical intuitions of mainstream Western civilization. However, Stout, like Ivan, Nietzsche and Williams, also rejects any hope in God. So, shy of some significant mitigating appeal, Stout should be asking "is it righteous to be?" and hearing only a devastating "No!" There is no significant mitigating appeal and no despair. Instead, Stout frames his argument within physicalist parameters and casts the ethical stakes in exclusively epistemological terms, thereby eliding the

---

44. Taylor, *Sources of the Self*, 521.

axiological challenge of affirmation, the dilemma of mutilation, conscious confrontation with the abyss—the entire context within which the question of God and theological talk of the fall, original sin, grace and salvation are of signal moment apart from any metaphysics in the pejorative sense or belief in a literal heaven.

As Taylor discerned with his "dilemma of mutilation," apart from hope in God the predominant extant Western options are precisely the excruciating indictment of Ivan or annihilation of our deepest moral and spiritual aspirations (a la Nietzsche and Williams). So an evidently unconscious incoherence like Stouts'—which simultaneously affirms classic moral intuitions, denies God, *and* remains blissfully oblivious to the abyss—arguably reflects the influence of a highly motivated, if unconscious, interest in eliding the axiological challenge of affirmation.

It is the eliding of the axiological challenge, not profound insight or argument, which protects Stout from wrenching, give-back-my-ticket cosmic and self-condemnation. Notably, Dostoevsky makes clear the futility of denial and the reality of life lived on in honest but enduring self-enclosure from grace. At the close of *The Brothers Karamazov*, Ivan, having been confronted by circumstances that bring home his complicity, lives on in a coma. At this conceptual juncture, Stout's Emersonian perfectionism needs enriching. This correlates to a point where Stout offers a classic sign of unconscious denial: the bare assertion and uncharacteristic name-calling he offers as argument in defense of his Emersonian piety in Chapter One of *Democracy and Tradition*.

Confession, Grace and Affirmation: How Faith Matters

Stout begins Chapter One of *Democracy* in a friendly tone. He notes that Emersonians and Augustinians, in contrast to mainstream twentieth-century political theorists, agree that piety, a spiritual virtue in the sense of "a morally excellent aspect of character," is critical to the health of a democracy.[45] But, he asks on behalf of Augustinian critics, do not Whitman and Emerson famously advocate a self-reliance that is incompatible with piety? No, responds Stout. To the contrary, they affirm profound "gratitude" as virtuous insofar as it is a "fitting or just response to the sources of our existence and progress through life."[46] But, Stout continues, was not just this form of piety rejected by Nietzsche, since it imposed a crushing existential burden

---

45. Stout, *Democracy and Tradition*, 20.
46. Ibid., 37.

insofar as "we owe more to the sources of our existence ... than we could ever repay"?[47] Yes. But Nietzsche was confused, for:

> No genuine virtue requires more of a human being than a human being could conceivably do. It is not an expression of justice but a mark of sadomasochistic pathology to demand perfect reciprocation where only imperfect reciprocation is possible."[48]

Sadomasochistic pathology is debilitating, which is why, "Above all ... the idea of original sin is blight on the human spirit."[49] By contrast, Emerson's genius lies:

> in the grateful but life-affirming spirit in which he was able to receive—and acknowledge dependence upon—gifts that could not be fully reciprocated. He knows full well that he is indebted, beyond all capacity to repay, to the sources of his existence and progress through life, but his is a piety cleansed of sadomasochistic tendencies by democratic self-respect ... He is saying that what he really does deserve to be praised for, whether it be his genius or his character, is itself conditioned. His merit does not go all the way down. It is rather part of the receiving, part of the gift.[50]

Stout notes, quite rightly, that "it would be foolish to expect Augustinians to read such a remark in context and not detect in it a trace of pride," for Dewey's "self-respect" and Emerson's "self-reliance" are "the fruit of a perfectionist spiritual practice that self-consciously refuses to be disciplined by Augustinian warnings."[51]

It is hard to imagine a more profound rejection of Christianity. The correlate ideas of original sin and humanity's final dependence upon divine grace for salvation (i.e., for affirmation, for "yes"), which Stout bluntly declares a "sadomasochistic pathology," lie at the heart of Christian faith. Astoundingly, given the severity of the attack, Stout's argument turns upon sheer assertion: "No genuine virtue requires more of a human being than a human being could conceivably do." Not only is this not self-evident, but as Pascal, Dostoevsky, Nietzsche, Levinas, Taylor, and Williams all agree, our most profound moral intuitions strip us of any such pretension to innocence.

47. Ibid., 38.
48. Ibid., 39.
49. Ibid., 20.
50. Ibid., 39.
51. Ibid., 39–40.

Stout, however, needs to elide the question so that Emersonian "grace" might suffice. Note how Stout subtly neuters the axiological dimension of Nietzsche's struggle. Stout speaks of us "owing more than we can pay," but the nature or currency of this "indebtedness" is never delineated. As a result, talk of our "debt" to the "sources of our existence" quietly strips our reflection of the concrete Levinasian moral dimension that relates us to our neighbors. Having dimmed the crushing axiological dimension of the question, Stout offers Emersonian grace. Emerson achieves a "life-affirming spirit" despite his recognition of impossible indebtedness, Stout claims, because his piety has been "cleansed" by "democratic self-respect." Unfortunately, "democratic self-respect," which here emerges as the pivot of Stout's entire case for existential affirmation, is never further explained or even mentioned. It can appear to suffice not because of its profundity, but because the axiological challenge to self and world affirmation has been elided.

Meanwhile, the resonance of Stout's talk of Emerson being "grateful" for "the gift" is parasitic upon the theism he rejects. Gratitude is not something one extends to inanimate objects or evolutionary process. I may say I am "grateful" that it did not rain. But if you later discovered me outside sincerely thanking the clouds for not raining that afternoon, then you would most likely think that while I was right to be glad, I was confused in my gratitude. Far from attempting to articulate an alternative understanding of "gratitude" with adequate subtlety and power, Stout continues in the vein that aligns Christian gratitude with sadomasochistic pathology and so immediately qualifies "grateful" with "but life-affirming." For "grateful" alone suggests dependency, and above all Emersonian self-reliance requires rejection of any such dependence (e.g., upon divine grace).

Consider the paragraph with which Stout closes Chapter One:

> What is it about a human being that freedom of conscience honors? For that matter, what is it about a human being that the prohibition of murder honors, or the prohibition of cruel and unusual punishment? Christians answer these questions by telling a story about souls created in the image of God. Emerson and Whitman also often talk about souls and about something divine and wondrous that can be discerned in a human being. They are self-consciously waxing poetic at those moments. They think of the Christian story as ossified poetry, and are striving for fresh images of their own. Their intent is not to take dogma and argue with it on its own terms. Their intent is simply to express faithfully something they have experienced and to enliven a similar capacity for awe and love in their readers.[52]

---

52. Stout, *Democracy and Tradition*, 41.

First one notes Stout's uncharacteristic lack of generosity. From the Psalmists to Augustine to Schleiermacher to Bonheoffer, the great theologians have been precisely about "striving for fresh images" so that they might "express faithfully something they have experienced" in the hope of opening their readers to like experiences of "awe and love."

Far more significant, Emerson and Whitman's experiences are such that they too talk of "souls" and "the divine." It is hard to see "self-consciously waxing poetic" as anything but a dampening of the clear intuitive power of their originating experiences in response to Stout's competing interest, namely, to his physicalist conviction that precludes affirmation of realities—for instance, souls (i.e., trans-empirical selves, what Levinas calls "faces"), transcending love, the divine—beyond the ontological boundaries of modern science (here again, one wonders what to make of Stout's appeals to "horrendous" violations of "the sacred"). Such denial of moral reality *may not* be unreasonable, but it is far from being obviously true. Neither, as Stout explicitly acknowledged, is it unreasonable to trust one's sense that the reality of animal being, let alone of the divine, is not confined within the bounds of the ontological order of the thing.

Christians believe that both their moral apprehensions and their experiences of transcending benevolence, of "yes" are real, if fleeting. They cannot reject the logical possibility they are misled, but they see no reason to conclude that they are waxing poetic. They quite reasonably embrace their hope, affirmation, confession of complicity, and sense of responsibility. Of course, even after the physicalist ontological exclusion is set aside there remains Stout's objection that Christian faith is hostile to life (i.e., because a core doctrine is blight on the human spirit). This objection turns, *contra* Levinas, upon preferring that which assures being over that which justifies it or, as is the case apart from grace, that which renders it unjustifiable.

Christians, in the spirit of the Talmudic scholar (i.e., Levinas), refuse to abandon their most profound moral convictions. Thus they not only judge the world fallen but also confess original sin. From a Christian perspective, *contra* Nietzsche or Emerson, this cultivates and sustains not sickness, but moral honesty. The honesty is painful, for it immediately turns in our hands and condemns us. Is it righteous to be? No, for the world is Fallen and as a result I appear from the first already complicit with all the suffering and evil (original sin). However, at the same time Christians proclaim *iustus*, they testify to their experience of the ultimacy of a divine "yes," of having been seized by a benevolence that transcends every economy, that ever overcomes the enduring *peccator*.

It is the *iustus* side of Luther's *simul* that Emerson and Nietzsche, like Ivan, evidently did not or would not experience. As Ivan illustrates, the immediate yield of retaining only the *peccator* (i.e., no *iustus*) is world and self-condemnation. One might admire a love so offended by suffering that it cannot but become hostile to real life taken whole (mirroring what Nietzsche considered the pathological intolerance for suffering which distinguished the *evangel*).[53] Without mitigation, such love makes it impossible to embrace those portions of life, however slight and unjustly distributed, which are good and joyful. Taken on their own terms, closed off from grace, Nietzsche and Emerson were quite right to attack the *peccator*, to attack the Western mainstream's most profound moral intuitions, to attack *mauvaise conscience*. But it is not the case that, taken on Christian terms, such love entails Ivan's excruciating stance (as Nietzsche also noticed but failed to understand, the *evangel* wanted to share his extant experience of glad tidings, that is, his extant experience of a transcending "yes").

In sum, Christian faith in God, faith even that our most profound ethical convictions reflect God's own convictions, is not anything we can "use or apply" in order to resolve specific ethical quandaries. So Stout rightly attacks metaphysics in the pejorative sense. Nor is faith in God affirmation of the proposition "God exists," let alone the product of some theistic proof. So Stout also rightly attacks the God of analytic metaphysics. Faith in God is life lived in the light of Luther's *simul*, it is living the despair trumped by joy of *simul peccator et iustus*. It is the *mauvre conscience* that nonetheless experiences itself redeemed. Faith is utter surety that despite my sinfulness I am embraced by a transcending benevolence (Calvin).[54] Whatever else "God" may signify, then, it signifies the experienced reality of a redemptive "yes" which is enabled without denial of evil or Nietzschean transvaluation—and if this is the case then God is most reasonably understood to be something more than an "imaginary projection."

Contrary to a widespread supposition that Christianity quite automatically tends toward an escapism that directs attention away from evil (e.g., Marx's "opiate,"), the opposite is the case. The profundity of Christianity turns precisely upon unmitigated naming and confession of evil, including evils done "in the name of faith." On the other hand, for those striving for self-reliance, the need to escape Ivan's fate quite automatically tends toward a need to deny evil and complicity. At this juncture, then, a legitimate moral realist dimension of Christian faith, though nothing that grants epistemic privilege vis-à-vis one's position on ethical quandaries, comes into view.

Consider that insofar as Westerners are in fact existentially constituted by a classically Jewish and Christian moral orientation but now find

---

53. Nietzsche, *Anti-Christ*, remarks 29, 30, and 35–37.
54. See Calvin, *Institutes*, III.ii.7.

themselves incredulous over classic theistic hope in divine grace which allowed affirmation in the face of the abyss . . . well, here is Stout's ample "focal point for widespread cultural angst." This angst is sustained by classic moral sympathies, so the angst would subside to the degree we achieved Nietzschean transvaluation and self-overcoming (i.e., eliminated all moral conviction).

However, and here the concrete consequences of the question over moral realism become evident, if moral reality is not wholly a function of socio-cultural conditioning, if reality itself has an ineradicable moral dimension, then successful self-overcoming of all moral sensitivities would amount to self-mutilation of our inherently moral being. It would require continual denial of reality. It would require firm reinforcement of the fantasy that one is not guilty of original sin, not part and parcel of this Fallen world, that one somehow stands alone and innocent. Relative success in eliminating all of one's moral compunction would mark massive, immoral denial of the fundamentally moral character of reality.

Notably and to the contrary, Stout's moral sympathies throughout *Democracy* and *Blessed* are far more redolent of the prophets and Jesus than of the spiritual isolation he reads and recommends in Emerson.[55] It is hard to see how lessening or eliminating classic moral sympathies cannot but make realization of Stout's ethical ideals more difficult. For if all sense for profound responsibility to and love for neighbor is overcome, from whence motivation for preferring that which justifies life to that which assures it, for preferring not only justice but grace and kindness, for a desire to work and even to sacrifice for the good of others?

To the contrary, does not secular rationality run the risk of being not merely amoral but immoral insofar as it equates rational action with self-interested action? Is not the idea that everyone's self-interests, sufficiently enlightened, will urge us to an adequate vision of moral reality and the common good: is that not utter fantasy? Do not a multitude of justifications for illicit actions of nations or multinational corporations end with appeal to survival or profit (self-interest), period? Do not all the complaints about religion as the root cause of all wars (which wars, precisely?) distract us from the political and economic oppression and/or greed and drive for power that actually foments most wars and terror attacks? Are not attacks upon religion (upon "sermonizing" or "moralizing") actually attacks upon the idea that we may be called by and be subservient to moral reality? Does Stout really want to follow Alinsky and place "self-interest" and "anger" at the motivational heart of the struggle for justice, when the overwhelming

---

55. Emerson, "Self-Reliance," 144–45.

majority of activists we meet in *Blessed* explain themselves in terms of faith, heed Augustinian warnings, and center themselves upon love of God and neighbor?

Does Stout not, despite his prophetic impulses, remain caught within the grasp of a metaphysic that reinforces a greedy, immoral world-view that runs exactly contrary to his passions and concerns? Does not denial of original sin actually amount to assertion of Pascal's "my place in the sun?" Have not many transnational elites, in the devastating, socio-economic sense of the Deuteronomist and the prophets, forgotten God? Is it surprising that elites with no sense for grace readily express disdain for all faiths and moral realism? Does not Taylor's dilemma of mutilation explain why, once grace is discounted, the denial of moral realism is attractive to those who want to shield themselves from an ontological reality that brings condemnation?

Stout realizes (in theory, at any rate) that physicalism remains provisional. He is inarticulate regarding moral sources and reality. His blending of morally realist *mauvre conscience* (with its need for grace) and Emersonian self-reliance (which has no room for grace) is unstable. But he is nonetheless seized by the moral convictions of Jesus and the prophets. In *Blessed*, Stout literally walks with the oppressed and writes on behalf of their struggle. But physicalism blinders his understanding. So I close with a call to overt awakening.

When Stout sees the oppressed and exploited, he has no real doubt that moral reality has been violated. He is also fully aware that biology and history tell overwhelming tales of suffering and exploitation, that we all find ourselves thrown into being already complicit. In other words, Stout realizes the essential truth of the Christian doctrines of fall and original sin. A critical question: when Stout considers those who do evil, is he overcome with love for them? Would he (and would we) love to see them freed from their bondage to oppressing?

If so, then we know the reality of a transcending love that is alpha and omega, we know the reality of a love that condemns evil but still loves the enemy, the enemy we struggle against as enemy, the enemy that we too are. If so, then we abide in love, in a gracious, transcending love that both provokes and transcends awareness of fallenness and sinfulness. Insofar as to live by faith is to live in the light of this love divine, sure of divine benevolence towards myself and all, then I can quite reasonably and without any real doubt confess that we live by faith in God. In sum—and analogous faith may be found in other faith traditions—given Stout's professed ontological openness, it would be most consistent and reasonable for Stout to affirm that the central Christian confessions I have discussed are *reasonable* (violate no established metaphysical boundaries and accords with personally passionate, historically deep, and cross-culturally wide moral affirmations), and *prophetic* (provoke struggle against oppression), and *saving* (alleviate despair by allowing for affirmation).

Bibliography

Brandom, Robert. *Making It Explicit: Reasoning, Representing, and Discursive Commitment*. Cambridge: Harvard University Press, 1994.

Calvin, John. *Institutes of the Christian Religion*. Edited by John T. McNeill. Translated by Ford Lewis Battles. Philadelphia: Westminster, 1977.

Dostoyevsky, Fyodor. "Rebellion." In *The Brothers Karamazov*. Translated by Richard Pevear. New York: Farrar, Strauss & Giroux, 2002.

Emerson, Ralph Waldo. "Self-Reliance." In *The Essential Writings of Ralph Waldo Emerson*, edited by B. Atkinson, 144–45. New York: Modern Library, 2000.

Frankenberry, Nancy. "Preface." *Radical Interpretation in Religion*. Cambridge: Cambridge University Press, 2002.

Gaston, William. "Augustine or Emerson?" *Commonweal* (January 30, 2004) 25.

Hauerwas, Stanley. *Performing the Faith: Bonhoeffer and the Practice of Nonviolence*. Grand Rapids: Brazos, 2004.

Kant, Emmanuel. *Ethics and the Limits of Philosophy*. Cambridge: Harvard University Press, 1985.

Levinas, Emmanuel. "Ethics as First Philosophy." In *The Levinas Reader*, edited by Sean Hand. Oxford: Blackwell, 1989.

———. *Otherwise Than Being or Beyond Essence*. Translated by Alphonso Lingis. Pittsburgh: Duquesne University Press, 1981.

Long, D. Stephen. "Jeffrey Stout: Democracy and Tradition." *Contemporary Pragmatism* (June 2004) 171–74.

Lovibond. Sabina. "Religion and Modernity: Living in the Hypercontext." *Journal of Religious Ethics* 33 (2006) 617–31.

Lovin, Robin. "Christian and Citizen." *Christian Century* (May 4, 2004) 34.

Meilander, Gilbert. "Talking Democracy." *First Things* (April 2004) 25–30.

Nietzsche, Friedrich. *The Anti-Christ, Ecce Homo, Twilight of the Idols and Other Writings*. Edited by Aaron Ridley and Judith Norman. Cambridge Texts in the History of Philosophy. Cambridge: Cambridge University Press, 2005.

———. *Human, All Too Human: A Book for Free Spirits*. Translated by Marion Faber and Stephen Lehmann. Lincoln: University of Nebraska Press, 1984.

Rawls, John. *Political Liberalism*. New York: Columbia University Press, 1993.

Stout, Jeffrey. *Blessed Are the Organized: Grassroots Democracy in America*. Princeton: Princeton University Press, 2010.

———. "Comments on Six Responses to *Democracy and Tradition*." *Journal of Religious Ethics* 33 (2006) 713.

———. *Democracy and Tradition*. Princeton: Princeton University Press, 2004.

———. *The Flight from Authority*. Notre Dame: University of Notre Dame Press, 1981.

Taylor, Charles. *Sources of the Self: The Making of the Modern Identity*. Cambridge: Harvard University Press, 1989.

Williams, Bernard. *Truth and Truthfulness: An Essay in Genealogy*. Princeton: Princeton University Press, 2004.

PART 4

Reformed Theology and Practices of Faith

11

Reformation and Bodily Proprieties
Disrupting Rituals of Hospitality

Mary McClintock Fulkerson

THERE IS AN ONGOING racial homogeneity in most Protestant churches in the United States. Of course, African American churches have a historic reason for being comprised of one "race"—minimally it was a survival strategy. However, it is important to look at predominantly white churches to consider this question: why do we go to church with people just like ourselves with regard to race (and, typically, class)?[1] The PC(USA) is over 90 percent white and 3 percent African American, so most of our churches are predominantly white.[2] Of course, most white churches would insist that they are not exclusive, but welcome all people. A very common mantra is "we don't see color," just people (We're not racists!).[3] "Loving our neighbor as we love ourselves" would seem to be a standard biblical theme that few churches would deny. I have yet to find a church webpage that explicitly rejects non-white persons. Furthermore, the PC(USA) has national entities such as the Office of Multicultural Congregational Support, the National Black Presbyterian Caucus, Racial Ethnic and Women's Ministries, and

---

1. While I will not explore other ethnicities, the general rationale for all-Asian-American or all-Hispanic-American churches would be similar. As minority groups, they gather together for mutual support and solidarity in a predominantly white culture.

2. According to a summary at a Montreat conference on multiculturalism. Hawkins, "Ties that Bind."

3. Among others, Edgardo Bonilla-Silva has written much on white comments to this effect. See *Racism without Racists*.

ALWAYS BEING REFORMED — PART 4

Racial Justice Ministries. It has organized conferences on the topic.[4] Indeed, in 2008 the General Assembly committed to "Grow God's Church Deep and Wide" in relation to multiculturalism, a goal extended through 2011.

Given administrative and structural goals, and the ostensible prominence of hospitality in Protestant churches, what might be examples of contradictions? Let me look at another denomination. Given the explicit mission of a particular United Methodist church to be inclusive of people "not like us," one example in that church would seem to suggest an unusual contradiction. I did an ethnographic study of a multi-racial church that formed in the early 1990s around the biblical story of welcoming the "other."[5] What was originally a small white community came to include African Americans, Africans, and people with disabilities from group homes. The church members really did "practice what they preached," as the saying goes. The founding minister, a white male, made every effort to bring in people of other races and ethnicities. One Sunday, however, the white minister was out of town and had gotten an African minister to preach in his place, and some of his African friends came to the service. A few white members of the church later complained to the regular pastor that the church was getting "too black," even as numerically, whites continued to outnumber persons of color. Later when the United Methodist District Superintendent replaced the white pastor with a black man who was originally from Jamaica, some of the whites simply left the church without giving any explanation.

Another example of a disconnect between so-called Christian hospitality and reality involves an African American pastor in the United Methodist Church. He tells of his ongoing experience in the United Methodist Church of being assigned to all-white churches over the years and consistently getting the negative kick-back over and over again from church members who said that they were "not ready yet for a Black pastor." While this began in the 1980s, it continued into 2008 and afterward. This minister was rejected even by white churches over which he had served as the District Superintendent for eight years.[6]

According to a report given at a conference entitled "Ties That Bind: The Presbyterian Church and Race," the Presbyterian Church (U.S.A.) remains quite segregated. An African American Presbyterian pastor said this

---

4. "The Ties That Bind: Race in the Presbyterian Church." This event was the 6th annual gathering on Presbyterian History and Reformed Theology, meeting at Montreat from July 18–21, 2011. It was supported by Johnson C. Smith Seminary and Columbia Theological Seminary, as well as the Montreat Conference Center.

5. Fulkerson, *Places of Redemption*.

6. These stories come from an interview I did with the pastor, who requested that his identity remain anonymous. February 9, 2014.

was not only because "blacks fear a takeover of their churches if too many whites join and some even want to be away from whites in worship." Similar to the Methodist clergyman's experience, not only are whites reluctant to worship with blacks, there is an even greater impact on the denomination due to whites' attitudes toward churches led by persons of color. "Whites are reluctant to accept blacks as their pastors. It is far easier to find a black person who resides in an area where there are no African American Presbyterian Churches who will go to worship with a white congregation than to find a white Presbyterian who will join a black church . . . There are few whites who will cross the color line and worship with a congregation not of their racial heritage."[7]

While the incidents mentioned above are anecdotal examples rather than summaries based upon social scientific surveys, they seem to suggest that for many white people black bodies are perceived as problematic. Now, of course whites have long been used to black bodies—whether as slaves, maids or janitors, or more recently, as the minority "add-on" at work so as to fulfill requirements for diversity in the workplace. In my examples, black bodies are perceived as problematic when granted positions of authority[8] *or* when they seem to grow in numbers such that the majority group might feel in danger of being (even potentially) outnumbered. These "disruptions" of the white comfort zone would appear to contradict claims about welcoming and loving the stranger that are ostensibly central to a Christian call to follow Jesus. Indeed, they are a reminder of a rather common reality that is most simply described as a disconnect between our beliefs and our actions. Put more subtly, this disconnect is between what we think and say and what our bodies experience as comfortable and normal. On such terms, whites will not typically say they do not like to be around persons of color, even as they may well feel uncomfortable if the persons of color are the majority in the room. Many white people are simply not used to being a minority population when it comes to race.[9]

---

7. Hawkins, "Ties that Bind."

8. A secular example: "(T)his pattern of privileging white voices is so well known that some people of color working with nonprofit organizations or service projects occasionally bring a 'buffer' to meetings with institutional decision makers. The buffer is a white person who acts as the spokesperson for the group and appears as the leader, even if the person in the top position is actually the person of color sitting to the side." Tochluk, *Witnessing Whiteness*, 195.

9. This generalization about whites is, of course, complexified by gender. Many white women would confess to feeling minoritized. And it is important to acknowledge that there are a number of other ways to further specify difference relative to ethnicity and sexual orientation, even as that topic is beyond the scope of this discussion.

Acknowledging the complexities of human beings invites attention to hospitality and recognition that hospitality is inevitably complicated as well. I begin with the question, how does our Reformed tradition as an ongoing and potentially redemptive logic invite new ways of thinking about hospitality? Pursuit of this question requires a brief clarification of the notion of logic when applied to theological thinking. While it would be typical to think through the question of hospitality by attention to Reformed doctrines, attempting to discern the orthodox Reformed definition of "hospitality" that one can employ to authorize a contemporary practice, this is not the most useful approach. Recognition of the inevitability of change in contexts of faith does not discredit the use of tradition. However it does call for a way to see continuity in change. And "logic" offers a way to think about the normative function of our traditions in a way that allows for change and continuity. How are different key themes of the Reformed faith connected? How can they be linked in new ways? One metaphor for these connections—for a logic—has been the use of "grammar" to allow for the way theology is contextual, always changing, but has deeply embedded rules for how themes need to function.[10]

Although Reformed theology is not one thing, let me appeal to a Reformed logic.[11] First of all, there is a logic that connects the theocentric nature of human beings with our finitude and propensity toward sin. To say that human beings are theocentric is to define us as dependent upon that which is truly God. No worldly thing can secure us ultimately, for we must depend upon God for our security. As finite, and always subject to loss and failure, we are insecure and have a propensity to look for security in things of the world. Such "things," like safe homes and neighborhoods seem to make sense; they can be easier to latch on to, rather than being grounded in that which is truly God. The complexity of our nature—as created in the image of God, to be in relation to God, yet as finite and fallible—leads to a tendency toward idolatry. Such is a tendency to find something that can protect us from risk and harm and loss; in other words, something that is itself not finite or fallible. Yet nothing worldly qualifies, so our tendencies can become idolatrous. It is only when grounded, when absolutely dependent upon God that we are free to accept and live with the threats and losses that come with worldly existence, a freedom that gives us the courage to love the stranger and creation as God's.

---

10. See Lindbeck, *Nature of Doctrine*.

11. As Amy Plantinga Pauw and Serene Jones point out "Reformed theology has always been polyphonic—which is why it is more accurate to speak of Reformed *theologies* and *traditions*." "Introduction," xi.

The connection between being created in the image of God and idolatry, as in broken relation to God, is ordered by a logic that refuses to allow the total vilification of human being, such that our very embodiment, our desires, our sexuality are inherently sinful. The Reformed logic also entails a rejection of the other extreme, that if we work hard enough, are righteous enough, we can save ourselves: in other words, the refusal to recognize that we are saved by a gracious God in Jesus Christ. This logic is connecting our understanding of human nature and our understanding of God. As a logic it creates a kind of paradox: that we are responsible worldly, finitely good creatures, who nevertheless need to be redemptively grounded in that which is truly God, and it was crucial to the insights of the Protestant Reformation.[12]

These themes and their connections require from the Reformed tradition an ongoing commitment to "reformed and always reforming," a longstanding clear articulation of a founding logic for this theological tradition. Simply put, the anthropological logic operates upon the beliefs that human beings are created in the image of God, a status that entails the inevitable ongoing redemption of human lives, along with the inevitable ongoing need for confession, change and hope, grounded in that which is truly God. Secondly, this theocentric posture is not a move away from the world but a liberative move toward it. A God-centered posture toward the world must honor all worldly entities in their finitude and creative plural determinacy. The linkage of iconoclastic honoring of the world is well displayed in Calvin's conviction that "the imago Dei is a *task* characterized by the display of gratitude." It compels reformative moves such as disengagement of "the human 'likeness' to God from narrow identity with such historically male-associated features as reason. To enact the imago Dei is not to have a particular (gendered, racialized, etc.) identity, but to live in a mode of thankfulness and dependence on God."[13] Thinking of this as a logic rather than specific concrete beliefs and behaviors allows for recognition of the inevitable *change* in our realities. What is idolized will always change; the realities in need of honor for their finite goodness will change as well.

---

12. These logics are seen in the rejection of what became the views of Manichaeism, works righteousness, and humanitarianism. The Reformation employed this logic as a way to criticize what were perceived to be the Catholic practices that were supporting Pelagianism, a kind of works righteousness, sacralizing of finite worldly goods, and such practices as the selling of indulgences, a way to pay for permitted remission of sins.

13. "Reformed linkage of sin against God with sin against the neighbor . . . (his) warning that an account of God can function as an idol when it comes 'at the expense of humanity' is a Reformed version of feminist . . . concerns regarding use of . . . historical tradition to denigrate human identities . . . de Gruchy insists, such idols must be smashed 'in the service of human & social liberation.'" Fulkerson, "The *Imago Dei*," 99, 101. See de Gruchy, *Liberating Reformed Theology*.

Thus, new forms of denial of and damage to the imago Dei can be surfaced, identified and addressed by a Reformed logic. The observation that the image of God cannot be hierarchalized based upon gender is a relatively new and modern display of the Reformed logic, since for centuries women were granted a lesser status by Christian authorities who were predominantly male. As contexts change, the Reformed logic must always be applied in new ways. Surfacing and recognizing such damage is not simple, however, and we cannot simply add the formerly excluded to our "love the neighbor" list. To explore the harm and redress needed for the problems identified thus far invites a complicated version of iconoclasm. As pointed out, given the Reformed logic of an "always being reformed" imperative, use of this logic requires critical assessment through the lens of iconoclasm of any tradition that is employed to support these exclusions. All traditions are finite and created, even scripture. This challenges us to view any false requirement upon participation in churches as idolatrous, as sin. Thus, we might want to say that a valorizing of "whiteness" is akin to an idolizing of a group identity.

And those false qualifications can be embedded in social structures, not simply identifiable in individual biases. An example would be a valorizing of "whiteness" as akin to an idolizing of a group identity. Never simply reducible to malicious individual acts, this idolizing inevitably entails the vilification of a group perceived as threatening that identity; and such vilification occurs at the social institutional level—in stereotypes and negative images of blackness that become deeply embedded in white consciousness. Even when not explicit or even intentional, such white racism is idolatrous and needs to be "reformed." While the case is pretty clear that we have inherited and continue to be shaped by this social/institutional form of sin, I want to focus on other elements in our theological tools that need disruptive attention.

The "tradition" that needs disrupting is a notion of hospitality that confines "tradition" to correct beliefs, rather than recognizing the deeply embedded incorporative traditions that continue to reproduce class and racial homogeneity, among others.[14] We need to surface the bodily aversiveness that has shaped many whites and contributed to forms of boundary maintenance that continue to have impact in churches as well as so-called "secular" society. And we are shaped not simply by the "traditions" of Scrip-

---

14. Among other identity markers that generate discomfort would be what is typically called "disability" and LGBTQ or so-called "homosexuality." "Gender" is still an issue, as well, but often less explicit, since women have made up a majority of congregations in the US for most of our history. I do not want to reduce the problem to "race," but am starting with it.

ture, of creeds such as the Westminster Confession (1647), the Barmen Declaration (1934), Confession of Belhar (1982), Confession of 1967, but also by social traditions that shape our bodily habits.

There is, to be sure, a growing concern by theologians and ethicists for "practices" rather than beliefs, which leads to emphasizing the priority of practice over rules. Stanley Hauerwas has come close to romanticizing the ethical power of worship, saying that along with baptism the sacrament of Eucharist is "the essential rituals of our politics; indeed, "liturgy *is* social action."[15] He invokes liturgical scholar Donald Saliers who "has tried to help Methodists recover the way worship is evangelism and ethics by reminding us how worship is about the shaping of the affections."[16] Another liturgical scholar, John Baldovin says, "One of the (many) functions that rituals (and therefore liturgy) perform is to help a group of people experience solidarity, identity and common purpose. And the very reason they need ritual is to express that identity bodily and communally. My point here is not to persuade people to sign themselves with the cross at the liturgical proclamation of the gospel so much as it is to argue that what we do communally with our bodies at worship makes a great deal of difference when it comes to one of the main reasons for public worship in the first place—namely, to express who we are as a community in the presence of the living God."[17]

Bodies Matter: Forming Our Bodies for What?

Given the overwhelming significance attributed to the formative function of liturgy, the role of racial/class homogeneity matters even more. If we continue to do the Eucharist with bodies that are basically just like ourselves, what kind of "radical hospitality" are we reproducing? What kind of "social action" are we performing? To get at these questions, let me turn first to an account of Eucharist that illustrates the complexity of messages

---

15. Hauerwas, *Peaceable Kingdom*, 108.

16. Hauerwas, "Worship, Evangelism, Ethics," 97. Hauerwas agrees with Saliers that "in worship 'form matters' for the truthful shaping of our emotions. The words we use matter. It matters that the Word should be followed by table if we are to be rightly formed as Christians. It matters what kind of music shapes our response to the psalms, since what the psalm declares is not separable from how we as the Church sing that declaration... In this respect, there is an interesting parallel between liturgy and ethics as disciplines... As the quote from Augustine reminds us, it is not any God that Christians worship but the God whose justice is to be found in Jesus' cross and resurrection. To learn to worship that God truthfully requires that our bodies be formed by truthful habits of speech and gesture. To be so habituated is to acquire a character befitting lives capable of worshiping God." Ibid., 98–101.

17. Baldovin, "Embodied Eucharistic Prayer," 3.

communicated in the sacramental practice. Amy Plantinga Pauw describes her grandmother's Reformed church doing the Lord's Supper:

> I watched her receive the bread and wine from a phalanx of white men in dark suits, who would stand, hands folded, guarding the communion table until the minister in his long robe gave the authoritative nod to distribute the elements. As far as I could tell, my grandmother had thoroughly internalized the theology behind these liturgical arrangements. Along with her communion wine, she drank in potent assumptions about gender and grace, about divine rule and male authority. Denied the possibility of holding ordained office, or even the right to vote in congregational meetings my grandmother was largely shut out of the communal discernment of God's call to ecclesial faithfulness. Yet the church was at the center of her life . . . My grandmother's story is a common one. Life in the church has often been a jumbled experience of nurture & repression, identity formation & alienation for women. How do the resources of Reformed theology make sense of women's ambiguous ecclesial experience and empower them to seek the church's faithful transformation?[18]

Plantinga Pauw's story is an excellent example both of how we should not completely "diss" our traditional practices, and how we need to explore the other dimensions of tradition and what traditions are reproducing. Even as women have continued to hear gospel, the gendered messages sent to Plantinga Pauw's grandmother are and have been sent in churches for years and years—that is, the deeply habituated sense that only male bodies can perform authoritatively. To begin to explore how we might surface a fuller concept of theological "tradition" and its heretofore unacknowledged role in reproducing problematic boundaries I turn to sociological categories of cultural/social identity and the reproduction of that identity.

Sociologist Paul Connerton argues that both cultural identity and memory are constituted by shared practices—practices of inscription, defined as written and savable meanings, *and* incorporative practices, defined as bodily practices that convey meaning in their performance.[19] These incorporative or bodily practices are typically ignored in Christian accounts of tradition. In other words, "tradition" is not simply the "beliefs," doctrines, creeds and scripture that have normative roles in our faithful life as "church," it is also the pre-reflective bodily habituations that have shaped the way we—a particular group—experience the world. In the story of Plantinga

---

18. Pauw, "Graced Infirmity," 189.
19. Connerton, *How Societies Remember.*

Pauw's grandmother, who had been traditioned as a woman to respond to (white) males as the authoritative figures in a church (and most likely in other social contexts), her incorporative practices were clearly gendered by a patriarchal social world. Of course how we experience the world can be categorized in numerous ways; what is helpful in recognizing this reality as bodily habituations, or what is termed "*habitus*," is a way to recognize particular dimensions of social memory that matter, even as they are not always noticed or acknowledged.

As Pierre Bourdieu defines it, habitus refers to agents as "socially informed bod(ies)" meaning that practices are a social enculturation which takes the form of "a system of lasting, transposable dispositions which, integrating past experiences, function at every moment as a matrix of perceptions, appreciations, and actions and make possible the achievement of infinitely diversified tasks." These habituations are durable dispositions that re-externalize social cultures in ever-new ways. As agents are "socially informed bod(ies)," practices on Bourdieu's terms are a social enculturation: "a movement from the externality of established customs and norms to the internality of durable dispositions, habituation is a matter of re-externalization—of taking the *habitus* that has already been acquired and enacting it anew in the place-world."[20]

A *habitus* would be the capacity to play tennis, or, more broadly, the bodily skills we need simply to operate in the world. These bodily knowledges are, of course, shaped by our particular cultures and include the status of different bodies as defined by those "cultures." There are, as Connerton notes, incorporative practices of ritual that help define culture and incorporative practices he terms "bodily proprieties," defined as the practices (movements, postures, gestures, etc.) designated as "proper" for particular kinds of bodies to perform.[21] An obvious example would be the contrasting bodily proprieties of a monarch in comparison with the serf in medieval times, or a plantation owner in comparison with the slave, who would typically perform submissive postures in the slave owner's house. Clearly bodily proprieties are connected to cultural power distribution, thus can to some degree be strategies of power and survival strategies.

There are obviously racialized, as well as gendered habituations, which embed in us the "knowledge" of how it is proper for our kind of body to act.

---

20. Bourdieu, *Outline of a Theory of Practice*, 16. See Calhoun, "Habitus, Field, and Capital," 61–88.

21. Connerton, *How Societies Remember*, 72. Examples he provides include medieval proprieties for serfs as well as monarchs. I am clearly invoking bodily proprieties as they are assigned to racialized groups.

So even if (typically) unacknowledged, "white habituations" are part of our social identities.

Complicating further Bourdieu's notion of the *habitus* as bodily memory for a skill, Paul Connerton's account of incorporative practice focuses on the function of bodies as nonsymbolic mediums of communication. This is an important indicator of what is sometimes a disconnect between what we say we believe or think, and how we have been habituated in relation to different kinds of bodies. I may not *intend* to communicate my discomfort around disabled bodies, or bodies of a different "race," but my white and "normate" habituations are deeply embedded; thus to be in a very different setting with bodies very different than my own can be unsettling—my discomfort in situations where I am the minority white person, or where I have to relate to twisted bodies in wheelchairs.[22]

The importance of attention to habitus is that it forces us to think more complexly about alternatives to the model of "rule application" (beliefs cause practices), which has been challenged by sociological research, *and* the romanticized alternative in theological thinking that liturgical practice without attention to social-cultural habituations does "the good."[23] The social conditions of communication, as Bourdieu would insist, have to be factored into a practice. A *habitus* of racial justice is not adequately defined by knowledge of principles (or stories) of love, or of what the church or even Jesus said in the past. Connerton's account of incorporative practice focuses on the function of bodies as nonsymbolic mediums of communication. Our "love the neighbor" stories are the sedimented meanings of a community's tradition; however, incorporative practices refer to the activation of meaning by bodily practices. These latter practices convey their own meaning in the performance; contemporary bodily activity is itself the communication. As Connerton says, "the transmission occur(s) only during the time that . . . bodies are present to sustain that particular activity."[24] Bodies are not simply expressing or enacting the values of a community in a secondary way, the concept of *habitus,* as one scholar puts it, assumes a notion of the "body as an assemblage of embodied aptitudes, not as a medium of symbolic meanings."[25] Again, I can be saying one thing about loving all people and

22. See my examples in Fulkerson, *Places of Redemption*, 3–7.

23. Mark Chaves' presidential address for the Society of Social Science, etc. makes this case.

24. Connerton, *How Societies Remember*, 72. This point is made more explicitly by Connerton than Bourdieu.

25. This view of body as medium of symbols, in contrast, relies upon what Connerton calls inscription practices and simply means that bodily practices pass on written or otherwise saved or stored meaning. This would seem to be all that MacIntyre suggests. Asad, *Genealogies of Religion*, 75.

calling racism a sin, but my deeply embedded racialized bodily propriety may communicate something very different when I react with fear at night when I encounter black teenage boys—or when white churches say they are "not ready for a black pastor."

So the postures of worship have their own communicative function; however, they may not be congruent with what we say we believe.[26] This is not to deny the significance of bowed heads or kneeling. It is to say that what needs more attention is not simply the affective and bodily messages sent and performed in our current worship practices, but of the racial and class incorporative practices entailed in them. Even as our propensity to think of practices as "normal," undistinguishable except, perhaps, by the adjective "Presbyterian," what I am referring to here is that there are "white" practices that are deeply habituated habits that we never acknowledge as such. Even though there are typically black, or ethnic and minority groups, national committees, and forms of worship, the adjective "white" is rarely, if ever, applied to a church or denominational entity. In a critique of the "Performances of Whiteness in the Jim Crow South" that looks precisely at the white habituations of the day Steven Hoelscher observes: "(d)enying white as a racial category, neglecting to see that whiteness has a history and geography—as Americans have long done—allows whiteness to stand as the norm . . . Such an erasure allows many people to merge their perceived absence of racial being w/ the nation, enabling whiteness to become their unspoken but most profound sense of what it means to be an American, and, by necessity, making all other racialized identities an Other."[27] While we are certainly beyond the Jim Crow south, Hoelscher is identifying one of the standard features of what is now termed "colorblindness as the new form of racism."[28] The more common version of this is obliviousness to white privilege and discomfort when we are not with people like us.

The complexity of attending to white habituations is clearly more than I can address here. And the intersections of gendered bodily proprieties, class and other markers with racialized bodily proprieties obviously require

---

26. Connerton, *How Societies Remember*, 73. The contrast entailed in the distinction begun with the notion of inscribing practices is not between signifying and pre-linguistic bodies, but between practices in which this storage is the primary way to pass on the communal memory and practices that focus primarily upon the passing on that occurs in face-to-face bodied encounters (which itself can include signifying)—incorporative practices.

27. Hoelscher, "Making Place, Making Race," 662.

28. The argument that colorblindness is the new form of racism is made by a number of scholars. It is characterized by reducing racism to individual, malicious acts toward a person of color, ignoring the social-structural forms of racism, avoiding any discussion or avowal of white privilege, etc. Bonilla-Silva, *Racism Without Racists*.

attention. (A homeless white man who comes into a middle/upper middle class white church can prompt certain negative bodily reactions even in a church with a ministry to the homeless.) Bonilla-Silva, a major critic of colorblindness as the new racism, found a prominent "white habitus," characterized by "a set of primary networks and associations with other whites that reinforces the racial order by fostering racial solidarity among whites and negative affect toward racial 'others.'"[29] A former colleague of mine identified this habitus as "ownership of space."[30] My question here is, if we take bodily habituation seriously—which we should, given a non-dualistic honoring of the imago Dei—the white habitus needs to be factored into a reading of the Eucharistic ritual of hospitality: are we simply reproducing our comfort and appreciation of bodies that look like us, even as we never acknowledge or talk about "whiteness"? How might we "disrupt" the way the ritual is too often done in order to enhance what we mean by hospitality?

Alternatives will be complicated and challenging. Racism and its legacies are not the only social wound that needs addressing in the church. But let me close with some themes for exploration:

1) Given that whiteness is typically ignored, how can the call for Johann Baptist Metz' "dangerous memory" associated with the Eucharist be employed to surface our own racial histories? Rather than simply "remembering Jesus" as a nod to the past, how can "remembering Jesus" serve to open up the contemporary situation of injustice/obliviousness and avoidance around these issues?[31] 2) How might "hospitality" be more than superficial encounters with the "other"? Can communal, face-to-face relations be generated between persons of different races as contexts for honest conversations around these issues? 3) How might the white habituation into "ownership of space," as an experience of being the "normal" and the dominant, not only be acknowledged, but altered in other ways, as well?

Reformed and always reforming is a challenging and yet hopeful communal commitment for the Presbyterian Church (U.S.A.) and, hopefully, for the broader world. We must always treasure one another and the wider, finite and fallible world, even as we are called to discern harm, confess our sin, repent and change as we are grounded in the loving and transforming God.

29. Bonilla-Silva, *Racism Without Racists*, 16.

30. William Hart, former professor of race theory and religious studies at Duke.

31. I am currently part of a predominantly African American group that has been meeting for four years at a multiracial church that discusses our racial family histories as we use the stories and history of Pauli Murray to discuss our own and the larger culture. This came out of the Duke Human Rights Center's Pauli Murray Project, which organizes public discussions on these issues through using Murray's writing and her history.

Bibliography

Asad, Talal. *Genealogies of Religion: Discipline and Reasons of Power in Christianity and Islam.* Baltimore: Johns Hopkins University Press, 1993.

Baldovin, John F., SJ. "An Embodied Eucharistic Prayer." In *The Postures of the Assembly During the Eucharistic Prayer*, edited by John K. Leonard and Nathan D. Mitchell, 1–13. Chicago: Liturgy Training, 1994.

Bonilla-Silva, Edgardo. *Racism without Racists: Color-Blind Racism and the Persistence of Racial Inequality in America.* Lanham, MD: Rowman & Littlefield, 2014.

Bourdieu, Pierre. *Outline of a Theory of Practice.* Translated by Richard Nice. Cambridge Studies in Social Anthropology 16. Cambridge: Cambridge University Press, 1977.

Calhoun, Craig. "Habitus, Field, and Capital: The Question of Historical Specificity." In *Bourdieu: Critical Perspectives*, edited by Craig Calhoun, et al., 61–88. Chicago: University of Chicago Press, 1983.

Chaves, Mark. "SSSR Presidential Address: Rain Dances in the Dry Season: Overcoming the Religious Congruence Fallacy." *Journal for the Scientific Study of Religion* 49 (2010) 1–14.

Connerton, Paul. *How Societies Remember.* Cambridge: Cambridge University Press, 1989.

De Gruchy, John. *Liberating Reformed Theology: A South African Contribution to an Ecumenical Task.* Grand Rapids: Eerdmans, 1991.

Fulkerson, Mary McClintock. "The *Imago Dei* and a Reformed Logic for Feminist/Womanist Critique." In *Feminist and Womanist Essays in Reformed Dogmatics*, edited by Amy Plantinga Pauw and Serene Jones, 95–106. Louisville: Westminster John Knox, 2006.

———. *Places of Redemption: Theology for a Worldly Church.* Oxford: Oxford University Press, 2007.

Hauerwas, Stanley. *The Peaceable Kingdom: A Primer in Christian Ethics.* Notre Dame: University of Notre Dame Press, 1983.

———. "Worship, Evangelism, Ethics: On Eliminating the 'And.'" In *A Better Hope: Resources for a Church Confronting Capitalism, Democracy, and Postmodernity*, 95–106. Grand Rapids: Brazos, 2000.

Hawkins, Jimmie. "Ties that Bind: The Presbyterian Church and Race." Columbia Theological Seminary Presbyterian History and Reformed Theology Series, July 18–21, 2011.

Hoelscher, Steve. "Making Place, Making Race: Performances of Whiteness in the Jim Crow South." *Annals of the Association of American Geographers* 93 (2003) 662.

Lindbeck, George A. *The Nature of Doctrine: Religion and Theology in a Postliberal Age.* Philadelphia: Westminster, 1984.

Pauw, Amy Plantinga. "The Graced Infirmity of the Church." In *Feminist and Womanist Essays in Reformed Dogmatics*, edited by Amy Plantinga Pauw and Serene Jones, 189–203. Louisville: Westminster John Knox, 2006.

Pauw, Amy Plantinga, and Serene Jones. "Introduction." In *Feminist and Womanist Essays in Reformed Dogmatics*, edited by Amy Plantinga Pauw and Serene Jones, ix–xvi. Louisville: Westminster John Knox, 2006.

Tochluk, Shelly. *Witnessing Whiteness: First Steps Toward an AntiRacist Practice and Culture.* Lanham, MD: Rowman & Littlefield, 2008.

12

Land, Exile, and the Spirit of God
Rebuilding Selves in a Globalized World

Grace Ji-Sun Kim

Introduction

For many people, modern life has become a life of transit. People continuously move from one place to another in search of work and a better life. Sometimes conflict, colonialism, and environmental devastation such as storms, blizzards, and typhoons displace people. With the added stress of climate change, many are forced to leave their homes and their land to safer areas. This has been problematic to many as people try recover from storms and other weather disasters caused by climate change. With the scientific consensus that climate change is due to our atmospheric pollution caused by greenhouse gasses, we need to rethink how we live and how we use the earth's natural resources. In these times, we need to reevaluate our ways of living and reconsider ways to live sustainably. We need to rethink theological stewardship and how we can become better caretakers of the earth rather than destroyers of land, air, and sea.

Due to many natural events and human actions, people are displaced. Postcolonial biblical scholar, R.S. Sugirtharajah states how transgressing boundaries, exile, return, immigration, deterritorialization, and inhabiting in-between spaces are all at the heart of many communities today.[1] Few communities are immune from the results of this situation. Since so many are affected, it is necessary to examine the context and how one can deal with the issues.

---

1. Davidson, *Empire and Exile*, 7.

The ongoing process of land lost and new land acquired is familiar to Old Testament biblical narratives. The search for a place to live concerns both contemporary communities and the ancient texts.[2] This chapter will explore the biblical texts that deal with land, exile and colonialism. This examination will give insight into our present fragmented lives that result from displacement, colonization, and subordination and from the environmental disasters that are the consequences of using up our natural resources.

Land in Israelite History

The land is important. We are created from the dust, the land. We live off the land; we live with the land. Each person and every people yearn for a place to call their home. We are people of the land, and therefore, must take care of the land. As good stewards, we must try to save and protect the land rather than destroy it. But since the industrial revolution it is becoming harder to take care of the land and easier to convert it into deserts. We have put harmful chemicals into the air and waters that will eventually destroy the environment, which in turn will destroy ourselves.

This is the harsh reality that we are coming to grips with as we try to work toward renewal energy in hopes of preserving a livable planet. The Bible provides an understanding of the attachment to, and importance of, the land. In biblical history, land refers to real property, "real estate" if you will, where people can be safe and secure, where meaning and well-being are enjoyed. Land represents prosperity, security, and freedom. Both in biblical and in contemporary understanding "land" represents material and symbolic intentions.[3] Land is symbolic as it gives people their sense of identity, culture, history, religion and belongingness. When their land was taken away during the exile, the Israelites lost much of their identity. The land defined who they were as individuals and as a people.

Land is never simply real estate. It is always real estate associated with social meanings. Imagine the loss of people whisked away from their plains, in sight of Mount Kilimanjaro or from the shores of the Atlantic, or from rich farmlands on the shores of the Mediterranean. We recognize the yearning for land is a serious historical enterprise concerned with power and belonging.[4] The land for which biblical Israel yearns is never unclaimed space but is a place with Yahweh. It is land that provides the central assurance to Israel of its historicity. Israel is always on the move from land to landlessness, from

---

2. Ibid., 7–8.
3. Brueggemann, *The Land*, 2.
4. Ibid., 2, 3.

landlessness to land. Israel's faith is essentially a journeying in and out of land, and its faith can be organized around these focuses. The land becomes an essential aspect of the people whose sense of identity was lost once they lost the land. The experience of exile had profound consequences.

History of Israelite Exile

The Bible contains many stories of exile. The exile was a painful time where the Israelites lost land and with it a sense of identity and culture. The *promised* land provided such an important part of their identity that to lose it was a devastating loss of their cultural, religious and social identity.

Before the Exile, the Hebrew people had gone through times of triumphs and defeats, successes and failures, and exaltation and humiliation.[5] In exile, the people were displaced, alienated from the place which gave identity. This event of landlessness evoked rage (Ps 137) but also deep yearning (Lam 1:2, 3, 6, 7, 21). It brought strength and boldness to who they were as a people. In their state of landlessness, God heard their cries. Exile was not permanent and they were allowed to return home. Exile equals death and restoration equals life.

Returned Exiles

Cyrus around 539 BCE, permitted the people to return to their land in a process that went on for about a century. The exile and the return represented fundamental changes in the experience of the people and posed major challenges to their ethnic identity. To survive as a people held captive in a foreign land without access to the ancestral cultic centre had required establishing a boundary between themselves and outsiders. With their return, security was needed as well as a return to important features of their identity: the Temple and its cult. They needed to restore what they had lost.[6] "We, ourselves will build" (Ezra 4:3), is the attitude of the returned exiles; hope for the future lay only with them, not with the residue remaining in the land. As they returned, they were in conflict with those who never left the land. Both claim themselves as the true Israelites and both disclaim the other as impure. Thus as the exiled returned to their land, there was much discontent, strife and trials. There was much work as they tried to define and redefine their community.

---

5. Myers, *Ezra Nehemiah*, xix.
6. Esler, "Ezra–Nehemiah," 416, 417.

LAND, EXILE, AND THE SPIRIT OF GOD

The returned exiles were all the Jews who were taken into exile by the Babylonian king, Nebuchadnezzar in 586 BCE, and returned back home with the assistance of the Persian king Cyrus in 539 BCE. The *am haaretz* are those Jews who did not go into Babylonian exile but stayed in Palestine. The term "returned exiles," *golah* in Ezra-Nehemiah, is used to refer to Babylonian Israelites who returned to Palestine from 539 BCE. This term does not only mean the deportation and captivity, but also the community of the deported and returned exiles (Ezra 1:11; 4:1; 6:16, 19, 20, 21; 8:35; 9:4; 10:6, 7, 8, 16; Neh 7:6).[7]

In Ezra 4, "the people of the land" (v.4) wished to join the Judean returnees from Babylon in rebuilding the Temple (v.2). However the people of the land were foreigners, not truly Israelites (vv. 2, 10). With this conflict comes a shift in the definition of Israelite. A further exclusion is directed against Judeans left in the land during the "exile." The returnees are regarded as the true Israelites. It is they and not those who had remained in the land who are said to constitute "Judah, Benjamin, and the Levitical priests."[8] This division between the ones who remained and the ones who returned created tension and differences of opinion over who the true Israelites are. This internal conflict illustrates the difficulty of forming identity and community. The returnees and those who remained in the land are working in a framework of purity and not hybridity. They are assuming that purity exists and hybridity is unacceptable. Thus conflict arose as to the identity of the people which became explicit in the building of the temple.

Before Ezra's arrival, the conflict between the returned exiles and the *am haaretz* had not been about ethnicity. It was Ezra who introduced this into the conflict by using exclusive terms such as "holy race" in reference to the returned exiles (9:2, NIV). Such a use of ethnic terms to describe the post-exilic community undoubtedly fuelled conflict. Moreover, Ezra failed to address the ethnic conflict in an even-handed manner. He effectively excluded the *'am ha-'aretz* from the *golah* community, through ethnic definitions. Thus, if reconstruction theology has to contribute to the resolution of ethnic conflicts, it has to take into account the voices of all groups involved.[9] The division of *am haaretz* from the *golah* is an unfortunate part of the Israelite history. This type of division strives to build barriers between groups of people rather than accepting, embracing those who are different from each other.

---

7. Farisani, "Use of Ezra–Nehemiah," 35, 36.
8. Smith, *Memoirs of God*, 69, 70.
9. Farisani, "Use of Ezra–Nehemiah," 45.

Exile in our Present Context

Exile is disaster and trauma that is inseparably connected to human actions related to power, dominance, and brutality. Modern exile has torn millions of people from the nourishment of tradition, family, and geography.[10] Just as the trauma of exile was debilitating for the Israelites, so is our modern experience of exile. Exile is a life of loss: loss of memory, goods, home, and family stability. Exile is strangely compelling to think about but terrible to experience. It is the unhealable rift between a person and a place. Its essential sadness can never be surmounted. There is a crippling sorrow of estrangement. Exile becomes a condition of something left behind forever.[11] Lives are overturned and memories become entangled in the web of the old life at home versus the new life in the land of exile. It creates a tremendous burden and has no regard for human dignity and life.

We need to be reminded of the pain inflicted upon the wrenching of people from their home so that it will not reoccur. Exile is fundamentally a discontinuous state of being, cut off from one's roots, land, and past. The experience of exile is the experience of living in an alien culture and is characterized by a sense of not belonging. Exiles feel an urgent need to reconstitute their broken lives, usually by choosing to see themselves as part of a triumphant ideology or a restored people.[12]

Our present reality of people losing land is a result of numerous problems that we have caused due to greed, selfishness, and irresponsible behavior. Rich countries and rich people are too often living off the land and believing that its natural resources will never be depleted. The rich continue to believe in the notion that the natural resources exist only for their own pleasure and benefit. They work under the incorrect myth of a "supermarket" that will continuously provide a supply for our demands. They believe that all natural resources will replenish themselves.

This has resulted in environmental disasters and damage that causes people to move from their homes. Greedy corporations continue to deplete the land and throw pollutants into the air, water and land. The causes are not limited to greed. They are also exacerbated by subsistence agriculture where conservation, the alternative to overuse, is death by starvation. On the edges of the Sahara, both north and south, the land is suffering desertification. Local farmers are over-using water resources and overgrazing in the attempt to feed booming populations. As with the HIV/AIDS epidemic, there is an

---

10. Said, "Mind of Winter," 50, as cited by Smith-Christopher, *Biblical Theology of Exile*, 21.

11. Said, "Reflections on Exile," 357.

12. Ibid., 360.

insufficient will in wealthy countries to assist these populations. This is all contributing to climate change and migration of the poor. Some feel exiled from their own land as they seek safer places to live.

Such a view has changed our way of living into a life of "consumerism." We consume more than we need and waste too many of the land's resources. Overconsumption has taken over much of the world and we are purchasing more than we are ever capable of consuming in a lifetime. Rather than become resourceful people, we have become destroyers of the earth. We live on a treadmill of consumption that has a dramatic effect on the quality of life for poor people,[13] causing stress on the natural world as well as terrible injustice. It has become such a negative cycle for many of us, but we are unsure of—or unwilling to—get off this treadmill.

Our consumerism lifestyle and the notion that there will be an endless supply of natural resources are contributing factors to migration and exile from the land. This usually occurs to the most vulnerable and disenfranchised people in the world. Their lives are damaged, their memories lost, and their cultures devastated due to the problems to which both they and rich nations and people contribute. It is now becoming clearer than ever that we need to remember the creation stories of the earth and remember our connectedness to God and God's creation. This may help us to work towards a life of salvation and redemption.

Context, Center and Identity

In Ezra, the people of the land are presented as foreigners, who are not truly Israelites. With this conflict, we witness a shift in the definition of who is an Israelite. In other words who is at the center of the new community being formed? A further exclusion is directed against Judeans left in the land during the "exile." The returnees are regarded as the true Israelites. The exiles now become the ones in the center of power and view those who were there as marginal. As we imagine the exiles and the ones who remained in the land, we recognize that there is a struggle of power and who occupies the center and the margins.

As relationships build and people move into the land, negotiations and recognitions need to happen and occur. There appears to be a physical and mental paradigm shift to decenter. The center is reimagined so that political, social and religious power is not held by just a few but by many, a continuous check and balance of redefining and re-imagination. This in turn will allow for creativity, newness and solidarity with those in the margins, rather

13. McFague, *Life Abundant*, 85.

than seeing them as the Other. In that space of radical "Otherness," the distinction between being silenced and withholding speech is learned and the ability to say no to the colonizer is rehearsed. In that context the colonized develops "a counter-language," which serves as a language of resistance, a language of refusal, the speech of the margins. The choice of living in the margins exists as a "critical response to domination" that permits new possibilities for shaping and encountering reality.[14] We need to work towards a more equal existence of those living with unreserved power and with those without power. The center and the margins that are defined by those in power need to be questioned and renegotiated so that all can live in a more equal society.

Marginality as a location of resistance carries with it certain essentialist notions that strategically produce acts of defiance and transgression against dominant power. It is a discursive strategy of resistance that provides the opportunity to expose the dominant positions and how they coerce consent for their rule. An adequate reading of marginality requires attention be paid to the construction of the center in the narrative and how chosen marginality serves as a location from which to articulate resistance. Essentially the reading of the passage from the perspective of marginality requires knowledge of both the center and the margin as a means of understanding the whole picture.[15] This recognizes the margin as a product of the center, created through the processes of advancing unchallenged claims to supremacy and dominance and the imposition of these claims upon the margins, while at the same time depleting the margins of their ability to act or react. Since the claims to dominance must always be exercised in relation to an 'Other' the center ensures its perpetuation through the production and reproduction of the margins.[16] A movement towards eliminating or reshaping the center needs to be accomplished to prevent the Othering of those in the periphery.

Rebuilding Selves in a Postcolonial World

By its nature postcolonial theory is multidimensional as it combines multiple competencies, practices and positions to theorize and create solidarity around present and past geo-political relations. It serves interdisciplinary purposes and engages themes such as conquest, invasion, occupation, displacement, exile and forced migration, and cultural assimilation. These

14. Davidson, *Empire and Exile*, 103, 104.
15. hooks, *Feminist Theory*, preface.
16. Davidson, *Empire and Exile*, 106.

themes do not exist in a vacuum but interact and intersect with issues such as ethnicity, gender, class and political power.[17] Imperial occupation of a country results in a reordering of the power structures. Dislocation is a result of imperial occupation which is more than physical inconvenience; it is the creation of refugees who must flee for protection. The refugee created from this experience possesses limited access to space, and needs to renegotiate a place in social relations, power structures and culture retention.[18] Postcolonial perspectives seek to identify the differential power dynamics and try to seek favor of the colonized in attempts to balance the power structure.

In a postcolonial context, identity is always contested. More directly relevant to contemporary readers, are the problems of ethnic and cultural identity involved in exile and migration, and in the process of globalization. Such issues have less impact on North Americans and Europeans, since it is their values that are spreading throughout the world, but matters are very different for the recipients of new ways of thinking and living. Christians turn to those sections of the Bible that portray Jews and later Christians trying to exist and survive in the shadow of dominant empires and cultures, often far from their homelands. Old Testament prophets and priestly leaders struggled violently against the religious contaminations that the children of Israel brought back with them from Mesopotamian exile, and they denounced interracial marriage in terms that today are quite unnerving. Issues of cultural survival and assimilation arose in many societies emerging from colonial rule. One such account is the book of Esther, the tale of a beautiful exile at the Persian court who conceals her Jewish identity and ultimately saves the Jewish people. In the book of Acts, we read about the critical importance of possessing the correct credentials for citizenship, of integration problems even within religious communities, of mixed marriages, and of people needing to be skilled in multiple languages.[19] This becomes a complicated way of understanding identity. It seeks to strive for purity and rightful citizenship which becomes difficult for those who are living in exile, colonialism and are displaced in other ways.

The construction of identity along borders involves the struggle to be one or the other in the midst of social clashes. People are aware of multiple ethnicities, multiple languages and multiple ideologies. From these options, people construct their identities with certain allegiances. The choices one makes may well constrain choices in other areas, or at least be taunted by

17. Ibid., 40–45.
18. Ibid., 88–92.
19. Jenkins, *New Faces of Christianity*, 83.

social pressures to conform to one group or another. The process of individual identity formation often disrupts such dichotomies. Even when leaders express a rhetorical either/or, people frequently make their lives into a bricolage of both/and. On a social scale, such individual choices add up to the diversity of a pluralistic culture.[20]

For the experience of strangeness is like abjection. The stranger has no soul as the condition of exile is a "space that ruins our resting place." Exile deprives people of a sense of possessing an interior space from which to reflect, to love themselves and to project themselves out towards an exterior through loving others. The exile's sense of space is so dislocated that they can no longer affirm either the security of a psychic interior of the comforts of a normatizing, "transcendent" exterior. There is no place that offers itself as home. Exiled from the community, the foreigner becomes an eccentric anti-humanist, and this strangeness as difference is a threat to the social fabric. Similar to the real foreigner, our alien status makes us abject, asocial creatures.[21] In light of these difficult ways of understanding and developing identity for those who are understood as foreigners, exiled, and displaced, we need to take greater precaution and sympathy for those who are suffering from loss of identity, personhood and social self.

In light of these negative consequences of abjection, loss of identity and source of pain, religion needs to become a positive source of identity formation a way to rebuild people who experience exile, colonialism and trauma. People who have lost their land and feel a sense of loss of identity need to be able to find solace, strength, and faith in religion. Religion needs to somehow become site of resistance for power and strength. Religion can be a way to rebuild selves, identities, communities and peoples who have lost so much during exile and loss of land.

Spirit / Chi

In a globalized world, we cannot remain in our own families and neighbourhoods. We need to be mindful of others around us. We need to engage with people of other cultures and faith traditions. We need to understand that we are all on this earth to live as partners and co-caretakers. We cannot exist by ourselves, but we need to co-exist and work with others to save this planet. The land is important and our lifestyle is causing people to live in exile. We need to work together in collaboration to live more sustainably

---

20. Berquist, "Psalms, Postcolonialism," 199.
21. Smith, *Julia Kristeva*, 23, 24.

and ecologically. This involves being in dialogue with other faith traditions and religions.

As we seek to turn our lives around, we turn to our friends of other faiths. It becomes clear that the understanding of the Spirit exists in other cultures and faiths. This concept of the Spirit can become an entry point of interreligious dialogue so that religious people of all faith traditions can work towards saving the earth.

One aspect of the Divine that can help us transform our understanding and living is the Spirit. An understanding of Spirit is found in many cultures. It is necessary to be open to other religious and cultural traditions to gain insight into the words used when others talk about the Divine and the Spirit. This openness can lead to further dialogue, acceptance, and welcoming of strangers. In Asia, Spirit is commonly understood as Chi, which is a life force that gives and sustains life.[22] As we search the globe, we discover understandings of the Spirit such as *prana* and *ha*, which are all versions of the life-giving Spirit. These various terms all point to the same Spirit that is life giving and life sustaining. This commonality between cultures and people will aid us in our attempt to embrace the other. This process of embracing the other—or reconciliation—is central to salvation/redemption. As Christians from different social locations begin to recognise a common thread, understanding *Chi, prana, ha,* Holy Spirit, and other terms for the Spirit as inter-related can be experienced as salvific for us as Christians and in our relationships with others.[23]

Spirit-Chi is salvific in that it saves us, within us and among us and with others. It is a spirit that bonds us to each other and pulls humanity closer to all other living creatures. It will sustain us and keep us aware of our interconnectedness to and inter-reliance upon each other and all of creation, without which we will not survive. Hence, Spirit-Chi is essentially what keeps humanity alive as it is the life-giving force within us. Spirit-Chi is salvific and negotiates a space to save those who live in the liminal spaces between us.[24]

As people of all faith traditions, we call upon the Spirit to renew the earth. We all need to be transformed by this Spirit to work for justice. The Spirit that pervades this earth, land, and waters and which lives in all of us, needs to change us to work to save the planet and each other.

---

22. For a more detailed discussion on Spirit and Chi, see Kim, *Holy Spirit.*
23. Ibid., 145.
24. Ibid., 134–35.

Bibliography

Berquist, Jon L. "Psalms, Postcolonialism, and the Construction of the Self." In *Approaching Yehud: New Approaches to the Study of the Persian Period*, edited by Jon L. Berquist, 195–202. Semeia Studies 50. Atlanta: Society of Biblical Literature, 2007.

Brueggemann, Walter. *The Land: Place as Gift, Promise, and Challenge in Biblical Faith*. 2nd ed. Overtures to Biblical Theology. Minneapolis: Fortress, 2002.

Davidson, Steed Vernyl. *Empire and Exile: Postcolonial Readings of the Book of Jeremiah*. Library of Hebrew Bible/Old Testament Studies 542. New York: T. & T. Clark, 2011.

Esler, Philip F. "Ezra–Nehemiah as a Narrative of (Re-invented) Israelite Identity." *Biblical Interpretation* 11 (2003) 416–17.

Farisani, Elelwani. "The Use of Ezra–Nehemiah in a Quest for an African Theology of Reconstruction." *Journal of Theology for Southern Africa* 116 (2003) 35–36.

hooks, bell. *Feminist Theory: From Margin to Center*. Boston: South End, 1984.

Jenkins, Philip. *The New Faces of Christianity: Believing the Bible in the Global South*. Oxford: Oxford University Press, 2006.

Kim, Grace Ji-Sun. *The Holy Spirit, Chi and the Other: A Model of Global and Intercultural Pneumatology*. New York: Palgrave Macmillan, 2011.

McFague, Sally. *Life Abundant: Rethinking Theology and Economy for a Planet in Peril*. Minneapolis: Fortress, 2000.

Myers, Jacob M. *Ezra, Nehemiah*. Anchor Bible 14. Garden City, NY: Doubleday, 1965.

Said, Edward. "The Mind of Winter: Reflections on Life in Exile." *Harpers* (September 1983) 50.

———. "Reflections on Exile." In *Out There: Marginalization and Contemporary Cultures*. edited by Russell Ferguson, et al., 357–66. New York: New Museum of Contemporary Art, 1990.

Smith, Anna. *Julia Kristeva: Readings of Exile and Estrangement*. New York: St. Martin's, 1996.

Smith, Mark S. *The Memoirs of God: History, Memory, and the Experience of the Divine in Ancient Israel*. Minneapolis: Fortress, 2004.

Smith-Christopher, Daniel L. *A Biblical Theology of Exile*. Overtures to Biblical Theology. Minneapolis: Fortress, 2002.

13

Epistemological Transformation in Theological Education

HENK VAN DEN BOSCH

Introduction

"Complaints about theological education are as old as theological education itself," according to Edward Farley.[1] Attempts to do better are just as old. One of the most recent efforts that I know of to address weaknesses in theological education is a South African project of epistemological transformation. This contribution looks at the relevance of the issues raised in that South African project for theological education elsewhere.

The Athens vs. Berlin Debate

The most recent thorough discussion on theological education in the United States, one that is still indicative for the current state of theological education, was initiated in 1983 by the publication of Edward Farley's book *Theologia*, a discussion "concerning what is theological about theological education. It is not only the longest-lived but by far the liveliest conversation theological educators have been able to sustain among themselves ecumenically about the nature and purpose of their common enterprise."[2] Two different types of perspectives can be distinguished in this discussion,

---

1. Farley, *Theologia*, 3.
2. Kelsey, *Between Athens and Berlin*, 95.

and following Kelsey we can label these types the "Athens" and the "Berlin" approaches to theological education. Generally speaking, the "Athens" approach centralizes theological wisdom and spiritual formation, while the "Berlin" approach focuses on *Wissenschaft*, on learning and science.

Farley is representative of the first approach. Although his book is thirty years old, his motivation to write it sounds very familiar to those involved in theological education today: "Complaints about theological education are as old as theological education itself. Today they sound forth from many quarters: alumni who say they were not adequately prepared for church work, faculty who bemoan their professional isolation and loneliness, students who experience the ministry fields as trivial and academic fields as irrelevant, laity who are sure that the gospel has long been absent from the schools' agenda."[3] Farley argues that the reason for this massive discontent is the fact that "'Theology' has long since disappeared as the unity, subject matter, and end of clergy education,"[4] and has been replaced by a focus on the training of the minister as professional, the so-called 'clerical paradigm,' which leads to an external-teleological approach: "the only thing which studies of Scripture, theology, history, and pastoral care have in common is their contribution to the preparation of the clergy for its tasks."[5] In order to understand where things went wrong, Farley engages in an "archaeological recovery of the historical strata operative in current theological study."[6] To start with, the term "theology" is fundamentally ambiguous: it is a term for "an actual, individual cognition of God and things related to God," and simultaneously it is a term for "a discipline, a self-conscious scholarly enterprise of understanding."[7] Under the influence of Pietism and Enlightenment these two understandings of theology undergo a radical transformation and become the practical know-how necessary to ministerial work on the one hand, and systematic theology (as one technical and specialized scholarly undertaking among others) on the other hand.[8] The final step in the development from the unity to the fragmentation of theological education we owe to Friedrich Schleiermacher. According to Farley, it is his proposal for a theological encyclopedia in *Kurze Darstellung des theologischen Studiums* (1811) that is responsible for the introduction of the fourfold pattern of biblical studies, church history, dogmatics and practical theology into the study

3. Farley, *Theologia*, 3.
4. Ibid., ix.
5. Ibid., 114.
6. Ibid., 23.
7. Ibid., 31.
8. Ibid., 39.

of theology, finding a sense of unity in the clerical paradigm, the training of the minister as professional.[9] And it is in this fragmented situation that we find ourselves today.

Farley's analysis of the current crisis of theological education is persuasive. His proposal for reformation of theological education is less convincing. First he argues that the only way to overcome its "enslavement to specialties, its lack of subject matter and criteria, its functionalist and technological orientation"[10] is by recovering the original idea of "theology," and he suggests ways to do just that. He continues by indicating how this idea of theology as personal knowledge of God can play a part in the course of theological studies. These suggestions and indications (the final two chapters of the book), however, lack clarity to serve as guiding principles in thinking about the transformation of theological education, mainly because "*Theologia* as the material basis remains maddeningly elusive."[11]

The challenge put forward by Farley is taken up by Joseph Hough, who opts for the vocational approach to theological education. Hough agrees with Farley with regard to the crisis in theological education, and with Farley's analysis of fragmentation as core constituent of this crisis. But that is as far as the agreement goes. Hough strongly disagrees with Farley's judgment that the growing dominance of the clerical paradigm is the source of all confusion in theological education. Hough claims that the study of theology has always been understood as professional study. "The specific purpose of the theological school is to prepare leaders for the churches, including those leaders who are required to be ordained. It is not only appropriate, therefore, but absolutely necessary for the sake of the churches, that theological schools take seriously what Farley has called the 'teleological' basis for the unity and coherence of theological studies. The theological school *is* a professional school."[12] The problem theological schools are facing is not that they are professional schools dominated by the clerical paradigm, according to Hough; the problem is that "the notion of what constitutes appropriate professionalism in the church at present is distorted and confused."[13] An important reason for this distortion is the rise of the modern idea of the profession as part of the emerging scientific-technical world view of the 18th and 19th centuries.[14] Hough refers here to the semi-

---

9. Ibid., 84–94.
10. Ibid., 156.
11. Hough, *Beyond Clericalism*, 57.
12. Ibid., 64.
13. Ibid., 64–65.
14. Ibid., 69.

nal work of Donald Schön, *The Reflective Practitioner*, who calls this the "technological program," "the idea that human progress would be achieved by harnessing science to create technology for the achievement of human ends."[15] The modern professional in this technical sense doesn't do his own thinking, but applies given research-based theory to generalized problem-solving. And this modern professional, with the primary focus on what the minister is actually called on to do, becomes the model product of theological education.[16] There is, however, a broad dissatisfaction with the modern professional paradigm, with Schön as one of the primary spokespersons. He is of the opinion that practice-based professional learning is more important to the professional than formal teaching or knowledge transfer, and introduces the ideas of reflection-in-action and reflection-on-action, both important concepts in the professional training of reflective practitioners today. Hough agrees with Schön's analysis and shows the failure of the technical concept of modern professionalism by pointing out that in the end the image of the practitioner is bereft of any normative identity. At this point he proposes his own concept of the minister as practical theologian with the primary task of giving reflective leadership to the church as it envisions its ministry in the world.[17] Since practical theology in this perspective is critical reflection on the church's practice in view of the gospel of Jesus Christ, the proposal does not mean that practical theology should be the exclusive prerogative of the minister. Hough identifies four tasks for the minister as practical theologian: leadership in the representation of the church's memory of Jesus Christ for the sake of the continuing renewal of the identity of the Christian community, leadership in the reflective practice through which that identity can be given concrete historical expression, institutional management, and counseling.[18] The theological curriculum should provide for the education of ministers as practical theologians in two ways, namely by allowing biblical and historical studies to focus on the critical presentation and re-presentation of the identity of the Christian community as it is formed and represented in the documents of that community's internal history, and a focus on the major issues Christians face in the world for systematical theology and ethics.[19] Hough concludes his proposal for a new ministerial paradigm and matching theological education by making a plea for the introduction of Schön's concept of the reflective practitioner in the

---

15. Schön, *Reflective Practitioner*, 31.
16. Hough, *Beyond Clericalism*, 71, 74.
17. Ibid., 79.
18. Ibid., 79–80.
19. Ibid., 80.

way we understand the relation between theory and practice in the education of ministers.[20] The idea of the congregation as focus for theological education is further developed in Hough's *Beyond Clericalism*.

※

In an attempt to flesh out the earlier proposals, mainly the one by Farley, Rebecca Chopp investigates the concrete reality of contemporary theological education. The task at hand, according to Chopp, is "not simply to understand the formal goal of *habitus* but to develop a *habitus* of God or ecclesial redemption in this particular age,"[21] assuming that this habitus will result in transforming practices. Utilizing central themes from feminist practices of theological education, namely justice, dialogue, and imagination, she approaches theological education as "a process of the intertwining of theology and education in and through practices, within which different voices reflect and construct practices of theological education" resulting in "some sense of how to move toward change and transformation of theological education."[22] She concludes by suggesting the inclusion of relationality and community, of crucial cultural problematics, and of the symbolic patterns of religion and culture as ways in which to transform our way of thinking of theological education: "the task for the subjects of theological education may be as much the doing of new relationships to God, self, others, traditions, and society as it is the articulation of right ideas."[23] We can hear an echo of Chopp's suggestions when later in this essay we will focus our attention on the epistemological transformation project.

Excluded Voices

Surveying the Athens vs. Berlin debate, Robert Banks concludes that "for all its breadth of coverage, in one sense the debate has a parochial flavor."[24] He substantiates this claim with two arguments. One is that the majority of theologians involved in the debate are divorced from grassroots ministry in the church or the world, a fact that results in proposals that are less concrete than required. The second and for this contribution more relevant

20. Ibid., 82.
21. Chopp, *Saving Work*, 14.
22. Ibid., 113.
23. Ibid., 111.
24. Banks, *Reenvisioning*, 60.

argument is that a significant number of voices are not heard in the debate: women, minorities, students, pastors, lay leaders, parachurch figures, and Third World theological thinkers and practitioners.

In the past decades, several attempts have been undertaken to assure the inclusion of excluded voices in academic discourse. However, when looking at the curricula used in centers of theological education, the impact of the various branches of critical discourse seems to be disappointing. Most curricula in use are variations of the traditional fourfold pattern, in which the various branches of liberation and local theologies are no more than electives.

The fate of African theology is a case in point. Over half a century has passed since a group of Roman Catholic priests published *Des Pretres noires s'interrogant* in 1956, an event often marked as the start of African Christian theology. In this half century a lot of work has been done: scores of African theologians have contributed to the development of African theology by studying and reflecting, by publishing articles and books, by teaching and preaching. Since by now some 400 million Christians, approximately 20% of the world total, are African Christians, and since, generally speaking, African Christianity is growing where Western Christianity is in decline, one would assume this theological output to have a significant impact on the theological scene. Yet most of African theology never makes it to the agenda of what, for lack of a better term, is usually called "mainline theology." The curricula of most theological faculties and seminaries are still dominated by Western theology, Western theological issues and Western theologians. Unfortunately this is not only true of Western theological institutions: even the curricula of African seminaries are still dominated by Western theology. Equally significant is the fact that precious little of the output of African theology gets published in leading academic journals or by leading academic publishing houses; African theology is a so-called niche-market, served by specialized journals and publishers and read only by a small number of interested theologians.

One of the attempts to address this issue of West-centrism, of a universalized West and a subalternized non-West, is undertaken by postcolonial discourse. Point of exit is the nineteenth century package deal of colonialism, Western superiority, and Christian mission. In this approach the missionaries simply proved themselves to be children of their time: a millennium of Christian presence in Europe had led to a thorough identification of Christianity with Europe, in the sense that being Christian meant being European, and the spectacular developments of the nineteenth century in science, industry, economy, etc., only added to the sense of European superiority and ethnocentrism. The result of this European ethnocentric missionary approach was that for non-Europeans to become Christians they first had to become Europeans. "The Western colonizers, along with Christian missionaries, preached the vision of modern Enlightenment of human equality, autonomy, reason, and Christian love and dignity of all individual human beings created in the *imago dei*, but they, at the same time, denied those visions for humanity in their very colonial practice of sub-alternization of the colonized and their knowledge."[25] As a result, for the longest time Western theological discourses have been considered as normative and universal, over against indigenous discourses that were only locally applicable. The aim of postcolonial discourse, according to Kang, is not to replace Western universalism by non-Western universalism in an act of "postcolonial revenge"—this would simply mean replacing one form of subjugation and exclusion by another. Postcolonial theological education is about "speaking *to* and engaging *with* significant socio-cultural and geo-political issues from a perspective of radical justice and equality, a perspective that is against any type of domination and control, which compose the fundamental nature of colonial mentality."[26]

One of the issues to be engaged is the use of language as an instrument of power, of "linguistic imperialism." According to Kang, English has become the global language in theological education to such an extent that those who are not native speakers of English are considered second class: "Even when they write and speak in English, people often categorize it as 'indigenous,' 'local,' 'contextual,' or 'particular' and often it turns out to be simply '*as-discourse*' because they write only 'as-Asian,' 'as-African,' 'as-Latin American,' and so forth."[27] Language thus becomes an instrument of power and exclusion. This discursive hierarchy between those who speak English and those who do not or at least not flawlessly, a hierarchy Kang labels as "discursive colonialism," is elsewhere referred to as "linguistic imperialism," a term denoting the "ideologies, structures, and practices which are used to legitimate, effectuate, and reproduce an unequal division of power and resources (both material and immaterial) between groups which are defined on the basis of language."[28] What is needed in the face of this exclusionary use of language as a criterion for quality is not a superficial curricular or organizational fix, but a fundamental rethinking of the nature and purpose of theological education.

25. Kang, *Envisioning*, 34.
26. Ibid., 36.
27. Ibid., 37.
28. Ibid., 37.

A similar argument, applied to the methodology of doing theology, we find in an essay by Kevin Vanhoozer: "By and large, the voices that we think are authorized to speak of God belong to those who have been trained according to Western notions of theological reason."[29] He starts by criticizing the monological rule of the one-size-fits-all approach of western academic methodology ("our big fat Greek method"), the firm belief in the universality of instrumental reason. This methodology is also reigning supreme in academic theology, in the conviction that the truth of God can be discovered by induction and deduction. Non-Western theologians have voiced strong protests against this way of doing academic theology that is divorced from action. Now the question is how to do theology "after method," and "the single most significant methodological development that stems from the changing demographics of Christianity is the new appreciation for context":[30] the hermeneutical necessity to acknowledge an interpreter's situatedness in history, the praxis necessity to transform unjust social structures and dynamics, and the rediscovery of cultural identity.

This "turn to context" is emphasized by Scottish missiologist Andrew Walls, who adds a specific theological aspect to the argument. In various articles and essays he has emphasized the importance of the concept of translatability for the history and transmission of the Christian faith, and he links this importance to the centrality within the Christian faith of the doctrine of the incarnation. Walls claims that whereas at the heart of religions like Judaism and Islam is the prophetic word of God speaking to humanity, at the heart of the Christian faith is the incarnate Word of God becoming human, and he considers the incarnation thus as an act of translation: "Christian faith . . . rests on a massive divine act of translation, and proceeds by successive lesser acts of translation into the complexes of experiences and relationships that form our social identities in different parts of the world."[31] He then goes on to relate this concept of translation as incarnation to conversion: just as in the incarnation God became human in a specific time and place, in a specific language and culture, in order to transform humanity (in general, but of course always in its historical and cultural specificity), so does every successive translation bring Christ into a specific language and culture to transform it. "Conversion to Christ does not isolate the convert from his or her community; it begins the conversion of that community . . . This means that the influence of Christ is brought to bear on the points of reference in each group. The points of reference are the things by which

---

29. Vanhoozer, "One Rule," 85–86.
30. Ibid., 93.
31. Walls, *Culture and Conversation*, 47.

people know their identity and know where, and to whom, they belong."[32] In other words, the rejection of the universalist claim of Western theology and the acceptance of the fact that all theology is ultimately contextual and local, are theological necessities.

The turn to context, the conviction that all theology is ultimately contextual and local, will raise different questions in different contexts. In present-day Dutch society, for example, some of the major contextual issues a student of theology has to engage with could be the rapid marginalization of the Christian faith, and in its wake of the Christian churches, a lack of shared moral values and a shared moral compass, and the challenges that come with living in a multicultural and multi-religious society. In all of these major societal issues, theologians and ministers could and perhaps should play an important role as religious leaders. To give just one example: the multicultural experience is defined as "a particular moment within the experience of the multicultural community where 'culturally defined' groups engage each other in intentional ways in order to develop strategies to live together and to work together as distinctive members of the same community."[33] These intentional engagements, however, require mutual recognition, awareness and familiarity, and tolerance. For this reason, the minister as religious leader is in a position to play an important, facilitating role in these engagements. But how are students to be prepared for this role; or, on a more epistemological level, what are the implications for the theological knowledge with which theological education equips the students?

Epistemological Transformation

The developments described above can be interpreted as indicative of the need for a thorough transformation of theological education. The question then is how this transformation, if it is to go beyond the usual shallow cosmetic rearranging of curricula, should be done. One of the most recent proposals for change in theological education is the process of transformation currently undertaken by South African educational institutions.

In 2009 Jonathan Jansen, a scholar of Education Studies and current Vice-Chancellor of the University of the Free State in Bloemfontein, South Africa, published a book in which he described his experience as first black Dean of Education at the mainly white, Afrikaner University of Pretoria. The book title, *Knowledge in the Blood*, refers to "knowledge embedded in the emotional, psychic, spiritual, social, economic, political, and psychological

---

32. Ibid., 51.
33. Irizarry, *Toward an Intercultural*, 29.

lives of a community . . . It is not, therefore, knowledge that simply dissipates like the morning mist under the pressing sunshine of a new regime of truth."[34] Knowledge in the blood is emphatic knowledge that does not tolerate ambiguity, and it is defensive knowledge that reacts against and resists rival knowledge. Knowledge in the blood, in other words, is not easily changed. This knowledge in the blood is fairly similar to Pierre Bourdieu's concept of *habitus*, the mental structure developed by individuals in a certain social context, the way in which they view and value the world and act in it. Individuals within a shared social context will develop a shared *habitus* that they will consider to be self-evident and that they will reproduce in their thinking, judging, acting. It thus becomes a self-generating and self-sustaining reality. One of the ways this *habitus* or knowledge in the blood takes shape and is handed down to next generations is in the institutional organization of knowledge in the curriculum. Jansen distinguishes between the tangible curriculum (for example, course outlines) and the intangible curriculum (discursive patterns), the "shaping force in the lives of those who teach, learn, administer, manage, and lead within the institution."[35] The transformation of the South African educational system after the 1994 caesura, Jansen found, is usually done on the first level of curriculum, but needs to be done at the second, intangible level, if any real transformation and change is to be achieved. Curriculum can be simply defined as "an organization of knowledge that establishes what is to be known, in what order and to what purpose or results" and which also measures "the successful acquisition of that knowledge."[36] This simple definition, however, does not do justice to the complex nature of curriculum as organization of knowledge, since knowledge is contested: "Who governs what knowledge? Who decides what constitutes knowledge in the disciplines and professions? Who has access to it? Who can distribute it? Whose knowledge is included in the curriculum? As socially organized knowledge, curriculum reflects both the distribution of power and the principles of social control and reproduction in a given society."[37] Transformation, according to Jansen, has to take place at this epistemological level.

After moving from the University of Pretoria to the University of the Free State in Bloemfontein, Jansen challenged the various faculties of that traditionally white university to work towards real transformation. The 1994 caesura, the change from an apartheid government to a democratic

34. Jansen, *Knowledge in the Blood*, 171.
35. Ibid., 173.
36. Lange, "Knowledge, Curriculum, and Transformation," 36.
37. Ibid., 36.

government, "represented a radical shift in politics, economics and society," but amazingly "this shift in state and governance was not accompanied at all by a change in university curricula"; on the contrary, "many professors and universities teach exactly the same old knowledge that they did under apartheid."[38] He calls for a transformation that is more than a replacement within the curriculum of one kind of content with another, more than some 'additive content' to an otherwise unchanged curriculum, because knowledge is more than a thing that can be included or replaced in the curriculum; knowledge is "the embodiment of values, beliefs, and commitments; it is a reflection of history, traditions and practices; it is a projection of ideologies and politics."[39] The kind of epistemological transformation he is aiming at will, for one thing, go hand in hand with replacing "the natives": "Received knowledge must be challenged, extended, engaged and enriched by other perspectives on knowledge. And the best way to do that . . . is through the appointment of academics from outside of the institution, or similar institutions, and through the immersion of upcoming academics in new worlds of knowledge."[40] This fact alone makes it clear that this kind of transformation will meet with considerable resistance.

Nevertheless, the Faculty of Theology of the UFS took up the challenge and engaged in an exploration of the notion of epistemological transformation of theological knowledge. From the start, it is clear that this kind of transformation has at least three implications. It implies accepting an openness of knowledge: "welcoming complexity, fluidity and the coexistence of breaks and continuity, the possibility of tension, contradiction and paradox, and the anguish and uncertainty of the search for truth."[41] It further implies the democratization of knowledge, the facilitation of access to knowledge by all who want that access and the production instead of the reproduction of knowledge. A final implication is the reconsideration of knowledge governance, the question who determines what constitutes acceptable knowledge.[42]

Considering the issue of how epistemological transformation of theological education can take shape, Rian Venter[43] identifies a number of questions that need to be answered. The first question to be considered is the question of *the legitimacy of theological knowledge*: we live in

38. Jansen, "Can the Theological," 10.
39. Ibid., 12.
40. Ibid., 16.
41. Lange, "Knowledge, Curriculum, and Transformation," 40.
42. Ibid., 39–41.
43. Venter, "Theology," 48–64.

a post-Christendom culture, and it is fair to ask whether there is a public need for theological knowledge, whether it contributes to the common good. Venter proposes to disengage the legitimacy question from narrow ecclesial motivation (like training ministers for specific denominations) and to frame the issue in terms of the dialogue between faith and science.[44] A second issue is *the nature of theological knowledge*. The work of philosophers like Heidegger and Foucault and of critical discourses like postmodernism, feminism and post-colonialism have taught us that knowledge "is not stable, objective, neutral and innocent."[45] This issue results in questions like: whose interests are served by theological knowledge as an instrument of social power and control, how are various traditions represented, how does theological knowledge contribute to the good of the other, etc. Then there is the question of *the location of theological knowledge*: in separate seminaries or within the university, as a separate faculty or included in the department of humanities, etc. Opting for separate seminaries or divinity school or faculties runs the risk of an increasing isolation of theological knowledge and continuation of the split between faith and reason. Arguments like accountability, interdisciplinary conversation, and epistemic integration persuade Venter to opt for inclusion of theology within the humanities.[46] Very significant is the question *whose theological knowledge is to be produced*: which religious traditions should be served, or even more bluntly put: should certain denominational traditions be epistemically privileged? Venter argues for extended hospitality towards and space-making for the denominational and religious other, thus allowing what he calls an "epistemic rupture": a shift of paradigm, new post-colonial and post-imperialist habits of the mind. Two obvious starting points are the appointment of new faces representing the excluded other, and the opening of the curriculum to the voices of the excluded other.[47] Another issue is the question of research: *what theological knowledge should be generated*? According to Venter, a lot of theological research output is trivial and provincial, lacking accurate research foci, reproducing and reconfiguring existing knowledge, addressing intra-ecclesial concerns, and therefore with negligible impact and recognition.[48] A shift to the significant, addressing issues that really matter, is imperative. Related is the question of *the identity of the theological knowledge produced*. Most institutions for theological education label themselves with

---

44. Ibid., 49.
45. Ibid.
46. Ibid., 51.
47. Ibid., 52–53.
48. Ibid., 57.

a single qualifier: Protestant, Roman Catholic, Presbyterian, Baptist, etc. Venter questions these identity constructions by reduction to a single essence as distortions of identity, and suggests instead to identify a number of epistemic values, like ecumenical openness, multi-religious respect, social concern, multidisciplinary dialogue, etc. Furthermore he suggests the consideration of the three publics of theology as identified by David Tracy and the development of theology as public theology.[49] An important addition is the distinction between self-identification and public image, a distinction that requires reflection about image projection and perceived identity. In line with the discussion regarding the unity and fragmentation of theological knowledge, *the encyclopedia of theological knowledge* is questioned: the various theological disciplines distinguish themselves by means of study object, methodology, etc., distinctions that turn into impenetrable borders of demarcation that hinder meaningful integration and that also have a demonstrable adverse effect on theological education, for example when students are asked to preach. Similar questions can be asked with regard to academic programs (which interest is served by a particular programmatic organization of theological knowledge?), the theological library (what knowledge and whose knowledge are considered worthy of preservation for current use and for future generations?), academic networks (do they serve intellectual inbreeding or the generation of new knowledge?), etc. Regarding all these aspects, hospitable openness and inclusion are to be actively pursued. A final issue raised by Venter is the question of *the performance of theological knowledge*: does theological education "cement forgetfulness, prejudices, myopic visions, or insular practices? Or do we facilitate identity formation, enabling people to live with practical wisdom, appreciating their contingency, embracing the Other, contributing to the common good, and accepting historical ambiguity?"[50] Venter concludes his considerations regarding the how of epistemological transformation of theological knowledge by tentatively indicating what this project might bring about. The trinitarian understanding of divine identity includes hiddenness, fullness, love, relationality, hospitality, and space; the narrative of Jesus Christ speaks of kenosis, of fellowship with the other, of resistance to empire, and views incarnation as the ultimate embrace of otherness; the Holy Spirit is God doing ever new, impossible, and beautiful things, constantly crossing boundaries. "This vision destabilizes our myopic systems and invites us to more beautiful identities, and to greater community."[51]

49. Ibid., 58–59.
50. Ibid., 64.
51. Ibid., 66–67.

Theology as Public Conversation

The background for the process of epistemological transformation described above is the specific South African context of transition from a racially divided to a democratic and inclusive society. The process itself, however, could very well be of some relevance to institutions elsewhere that are equally in need of change. The next step, then, is to take a look at what epistemological transformation, in the form of the questions raised by Venter, might mean for the organization of theological education. In what follows, the Dutch context and the author's involvement in theological education and ministerial formation in that context are used as primary points of reference.

The question of *the legitimacy of theological knowledge* is a pressing issue. In a secularized context like Dutch society the question of a public need for theological knowledge is a genuine one. For state-funded educational institutions (like, for example, the Protestant Theological University) to motivate the legitimacy of the knowledge they transfer in education on a strictly ecclesial or even narrow denominational basis (namely, the training of ministers for the Protestant Church in the Netherlands) could even be considered a slippery slope. It seems that the question of the identity of theological knowledge produced is closely linked to the issue of legitimacy. When, for example, identity is construed as explicitly Protestant (as is the case with the Protestant Theological University), this identity construction seems to indicate the exclusion of the denominational and religious other. And again, in a context as secularized as Dutch society, this is a risky strategy of identity construction.

According to David Tracy, the theologian functions in respect to three different "publics": the academy, the church, and society,[52] a suggestion extended by David Bosch to theological education.[53] In the Dutch context, the church as a public has become very small indeed. And not only the numbers have eroded, but also the sense of belonging of those who still see themselves as members of a church community: their grasp of the tradition of the church and the language and symbols of that tradition has diminished. When it comes to the church, soon there will hardly be a public left to be addressed by theological education. Leaving the academy as public aside for a moment (a topic that will be addressed below when dealing with the location of theological knowledge), this automatically means that the focus shifts to society as primary public. Here the notion of public theology,

---

52. Tracy, *Analogical Imagination*, 3–46.
53. Bosch, *Nature of Theological Education*.

suggested by Venter, as a way of doing theology in the Netherlands comes into view. But then we first have to be clear about what we mean by the term 'public theology.'

The notion of public theology has been in use since the 1970's, but is used in such a variety of ways that it is questionable whether everyone using the term is referring to the same thing. In an attempt to map the landscape of public theology, Jacobsen proposes a distinction between six models of public theology, grouped into two categories.[54] The first category is the category of the foundational models, emphasizing the importance and need for public theology. Three models are distinguished within this category. The model of disclosure takes its point of exit in the assumption that the public being of God reveals Godself to people in different ways, with the public testimony of its faith as role for the church. One of the proponents of this model is South African theologian Dirk Smit, who within this model distinguishes four different emphases, namely on God's public nature, on the church's testimony through words and deeds, on the church's promotion of reconciliation, justice and peace, and finally on the church's obedient testimony of the goodness and mercy of God.[55] The universal model starts with the universal 'religious questions' that are faced by any human being and to which the theologian seeks to provide answers. Jacobsen refers to Tracy as exponent of this model of public theology. The factual model, finally, represented by Ronald Thiemann, takes its starting point in the fact that theology, as reflection on how Christians live Christian lives, a reflection resulting for example in moral choices, is always political and therefore always public. Public theology, then, seeks to understand "the relation between Christian beliefs and the broader sociocultural context."[56] The second category, according to Jacobsen, is the category of action models, proposing ways for realizing public theology. Again, three models are distinguished. The audience model starts with Tracy's threefold public of theology: society, academy and church, and sees theology as interacting with these publics. Within society, theology interacts with the techno-economic realm, the political domain and the cultural field, the interaction with the academy focuses on the faith and science debate, and the church is the community of moral and religious discourse in which the theologian is embedded. The apologetic model formulates theology's truth claims in ways accessible to all by using methods of reasoning accepted by all. The contextual model seeks to demonstrate great interest in the contextuality of its theological task, arguing

54. Jacobsen, *Models of Public Theology*.
55. Ibid., 10.
56. Ibid., 13.

for the need to be attentive to the issues at stake in a society, in order to articulate the content specific to it in ways relevant to the context.[57] Jacobsen observes that, generally speaking, the models of disclosure and audience are most recurrent models in public theology, whereas North American public theologians like Tracy and Stackhouse favor the universal and apologetic models by equating public with universal, and South African theologians like Koopman, de Gruchy and Smit opt for the factual and contextual models, equating public with common and perceiving public theology as able to contribute toward the common good of society in the struggle against racism, poverty, violence, etc.[58]

In the Dutch context, various models of public theology present themselves as viable options for theological education. The traditional ways of self-identification and legitimization of the knowledge transferred in theological education are narrowly denominational and ecclesial and therefore no longer tenable in a society where the vast majority of people has no understanding of or need for this kind of theological discourse. Taking the secularized, multicultural and multi-religious Dutch context seriously in theological education would result in a fully public theology that considers not only the church but society in general as its public and that takes society seriously as conversation partner. The consequence of this epistemological transformation would be the transformation of Protestant theology to public theology, with significant ramifications for curriculum: not by introducing public theology as a new addition to an otherwise unchanged curriculum, but by placing society (major societal issues) as public in the forefront of all theological disciplines. To give just one example of what this could imply: hermeneutics would no longer have its central focus in the relation between the ancient text and the modern reader (since this reader is only the professional theologian), but shift significant interest and study to the relation between the theologian and modern society: how do we communicate what we consider to be of ultimate value in language and symbols the public in general understands?

The question of *the nature of theological knowledge* presents itself as an issue of relevance to theological education, also in light of what is stated above regarding public theology. The awareness that knowledge is not stable, objective, neutral and innocent, but always linked to power, authority, money,

57. Ibid., 18.
58. Ibid., 21–22.

etc., makes issues like the interests served by theological knowledge as instrument of social power and control, and the possible contribution of theological knowledge to the common good, appear on the radar screen of theological education. Closely linked is the question *whose theological knowledge* is to be produced, a question that results in the awareness that most institutions of theological education are epistemologically privileging specific denominational traditions. Venter argues for hospitality and space-making in response to this question. In line with his suggestions, the implementation of a form of dialogical theology can be contemplated. This label is sometimes used to describe the work of theologians like Joseph Ratzinger, and also to refer to the work of theologians involved in interfaith dialogue, like for example Wolfhart Pannenberg.[59] The use here is similar: society as public for theology is multiform, multi-layered and multi-religious, and the task of the theologian is to enter into dialogue with this multiform society. The multiform character of present-day society is encountered in the individual (who shapes individuality by sampling from various sources), in the church (where people from different backgrounds and with various interests meet), and in society in general (where people and groups of people clash over goals to be realized, interests to be safeguarded, spaces to be occupied, etc.). The role of the theologian is to facilitate dialogue by embodying hospitality and offering space. In itself this is not a novel suggestion: the history of Christianity and of theology is full of people with differing ideas engaging in dialogue over these differences. What is new, however, is that this dialogue is no longer limited to one denomination or to one religion, but that a multicultural and multi-religious dialogue is facilitated, that the gesture of hospitality and space-making is extended to people of other religious persuasions and to people without religious persuasion. This dialogical response to the epistemological questions of the nature and ownership of knowledge will impact curriculum of theological education in at least two ways. The student of theology will have to be prepared for a role in this dialogue by being secure in her or his own (theological, religious, spiritual) identity, and by being knowledgeable regarding the possibilities and necessities for dialogue in her or his own context. And simultaneously, the dialogical character of theological education will have to be brought home by the hospitable invitation of the other (the denominational other, the religious other, the societal other) into both the student body and the faculty, by appointing new faces representing the excluded other. In this way, dialogue will not be a mere extension of an existing and unchanging curriculum, but will shape the entirety of curriculum.

59. Hošek, "Towards a Dialogical."

Regarding the question of *the location of theological knowledge*, Venter fears that separate seminaries contribute to the isolation of theological knowledge and perpetuation of the split between faith and reason. He opts for a joint inclusion of theology and religious studies in a school of humanities, based on arguments of accountability, interdisciplinary conversation and epistemic integration. The gap between theology as a normative approach to religion and religious studies as a descriptive approach is not as wide as we are sometimes led to believe. On the contrary, the similarities are more significant than the differences. Theology and religious studies share a basic approach of reality, namely one emphasizing both the distinction and the coherence between spirit and matter, and furthermore they share basically the same hermeneutical method in approaching the object of study.[60] For theology, a close cooperation with Religious Studies is clearly beneficial: on its own it runs the risk of isolation within the scientific world, of losing itself in intra-disciplinary and intra-ecclesial concerns, of having negligible societal and scientific impact and recognition, and finally of becoming totally irrelevant. The issue of relevance reveals a close link with the epistemological question of *what theological knowledge* should be generated. Regarding this issue, Venter fears a loss of relevance if a turn to the significant does not take place. This turn to the significant, a focus on the big questions in a given context, requires an expansion of the mental worlds, both of the scholars and of the students of theology, by means of an interdisciplinary approach. Here the location of theology at the university is undeniably beneficial.

An echo of Farley's complaint about the fragmentation of theological education can be heard in the epistemological question of *the encyclopedia of theological knowledge*, the partition of theology in disciplines that hardly communicate let alone cooperate with each other and obstruct meaningful integration. The problem of fragmentation is difficult to tackle: academic faculty is expected to specialize in their respective (sub-) disciplines, and will be evaluated on the basis of research output (academic publications). In order to be able to publish sufficiently, specialization is taken to such a high level that the importance of interdisciplinary communication and cooperation is overlooked. As a result, integration suffers. One possibility to stimulate the integration of theological knowledge is by actively facilitating the interaction between theory and practice. This can be done by taking the students as soon as possible out of the classroom and exposing them to the differentiated contexts of their professional futures (in other words, the differentiated texts they will encounter). The questions and issues that arise

60.

from this exposure can then be brought into dialogue with the various theological disciplines. In this fashion, each discipline is able to demonstrate its own perspective on reality, and the student learns how to respond to the issues of the future professional setting in an integrated theological manner.

The final epistemological question to be addressed is the question of *the performance of theological knowledge*: what personal identities result from theological education, i.e., from our theological knowledge production and transfer? Do we work towards the formation of insular and excluding personal identities, or rather of ecumenical and inclusive ones? In what ways do we facilitate identity formation? Although it is difficult to come to general statements in this regard, it seems fair to say that there is still a lot to be desired. As we have seen above, part of the problem is in the insular ecclesial context students are being trained to serve and the fragmented theological knowledge with which they are equipped for this service. This is where transformation is called for. A number of characteristics of the personal identity embracing the kind of epistemological transformation of theological knowledge proposed here have already been mentioned: a generous hospitality for otherness, a fundamentally inclusive mindset, an ecumenical approach to religious traditions, an interdisciplinary attitude towards theology, a tolerance of ambiguity and uncertainty, a deeply dialogical frame of mind. Transformed theological education aims at forming personal identities that are relational, open to unexpected encounters and invitations and also capable of extending surprising invitations; that are willing to engage in disruptive discussions, face uncomfortable questions, and are also able to pose these disruptive questions; that are prepared to be called out of their comfort zone and have the guts to call others out of their comfort zones. And have the inspiration and the resilience to dream of and contribute towards a society and a church that fit these same descriptions.

Summarizing the above very briefly: the 'turn to context' and the 'turn to other' take shape by the hospitable invitation of the other to participate in dialogical theology, by allowing society and the most pressing societal issues to take the front seat in theological education, and also by the continuing exposure of students to the widest possible array of different contexts. The combination of dialogue and exposure can assist the student in developing a spirituality that is both robust enough and open enough to engage the challenges of her or his context. And this same combination of dialogue and exposure can function as a sieve, shifting between cerebral and living theological knowledge.

Conclusion

According to Andrew Walls, incarnation, the heart of the Christian faith, can be interpreted as an act of translation, as an act of enculturation. Every successive act of translation brings Christ into a specific language and culture, just like in the incarnation God became human in a specific time and place, in a specific language and culture. There is, however, a flip-side to this coin: one of the dangers inherent to the fundamental translatability of the Gospel is that the translation logic can be arrested or frozen and that we abuse our particular interpretation of Christian identity to justify our own (social, economic, political, and ecological) interests.[61] It is possible to consider the current state of theological education as an example of an arrested translation logic.

Epistemic progress is not linear but takes place in the form of paradigmatic jumps and ruptures. Some of our South-African colleagues have come to the conclusion that in their specific context it is high time for just such a rupture in their practice of theological education. The application of their proposal for epistemological transformation to theological education in another context results in a number of fairly radical suggestions and proposals. But it could of course very well be that radical transformation is exactly what is called for in order to "defrost" current educational practices.

---

61. Cf. Denaux, "Theologie en geesteswetenschappen," 47.

Bibliography

Banks, Robert J. *Reenvisioning Theological Education: Exploring a Missional Alternative to Current Models*. Grand Rapids: Eerdmans, 1999.
Bosch, David J. "The Nature of Theological Education." *Journal of Theology for Southern Africa* 77 (1991) 3–17.
Chopp, Rebecca S. *Saving Work: Feminist Practices of Theological Education*. Louisville: Westminster John Knox, 1995.
Denaux, Adelbert. "Theologie en Geesteswetenschappen: Tussen Geloof en Cultuur." In *De theologie gevierendeeld: Vier Spanningsvelden voor de Theologiebeoefening in Nederland*, edited by S. A. J. van Erp and H. J. M. J. Goris, 40–57. Nijmegen: Valkhof Pers., 2013.
Farley, Edward. *Theologia: The Fragmentation and Unity of Theological Education*. Philadelphia: Fortress, 1983.
Hošek, Pavel. 2008. "Towards a Dialogical 'Global Theology': Wolfhart Pannenberg and Wilfred Cantwell Smith." *Communio Viatorum* 50 (2008) 257–75.
Hough, Joseph C. "The Education of Practical Theologians." *Theological Education* 20 (1984) 55–84.
Hough, Joseph C., and Barbara G. Wheeler, eds. *Beyond Clericalism: The Congregation as a Focus for Theological Education*. Scholars Press Studies in Religious and Theological Scholarship. Atlanta: Scholars, 1988.
Irizarry, Jose R. "Toward an Intercultural Approach to Theological Education for Ministry." In *Shaping Beloved Community: Multicultural Theological Education*, edited by David V. Esterline and Ogbu U. Kalu, 28–42. Louisville: Westminster John Knox, 2006.
Jacobsen, Eneida. "Models of Public Theology." *International Journal of Public Theology* 6 (2012) 7–22.
Jansen, Jonathan D. "Can the Theological Leopard Change Its Spots? On the Transformation of University Knowledge." In *Transforming Theological Knowledge: Essays on Theology and the University after Apartheid*, edited by Rian Venter and Francois Tolmie, 9–19. Bloemfontein: Sun Media, 2012.
———. *Knowledge in the Blood: Confronting Race and the Apartheid Past*. Stanford: Stanford University Press, 2009.
Jenkins, Philip. *The Next Christendom: The Coming of Global Christianity*. Oxford: Oxford University Press, 2002.
Kang, Namsoon. "Envisioning Postcolonial Theological Education: Dilemmas and Possibilities." In *Handbook of Theological Education in World Christianity: Theological Perspectives—Regional Surveys—Ecumenical Trends*, edited by Dietrich Werner et al., 30–41. Oxford: Regnum, 2010.
Kelsey, David H. *Between Athens and Berlin: The Theological Education Debate*. Grand Rapids: Eerdmans, 1995.
Lange, M. L. "Knowledge, Curriculum and Transformation." In *Transforming Theological Knowledge: Essays on Theology and the University after Apartheid*, edited by Rian Venter and Francois Tolmie, 31–43. Bloemfontein: Sun Media, 2012.
Maluleke, Tinyiko S. "Black and African Theologies in the New World Order: A Time to Drink from our Own Wells." *Journal of Theology for Southern Africa* 96 (1996) 3–19.

Schön, Donald A. *The Reflective Practitioner: How Professionals Think in Action.* New York: Basic Books, 1983.

Tracy, David. *The Analogical Imagination: Christian Theology and the Culture of Pluralism.* New York: Crossroads, 1981.

Vanhoozer, Kevin J. "'One Rule to Rule Them All?' Theological Method in an Era of World Christianity." In *Globalizing Theology: Belief and Practice in an Era of World Christianity*, edited by Craig Ott and Harold A. Netland, 85–126. Grand Rapids: Baker Academic, 2006.

Venter, Rian. "Theology, the Post-apartheid University and Epistemological Transformation: Intimating the Shape of the Challenge." In *Transforming Theological Knowledge: Essays on Theology and the University after Apartheid*, edited by Rian Venter and Francois Tolmie, 45–72. Bloemfontein: Sun Media, 2012.

Walls, Andrew F. 1996. "Culture and Conversion in Christian History." In *The Missionary Movement in Christian History: Studies in the Transmission of Faith*, 43–54. Maryknoll, NY: Orbis, 1996.

www.ingramcontent.com/pod-product-compliance
Lightning Source LLC
Chambersburg PA
CBHW071248230426
43668CB00011B/1638